After the Holocaust

AFTER

THE HOLOCAUST

The Migration of Polish Jews and Christians to Pittsburgh

BARBARA STERN BURSTIN

UNIVERSITY OF PITTSBURGH PRESS

Published by the University of Pittsburgh Press, Pittsburgh, Pa., 15260
Copyright © 1989, University of Pittsburgh Press
All rights reserved
Feffer and Simons, Inc., London
Manufactured in the United States of America

Library of Congress Cataloging-in-Publication Data

Burstin, Barbara Stern.
    After the Holocaust: the migration of Polish Jews and Christians to Pitts-
burgh / Barbara Stern Burstin.
    p. cm.
    Bibliography: p.
    Includes index.
    ISBN 0-8229-3603-8
    1. Poles—Pennsylvania—Pittsburgh—History—20th century. 2. Jews—
Pennsylvania—Pittsburgh—History—20th century. 3. Immigrants—Pennsylvania—Pittsburgh—History—20th century. 4. World War, 1939–
1945—Refugees. 5. Poland—Emigration and immigration—History—20th
century. 6. Pittsburgh (Pa.)—Emigration and immigration—History—20th
century. I. Title.
F159.P69P72 1989
304.8'748'860438—dc19

                                                              88-20490
                                                                  CIP

For my parents, Mildred and Joseph Stern, and in memory of my brother, Howard

And for David, Andrea, Jeffrey, Deborah, and Nancy

Contents

Introduction   ix

1. Prologue to Blitzkrieg   3

2. Between Swastika and Sickle   9

3. Point of No Return   42

4. "I Lift My Lamp"   64

5. A Jewish Community Faces the Refugees   87

6. Into the Pittsburgh Crucible   115

7. Displaced No More   140

8. Postscript   171

Notes   183

Bibliography   197

Index   211

Introduction

>>> IT WAS MURKY IN PITTSBURGH IN 1945. The air was smoke filled, the three rivers framing the city were polluted, the houses were dreary, the streets were dirty. World War II was over and Pittsburgh looked as if she had long since exhausted her greatness. She was spent, staggering under a choked industrial economy, grossly inadequate social services, and ruled by a tightly knit power elite, which did not seem to care. She was an example of "what a city shouldn't be." Perhaps she was even "barbaric," as one crusading journalist described her.[1]

But as barbaric and uncivilized as Pittsburgh might have been before the renaissance that was to change the face of the city within a few short years, it was paradise, a veritable mecca of peace and security, compared to the conditions out of which Pittsburgh's newest round of immigrants were to come. These immigrants were survivors of a war that had unleashed some of the most destructive forces in history. Upwards of thirty million persons had been displaced as a result of the conflagration. An estimated sixteen million military personnel and at least an equal number of civilians had perished. The deliberate terrorism, dehumanization, and bureaucratic mass murder of civilians, particularly of Jews, was unprecedented.

The Polish people experienced, perhaps more than any other with the exception of the Soviets, the barbaric excesses of Hitler's Germany. Certainly they suffered through the longest and most severe Nazi occupation of any country, and their nation's death toll was second only to that of the Soviet Union. They were further victimized by the Soviets, who together with the Nazis viewed the Poles' personal and national existence with contempt. It was thus from a devastated Poland that thousands upon thousands of its people, Christian and Jew alike, left to build their lives anew. These two groups had been linked through many generations prior to the war, sharing a common land and history. Together they arrived on these shores, seeking to pick up the pieces of their lives and start again.

Yet despite the same homeland, common oppressors, the trauma of displacement, and the mutual fears and uncertainties of resettlement in the United States, Christians and Jews traveled along somewhat different roads. They each came to America with distinct "baggage," as immigration historians are wont to say, that is, with diverse backgrounds, traditions, expectations, attitudes, and skills. Being Polish meant different things to each group, both in Europe and in America. Moreover, their common roots in Polish soil did not preclude misunderstandings and even hostility between them, which developed in Europe and which have not yet been healed. Though similar in many ways they yet see themselves as very different.

There have been many studies of Jewish survivors of the Holocaust—the deliberate destruction of six million Jews by Hitler and his collaborators. Considerable testimony of what occurred has been amassed in oral history projects as well as in a wealth of published material. Yet very little testimony has been collected from Christian victims of World War II, particularly Polish ones, about their personal knowledge of this event and their reaction to it; and even less has been translated into English. This applies not only to those Polish Christians who lived out the war under German occupation but also to those who endured under the Soviet authorities. By exploring the prewar, wartime, and postwar experiences of both Polish Christians (the overwhelming number of whom were Catholic) and Polish Jews in the Pittsburgh area, that gap in the historical record can be addressed and light can be shed on the total impact of World War II on both of these segments of the Polish nation.

It is also hoped that by juxtaposing the saga of each group a contribution will be made toward bridging the gulf that has grown between them and that on occasion continues to dog their relationship in America. Dialogues at both the national and local level have been repeatedly rocked by charges of Polish Christian anti-Semitism. The movie *Shoah* occasioned the latest round of controversy. A frank examination of the feelings and attitudes of each group toward the other and toward its wartime experience is a necessary precondition to communication and rapprochement between the two groups.

While both primary and secondary sources were used for background illumination, this study focuses upon the recorded accounts of one hundred and twenty persons who came to the city of Pittsburgh after leaving Poland during or immediately following World War II. Sixty Polish Christians and sixty Polish Jews were interviewed at length (up to three hours) in their own homes (with two exceptions) throughout the greater Pittsburgh area. Whenever possible, related individuals were avoided so as to get as diverse a group as possible. Each was asked about a hundred questions, covering the life span. The material presented is not only a composite portrait of their combined experiences but represents an attempt to convey the feelings and experiences of the individuals themselves. Wherever possible, research into local archives and other interviews with appropriate people were conducted in order to further corroborate and elaborate on the testimony of the immigrants. This was particularly true in the Jewish community because of the extensive records available. There is a scarcity of materials from Polish Christian sources in Pittsburgh.

The local picture is presented against the backdrop of efforts made by national Polish, Jewish, and Catholic agencies in behalf of refugees. It is hoped that this use of both written and oral sources will add to the immediacy of the presentation and convey, not just the broad outline of important historical experiences, but the feel and texture of the personal traumas making up that history as well.

There are inherent problems in collecting and using personal testimony. First of all, there is the question of the representative nature of those interviewed. How accurately do their experiences and attitudes reflect the larger group? For this research, all interviews were conducted with those persons who had moved to Pittsburgh in the aftermath of the war and were living in the city in 1982–84. Certainly, those who were interviewed felt they were very much like the other Poles who had emigrated to the United States following the war, and they in fact appear to be so.[2]

In addition to choosing a group solely from Pittsburgh, there was also the issue of individual selection. Only one out of every three people who were called on the telephone, whether Christian or Jew, agreed to an interview. For the Jews, the reason often given for refusing was an unwillingness to relive the past because of the pain of memory. For the Christians, the reason for refusing (usually unstated) was a reluctance to talk to a stranger and some suspicion about the motives of the research. For both groups, there also might have been something in their wartime past they did not care to bring to light. A number of people who were interviewed voiced their concern that anything they said might get back to the government in Poland and affect their families there. In fact, because of that fear, it was decided not to publish the surnames of interviewed people with relatives in Poland.

Personal testimony is not always reliable. Memories fade, current mind-sets color historical accuracy, prejudices and opinions affect reality. Individual recollections must be viewed in the cold light of other historical evidence. Yet history is not an exact science; it deals with people. And it is enhanced by the perceptions of eye witnesses. Perceptions, whether they are "right" or "wrong," whether they accord with the historical "reality" or not, are part of the necessary documentation of history and can often provide important clues to unraveling the past. When it comes to understanding contemporary times and what we are to make of them, such testimony is essential.

This comparative examination of Polish Christians and Polish Jews begins in chapter 1 with a glimpse of their past in an independent Poland before World War II. Were there differences in their backgrounds and skills? Were they "at home" in their own country? This would be part of the baggage that each group would carry with it to a new land.

Chapter 2 is devoted to the experience of both groups under Nazi occupation. From their testimony, did the Nazi machinery operate with equal ferocity and in equivalent fashion on both groups? In their common suffering and deprivation were there gradations of evil? And what did life under the Soviets mean to them? Many Poles were forced to endure Soviet occupation as a result of the Molotov-Ribbentrop Pact of August 1939 splitting Poland between Russia and Germany. This agreement prevailed until June 1941, when Hitler's troops suddenly crossed the demarcation line in Poland on their way to a devastating invasion of Soviet Russia itself. The experience of Poles under the Communists contributed to their desire to get away from the Soviets after the war and to their continuing hatred of Soviet domination of the Polish government.

Chapter 3 attempts to explore the attitudes of Poles who after the war made the decision not to return to Poland or not to remain there. Were there different reasons for such a decision on the part of the Christians and Jews? Moreover, what did each group encounter during this time of transition? How did their experiences affect them as they immigrated to the United States?

The focus in chapter 4 shifts to the effort by the Jewish community and the Polish Catholic community in the United States to bring their compatriots to this country. It plays out against the backdrop of the debate over the Displaced Persons

Act of 1948. This act, which was blatantly discriminatory, nevertheless did alter American policy regarding refugees from Europe. For the first time since 1924, this country began again to hang out the welcome sign for refugees. As David Wyman and others have pointed out, thousands of would-be immigrants had the door slammed in their faces as the United States refused to fill even its lawful quota of immigrants in the midst of the Nazi assault.[3] After the war, America resumed its historic role as the "haven for the oppressed," a role it continues to play today.

Chapter 5 focuses on the efforts made by the Pittsburgh Jewish community to resettle refugees coming into the area. (There was no comparable local effort in either the Polish Community or in the larger Catholic community.) The testimony of Pittsburghers who were living in the city at the time is used, as well as archival material. The activity of the local community is set against momentous events abroad that were drawing the attention and concern of Jews in Pittsburgh. How did Pittsburgh Jews feel about the efforts to resettle refugees and about those persons coming into their community?

Chapter 6 deals with the question of how the refugees reacted to the reception they received in this country, particularly in Pittsburgh. How did they feel about the efforts made—or not made—in their behalf? What problems did they face? Were the reactions and experiences similar for both groups?

Chapter 7 brings up to the present the experience of the refugees. How have they adjusted to their adopted country? What is their outlook on life, on the United States, and on themselves? Do they share the same fears and concerns? Where do their children appear to be heading? Are they and their children more alike than unlike? Are they Americans? Or are they still Polish Christians and Polish Jews?

Chapter 8 is a postscript—the record of a meeting that occurred in Pittsburgh between six Jews and six Christians who came from Poland after World War II. The convocation was an attempt to explore their feelings toward one another at this point in their lives and what they needed to say to each other. Moreover, it was an opportunity to probe what they think they had learned from their experience and whether they share anything as emigrants from Poland and survivors of the awful destruction of World War II. It was a moving and revealing climax to their arduous journeys from Poland to Pittsburgh.

After the Holocaust

1

Prologue to Blitzkrieg

▶▶▶ THE POLISH JEWS AND POLISH
Christians who came to Pittsburgh after World War II
grew up in a country that had during their lifetimes been
liberated from foreign domination. No longer the hapless pos-
session of three masters—German, Austro-Hungarian, and
Russian—a sovereign Poland had been resurrected in the aftermath of World War I. But political independence was to last
only twenty years before Poland was once again overpowered
and swallowed by her towering neighbors. Moreover, that short-
lived period of self-government did not bring a profound
change or reversal in an economy that continued to be agricul-
turally backward and industrially underdeveloped. In fact,
being cut off from markets by her independent status was
economically detrimental. The country was still a poor man in
Europe, and the onset of the Depression in the 1930s only
increased the hardship both in the countryside and in the
cities. "Poland was and is a land of paupers," remarked
Kasimierz Bartel, prime minister under the famous General
Jozef Pilsudski, the World War I hero who led Poland until his
death in 1935.[1] For the Jewish minority in Poland, comprising
one-tenth of the population, it is estimated that as many as
one-third of them were almost entirely dependent upon the
relief provided by private Jewish charitable organizations in the
United States.[2]

While economic adversity was often a common denominator

3

in Poland in the years preceding World War II, there was a clear difference in those pursuits at which Jews and Christians toiled. In a country with 61 percent of the population in agriculture, only 4 percent of the Jews were so engaged. The predominance of agriculture among Christians was reflected in the fact that nearly 40 percent of the Christian group in Pittsburgh came from farming backgrounds, while only one Jewish refugee mentioned that her family had owned some farmland in Poland.

With so many engaged in agriculture, only 6 percent of the Polish population was involved with trade. Yet over 36 percent of the Jews of Poland earned their livelihood from commerce. This too was underscored in the Pittsburgh group. Three-quarters of the fathers of the Polish Jewish refugees were wholesalers, dealing in everything from cattle to shoes, from grain to coffee; the others were in a variety of retail businesses, such as a grocery store, a café, a fur business, a beauty parlor, a dry goods store, and the like. The size and success of these commercial ventures, however, varied considerably. Harry Rosen's father was a grain dealer from Luck, in Eastern Poland, and struggled to earn a living. So did Aaron Fox's (Felgheber) father, who bought and sold cattle to the meat market. Jack Sittsamer's father peddled Singer sewing machines in Mielec; and Fanny Lieberman's father was a small paper peddler in Czestochowa. Julius Aussenberg's father was an invalid who was given a concession for a tobacco kiosk on a street in Tarnow. On the other hand, Lucy Dafner's family in Sosnowiec owned a large grain warehouse and Morris Manela's father and uncles were wealthy leather wholesalers. Samuel Frost's father was a big importer of Bata Shoes, and Gabriel Hoffman's father was an important military supplier in Deblin. While some of these Jews in commerce did very well, the overwhelming majority were small shopkeepers or had a stall at a market. They often worked alone.

Small-scale operation was also the order of the day for most of those engaged in industry. Only 19 percent of the general population of Poland before the war was in industry, although 42 percent of the Jewish working population was so engaged. In the Pittsburgh refugee group, as in Poland, more often than not the typical Jewish father was a petty craftsman employed in a small industrial enterprise. He was likely to be either a shoemaker, tailor, or baker, for Jews predominated in the needle trades and food industry.

Among the fathers of Christians who came to Pittsburgh, most of those in industry worked in construction, primary industry, or mining. Five fathers were in building or cabinet-making, ranging from a one-man operation to a company that employed a score of construction workers. Other fathers earned their living either as an electrician, an engine maker, a blacksmith, a wagon-wheel maker, or a forester. Maria S.'s father was a mechanic, who had his own oil-drilling and farm machinery repair business. Joseph G.'s father was a coal miner in western Lipiny, while Mieczylsaw G.'s father was a steel mill laborer in Crakow. Generally, in Poland only 3 percent of the Jewish workers were in heavy industry, while 37 percent of the non-Jewish workers were, often at semiskilled or unskilled jobs.[3]

Christians were also much more likely to be employed by the government directly or in government-owned monopolies. This was not only because Jews preferred to be self-employed, but also because of the discriminatory policies that prevailed. Only one Polish Jewish father among the Pittsburgh group was a government employee (city engineer in Bielsko), while fourteen of the Polish Christians had fathers in government service: four earned their livings from working for the railroad two as station masters, one as communications clerk, the fourth as an engineer; one was a dam operator in a rural area in eastern Poland, another was a government clerk, three were police agents, and one was an army career man; Stanislawa's S.'s father was a wealthy salt mine executive in that state-controlled monopoly; Viktor H.'s father and Helena B.'s father were both teachers in the Polish public schools; Alina J.'s father was an important chemist from the town of Koscian, the director of a large sugar refinery (state owned), and became a member of the Polish parliament.

Contrasts between Jewish and Christian backgrounds in Poland were evident in the context of a rural-urban continuum, since Polish Christians were so often engaged in agriculture while the Jews were not. The 1931 census showed that, while only one out of every four Poles was an urban dweller, the figures were exactly reversed for the Jewish minority in Poland: three out of four Jews lived in towns or cities. This is clearly seen in the Pittsburgh contingent of Poles. Twenty-two out of fifty-nine Jewish families came from cities of 100,000 or more, twenty-three families came from towns or small cities of 13,000 or more, and only fifteen, or one out of four, came from small villages. By contrast, only five of the Christians interviewed had originally come from the largest cities in Poland. Ten were from smaller cities, and forty-three (more than two-thirds of the group) were from rural areas.

According to the Polish census of 1931, Jews numbered 3,113,933 and comprised 9.8 percent of the total population. However, nothing—not their numbers, or their deep roots in Polish lands dating from the eleventh century (when Jews fled from German lands to escape persecution), or the equal rights spelled out in the Minorities Treaty signed by Poland in the aftermath of World War I, or the Polish Constitution—guaranteed them equal opportunity let alone economic security and acceptance.

Many Jews remembered incidents of discrimination and expressions of hostility against them. A number of the Polish Jews now living in Pittsburgh commented how fearful they used to be, particularly during the Easter Holy Week, when the charge of deicide was made against them from the pulpits of the Catholic churches. Harry Friedman, among others, recalled being stopped on the street and asked whether it was true that the Jews used Christian blood to bake matzot. Jews were aware of the church support of the government in urging boycotts against Jewish businesses, boycotts that often led to violence. Dora Hausler, a teenager from Warsaw, remembered the signs outside of stores reading "Jews and dogs not allowed." Fela Morgenstern from Lvov recalled shouts of "Send the Jews to Madagascar," and in her public school she found the teachers more anti-Semitic than the children. Some called Jewish boys not by their real names but by the name "Israel," and Jewish girls by the name "Chaya." "We had to be excellent to get good grades, and when a Jewish student got into a fight, the Jewish student was never right if he was in a fight with a non-Jew." Helen Birnbaum, who lived in the city of Pultusk near Warsaw, spoke about the time a girl behind her in a class had copied her paper. When that girl, who was Christian, got the highest grade in the class and Helen received just a passing grade, she went to the teacher for an explanation. She was merely ordered back to her seat. Another Jew, Rose Perlmutter, told of the time when she was a child and someone wrote on the blackboard "to Hell with Jews." When she complained to the teacher about it, she was informed that "we shouldn't forget that we're not welcomed in this country."

Yet despite evidence of overt anti-Semitism and government discrimination with regard to hiring, taxation, educational quotas and the like, prewar Poland was not Hitler's Germany. The Jews never underwent the brutal suppression that was all too common in Germany. There was no widespread government-sponsored riot against the Jews, like *Krystallnacht*, nor a complete denial of citizenship from Nuremberg-type legislation. The National Democrats, who favored restrictive measures against Jews, always had opposition from the parties on the left, including the Socialists, Communists, and liberals, who as a whole were not supportive of any of the anti-Jewish policies. And no native Fascist party emerged in Poland as it did in Hungary and Rumania.

On the eve of World War II, both Jews and Christians in Poland were struggling through a Depression and toiling in an economy too long on agriculture and too short on industry and trade. The government was mired in a discriminatory and ineffective policy, which was doing nothing to change the underlying structure of the Polish economy or improve its productivity. Government-inspired anti-Semitism was not succeeding in driving the Jews out of an economy to which they contributed heavily but was instead succeeding in handicapping the Polish economy so that all suffered. Political extremism was growing as conditions worsened during the Depression of the 1930s and as the Nazis embarked on a propaganda campaign to soften Poland for their assault.

Amid all this, Jews and Christians continued their traditional pursuits, soon to be overshadowed and, ultimately, eclipsed by the Nazi invasion. Terror, dehumanization, and murder unlike anything either Christian or Jew had ever known before was to descend upon the land and profoundly change the lives of those people who would ultimately come to Pittsburgh.

2

Between Swastika and Sickle

ON SEPTEMBER 1, 1939, THE GER-
man army invaded Poland. "They attacked from the
air; there were so many planes, you couldn't even see the sky. I
just couldn't believe how they had built so many planes. We
kept retreating as they bombed; we lost our horses; we didn't
have any ammunition, so we attacked with bayonets. We retreated back to Warsaw, with no food or water. On September
27th the [Polish] army surrendered. The Germans told us that
any soldier who wanted to could go home. I didn't believe them,
but I had no choice. As soon as we gave up our rifles, they put us
on trains, seventy-five men in a boxcar, locked us up for three
days and three nights, and when they finally opened the car, we
were POWs [prisoners of war] in Germany."

These were the words of Francinski D., who had been in the
cavalry up close to the German-Polish border in anticipation of a
German attack. To him and many others like him, the German
invasion was indeed a blitzkrieg. Warsaw fell on September 28,
but some Polish units continued to resist until October 5. In just
a few weeks, disaster had befallen the Poles. Once again their
country was overrun, their independence crushed by a foreign
invader.

The conflagration that the Germans had unleashed was not
merely to be a conventional war of territorial aggrandizement.
Hans Frank, appointed by Hitler to head what became known as
the Generalgovernment, which encompassed the bulk of Polish

territory, made his intention clear "to exploit them [the con-quered Polish territories] ruthlessly as a frontline region and war prize; to turn their economic, social, cultural, and political structure into, so to speak, a heap of rubble."[1] By the end of 1939, Frank, who was later sentenced to death at the Nuremberg War Trials for his crimes against humanity, had imposed a forced labor obligation on all Christian Poles fourteen years of age and older.

Janina W., who lived in a village near Lodz, recounted how she was taken out of school along with the other fourteen-year-old girls and thrown onto a truck to work at an ammunition factory. Another fourteen-year-old, Henrietta P., whose father owned two grocery stores in Lodz, was picked up along with 200 other girls and women in 1940 and deported to Germany. Her parents did not learn of her whereabouts for two months, until she was able to write home.

Joseph G. was taken in 1941 to work on a farm near Hamburg. He escaped back to Poland, but in February 1942 he was drafted into the German army, and by the middle of May found himself on the front line in Russia, pushing on toward Stalingrad. In order to get away from the slaughter, Joseph shot himself in the hand on two separate occasions, making up a story each time so that he would not be shot for desertion. He managed to survive the war, marry an American who had responded to his ad for a war bride, resettle in the Pittsburgh area, and write his memoirs.

Poles could be seized at any time by the Nazis and sent to forced labor in Germany or within the Generalgovernment. By the end of 1943 the percentage of Poles working as slave laborers in the Reich was higher than that of any other country. All told, during the war years 2.5 million Poles were deported to Germany as slave laborers. Nearly one-third of the Christians interviewed in Pittsburgh were victims of the German forced labor policy. Some were conscripted very early in the war, particularly from the western areas of Poland.

Generally, work conditions in Germany were poor but not life threatening. There was communication with relatives back in Poland through the mail, and there was the occasional opportunity to meet on Sundays with other Poles working in the area. The Poles were often permitted to go to church. While food rations were meager, there was usually some possiblity of getting packages from home. And the Christian Poles since they often worked on farms, were able to obtain enough to eat. As one of the forced laborers commented, "we were always hungry, but we weren't starving." Some tried to escape, but others felt that it would be more dangerous for them to be hunted by the Gestapo in Poland than remain where they were. Most of the Poles forced to work for the Germans felt that the Allied bombing of Germany endangered their lives far more than their working conditions.

The plight of the Jews was in every sense as harrowing as that of the Christians and beginning in 1940 was to become even more so. In addition to the sufferings caused by expulsions, forced labor seizures (which could begin for Jews at age twelve), Nazi terror, and indiscriminate sadism, further havoc and disruption was caused among the Jewish population by orders to establish ghettos throughout Polish territory. Beginning in late 1939 and continuing throughout 1940, the Jews of Poland were encased in sealed ghettos within towns and cities.

Many Jews who later came to Pittsburgh had experienced the horrors of the Nazi ghetto in Poland. One was Rabbi Mordechai Glatstein, who had fled to Warsaw from the western city of Lipno in 1939 and found himself a prisoner within the city walls by November 1940, along with a half million other Jews. By pretending to be an ordinary blacksmith, he managed to avoid the Nazi brutality that was particularly directed against orthodox laymen and religious leaders. In April 1942, after two years of daily struggle and just three months before the deportation in July of the majority of the population to the Treblinka death camp, Glatstein was asked during a secret meeting whether the Jews should attempt an uprising against the Nazis. "The young people wanted to have one, but the rabbis had to weigh whether it was permissible, because we knew we would die—and our tradition tells us we shouldn't give up hope." Glatstein himself wanted to fight "like Samson who wanted to die fighting against the Philistines," but the decision was made against a revolt at that time for fear that everybody would be killed. A year later, in April 1943, when young people were the only ones remaining in the ghetto and death was seen as inevitable, the decision was made to fight in what was to become known as the Warsaw ghetto uprising. Glatstein was captured at that time, survived both a selection in Auschwitz and a death march to and from Dachau, and was liberated by the Americans just before he and a number of others were to be blown up by a dynamite charge set by the Nazis in a cave in the Tyrol Mountains.

Rose Turbiner was also trapped in the Warsaw ghetto. She had lived for one year in a bunker prior to the uprising of the ghetto in April 1943. In May of that year, she and her family were sent to Maidanek. They were immediately separated, and she never saw her mother, father, and three brothers again. She and her sister were in the camp less than a year before being sent to Auschwitz, where her sister died.

The beginning of Operation Barbarossa (the invasion of Russia by the Germans) was to mark the start of an even more deadly policy against Polish Jews. Poland had been partitioned between the Soviets and the Nazis ever since September 17, 1939, when the Soviets had marched in to claim their half of the country according to the terms of the secret Molotov-Ribbentrop Pact of August 1939. With the Nazi surprise attack on Soviet-occupied Poland on June 22, 1941, the Germans now embarked on "the Final Solution," the plan to murder all the Jews of Europe. Within six months, the Einsatzgruppen, which were SS killing squads, gunned down an estimated 500,000 Jews.

Dora Iwler of Pittsburgh had been living in Chodorow in eastern Galicia. Under the Soviet occupation, her father's fruit store had been appropriated, but when the Germans came into the town in the fall of 1941, "they killed people just to kill them. My sister was killed right then. My mother was taken away, and my father and two brothers hid and later joined the partisans, but I never saw them again. We buried my sister with a bottle with her name in it."

Dora escaped a second roundup of Jews and decided to pose as a so-called Aryan, because she was blond. She escaped with the help of a Ukrainian neighbor. For two years she lived with another Ukrainian family, constantly fearful that they would discover her real identity. In 1944 she was caught after being pointed out by an old Christian classmate, taken to a Polish jail, and threatened with death. "It was a moment in my life when I didn't care. I said, 'I'm glad you are going to have me on your conscience.' The Nazi hit me so hard on the ear, I didn't hear for three days."

She was eventually taken to the Janowska slave labor camp near Lvov, miraculously escaped, went from village to village as a Christian, and was able to stay with a farmer and his family until the end of the war, never revealing her Jewish identity to him.

Thelma Zimmett lives in McKeesport now (her husband died in 1985) but over forty years ago, as a newly married couple, she and her husband were living in Soviet-occupied Poland. When the Germans invaded, the couple was sent to the camp at Zaslaw. Somehow, they were able to learn that the Germans were planning to massacre the Jews at the camp, and they made their escape. For the next two years the young couple lived in the woods, cajoling or threatening farmers for food, wielding a stick that had been rubbed with coal to make it look like a rifle. During their ordeal, Thelma developed frostbite on her toes. Her doctor husband was forced to cut them off, using a crude knife and wooden instrument. Her nightgown served as gauze. Today, her foot looks as if the operation might have been performed in a hospital instead of in the dark cold of a Polish forest.

Gusta Relis was forced from her small village into the ghetto of Podhajce. On June 6, 1943, the ghetto was liquidated. As the Germans were marching the Jews to the outskirts of town, her mother pleaded with her to try to escape through a nearby side street. In a desperate effort, the twenty-two-year-old girl was able to elude the Germans and go into hiding with the aid of Polish neighbors. The rest of the Jews, including her mother, were shot and dumped into a mass grave on the edge of town. "The earth moved for three days because many in the grave were not yet dead."

Ruth Weitz and Fela Morgenstern both were living in Lvov. Fela, a student at the time, remembered how exams were scheduled for June 22 (the date of the German invasion of Soviet-occupied Russia). "That's how ignorant and unprepared they were for any German attack. Right away, the Nazis separated Jews and non-Jews waiting on food lines, so we got less or none at all. By 1942 it was very bad for Jews. My father got me a *Kenncard* so I could be identified as an Aryan and escape from the ghetto. The last thing he said to me before I got out was for me to remember that I was a Jewish girl. I never saw him again."

Ruth Weitz was warned by a German soldier about what was going to happen to her and her family. He told her to tell her father to sell what he could in order to have cash in the ghetto. They were taken to a work camp to help lay asphalt on a road. "We were numb. People were killed every day and night and nothing bothered anyone anymore. I saw my parents and brother shot. My sister was shot in the woods. A German asked me, 'Why aren't you screaming? Why don't you care about whether you get shot or not?' 'Because, if you shoot me today,' I said, 'tomorrow I will not suffer.' " In 1943 with about 100 others and with help from the Polish underground she escaped and lived with the partisans until her liberation by the Russians.

One Christian refugee recalled the agony of the Jews in eastern Poland in the aftermath of the Nazi invasion. Jan P. worked in the town of Lutowiska, which was near his hometown of Polana in east Galicia, the same town that the Zimmetts were from. "There were many Jewish merchants in the town, and there was good relations, although right before the war there was propaganda to hate the Jews. The Germans marked all the Jewish homes. Later they shot all the Jews from the town and put them in a mass grave even if they were still alive. They threw babies up in the air and shot them! When two Jewish brothers escaped, my mother hid them for two weeks. But she was scared that if she was caught, we would all be killed. Another neighbor hid them for a month, but a Ukrainian found them and turned them over to the Germans. I had to bury them. . . . There was much sympathy. People used to say that they started with the Jews, but they're going to finish with the Catholics."

In January 1942, at the Wannsee conference held in a suburb of Berlin, Nazi brass, including Hans Frank, drew up plans for implementing the Final Solution on orders from Hitler. It had become clear that the methods used by the Einsatzgruppen to kill 1.4 million people in Poland were insufficient to kill the millions of Jews throughout Europe who were marked for death. While the Jews caught by the Einsatzgruppen were the first to die en masse, the 1.2 million Jews of the Generalgovernment in addition to the 1.8 million brought into the area from towns and cities all over Europe were soon to be confronted with the horrible efficiency of the Nazi gas chamber, a facility that, using the latest developments in science, could kill as many as one thousand people at a time in a matter of minutes. In December 1941 the first gas chamber began operation at Chelmno in Poland. By mid-1942 the death centers of Treblinka, Sobibor, Maidanek, Auschwitz, and Belzec, in addition to Chelmno, were in full operation. Four of these camps— Treblinka, Sobibor, Chelmo, and Belzec—were solely for Jews, who were gassed as soon as they arrived.

While the Jews from the ghettos in the western areas of Poland were the first victims of the gas chambers, by February 1942 the gassing of the Jews of the Generalgovernment had begun. Tarnow and Radom were the first cities to be targeted.

Julius Aussenberg was living in the ghetto of Tarnow. In 1942 his mother was shot, while he was taken along with other able-bodied men to the labor camp of Szebnie. "When I came there it was horrible. There was random shooting, hanging for anything, just massacres." In the late fall of 1943 he was shipped to Auschwitz. "The older inmates pointed to the smokestacks and told me that's where I was going. I worked outside the Buna rubber factory run by I. G. Farben until I got sick with boils and was taken to the hospital, which was really the way to the gas chambers. I was a *musselman* by then—a zombie, more dead than alive."

A Polish Christian friend of Aussenberg's saved his life by bringing him food and clothing and recommending him to the care of a Polish doctor at Buna. The doctor, in turn, did indeed save Aussenberg by making him a male nurse so he could get better provisions. However, in late 1944 Aussenberg was marched out of Auschwitz to Gleiwitz, taken by train to Buchenwald, and then later forced on a death march from that camp in the spring of 1945. He decided on an escape attempt.

"I don't know where I got the strength. I had the sense to run zig-zag. I just kept running until we just dropped down on the wet ground. We covered ourselves with branches, and in the morning I got up, grabbed my friend, and gave him a little pep talk that we are almost like free men! Soon afterward we were liberated by the Americans at Halberstadt."

The mother of Harry and William Friedman was in charge of an orphanage in the ghetto at Radom. When she was warned by a kindly SS captain that deportation was imminent, she refused to leave the children. Her husband refused to leave her. The couple and their thirty-six charges were taken out of the ghetto in August 1942 and never seen again.[2]

Harry Feldman was married, with two children. For one year he lived and worked in the ghetto in Crakow. When his second child was born in the ghetto, a Polish woman exchanged her dead newborn for the Feldmans' child. In 1942 Harry, his wife, and older son were taken to Auschwitz. They were held at the entrance to the camp for three days without water waiting to get in, but the camp was filled and they were finally taken to Maidanek. His wife was taken off the train and immediately gassed. "I saw the smoke from the crematorium with my own eyes." His son was fortunate; he was taken by the Red Cross in a deal with the Germans to exchange children for medicine. Harry himself was beaten unconscious when he tried to get some food from a garbage can. "I was a half-face." Ironically, he was saved by the father of another man who was to survive and come to Pittsburgh. Michell Borke's father had been a prominent surgeon before the war. Despite a prohibition on helping Jews, he was able to save Harry before his own death in 1943 at the Maidanek camp.

Harry was later able to escape from a truck outside Maidanek and in 1943 joined a partisan unit made up of Russians, Ukrainians, Jews, and Poles. They were directed by the Polish underground and supplied by English parachute drops. On one mission, he was captured by the Nazis and bound with his hands behind his back awaiting execution. Just before he was to be shot, his buddies attacked with hand grenades and automatic weapons. Afterward he complained to them that they nearly had come too late! When the war was over, Harry returned to Crakow to see what happened to the Jewish girl he had loved, but had not married because of her father's opposition. A strange man was living in his former girlfriend's apartment and showed him the wall against which her whole family had been lined up and shot. The bloodstains were still there. "I pricked my finger and mingled my blood with hers," he mournfully recalled. "But if I had married her, I would have been shot too." After the war, Harry was able to retrieve both his children. Given the odds against Jewish children surviving, he was a very fortunate man. "Everything was a miracle," he sighed.

Jack Sittsamer lived in Mielec, the town where thirty-six Jews were burned in the slaughterhouse in the early days of the

Blitzkreig. His father was killed in the first selection of Jews in 1942. In the second selection, Jack was sent to work at the airplane factory in town. He lived in the barracks just inside the compound and risked his life continually to steal potatoes from the field outside. He contracted typhoid and was saved by a Jewish supervisor, who hid him for one month. In July 1944 he too was sent to Auschwitz, but "they wouldn't let us in." He was finally marched five miles uphill to Flossenberg. "German civilians were spitting at us and making fun of us. It was like a party for them." He was later shipped to Leitmeritz and then to Gussen II near Linz, Austria, outside of Mauthausen. On May 5, 1945, it was overrun by the Americans. "I don't think if they would have come five days later, I would have made it. I had given up. . . . I was just too weak."

The memories of the final days in the ghettos and the mass gassing of millions are seared not only into the minds of Jews but into the minds of some Christians as well. Joanna G. had been expelled to Tosie, a small town east of Warsaw and right next to Treblinka. She recalled the day when the Jews were taken out of Tosie to be marched into the ghetto at Warsaw. Over 200 people were shot, and she saw a German smash a Jewish baby against a wall and shoot the mother. In 1942 when Treblinka B, the special gassing facility, was built, she heard the train whistles of the cattle cars transporting the Jews into the camp. She could hear the screaming of the people as they were unloaded and she could smell the odor from the crematorium. "Sometimes, the stench was so bad I couldn't go out. I drove with a Polish farmer one day past the camp and saw mounds of clothes piled up. Many people hid Jews because we all lived together; we were friends. I used to make moonshine in order to cope with what was happening. To this day I still wake up with nightmares and hear the sirens of the incoming trains."

Stanley K. worked in a bakery right next to the marketplace in Miezyrzec in 1942. On the eve of the war, the town had 12,000 Jewish inhabitants, representing 75 percent of the population. In 1942 when these Jews met their abrupt end, Stanley was an eyewitness. He saw the Jews being marched all day long through the marketplace and then separated to the right and to the left. His vantage point was a secret window that was painted on the outside. "A man tried to run into our yard, but we heard gun shots, and he fell dead. They marched the old people till they were exhausted, and then they shot them. Jews always tried to escape, but they were shot. They took my father's wagon to carry the bodies."

By the spring of 1943 approximately 2.7 million of the 3.3 million Jews of Poland were dead. Those Jews still alive in Poland were either in concentration camps, in hiding, or had been able to join partisan units. Only two ghettos remained—Bialystok and Lodz. However, in August 1943 the Bialystok ghetto was destroyed and the Jews murdered. Lodz remained with its remnant of 69,000 Jews until early 1944. Because of this, it is not at all surprising that eight Jews in the Pittsburgh group were from Lodz. The people in Lodz had a better chance of surviving precisely because they were able to remain in the city longer than other Jews, who had long since been taken to death camps or slave labor facilities.

Aron Goldman was one of those future Pittsburghers from Lodz. He was able to stay in his home as the ghetto was formed around him. He worked with his father, who was a skilled tinsmith employed by the German government, and shared his rations with his mother and two younger brothers. He remembered hangings in the street, raids, and the synagogues being burned when the Germans occupied the city. "There were two beautiful synagogues which were ten stories high with gold-embroidered stained-glass windows." Later he and others used to smuggle the wood from the destroyed synagogues in order to have some fuel. "I remember when they emptied the hospitals and the Germans threw the patients from the sixth and seventh floors. My father had a German friend who warned him to get out, but where were we going to go? My father was beaten by the

Gestapo and was incapacitated for three months. In 1943 people were dying in the streets like flies. We used to kill dogs and eat them."

Aron and his brother were eventually sent to Auschwitz. In one selection, the two boys were directed to the right while their parents were sent to the left. Aron was in Auschwitz for six weeks and then was transported to Gerlitz, Germany, to make ammunition. When the Russians were approaching, they were forced on a three-week death march. Of the 1,200 who started the march, only fifty lived to see their day of liberation—on May 7, 1945. Aron's brother, Melvin, who also had been at Auschwitz, was able to hide in the toilets when the Jews were being marched out. A German Communist who had been involved with the resistance at Auschwitz succeeded in placing him on a transport to Braunschweig. From there, he was transferred to Ravensbruck. "I had no food for four days. When the Americans of the eighty-second Airborn Division came in, I was given thirty pints of blood. I was 90 percent dead."

Henry Mangurten, from Lodz, was nine years old in 1939. He worked as a helper in a steel-fabricating plant in the city, assisting Arnold Zweig, a Jew a few years his senior, who also survived the war and coincidentally also wound up in Pittsburgh. Henry was taken out of the ghetto in 1942 when the Nazis were weeding out the young and the old from the population. Somehow, he was able to escape and get back home.

"It was a miracle. . . . There wasn't a soul on the streets except the people hanging in the gallows." The young boy was later shipped to Auschwitz on one of the last transports out of the city. He survived the selection conducted by Dr. Mengele and remained in Auschwitz two months before being taken to Katowice to work in a coal mine. In the winter of 1945 he was sent to Mauthausen, Austria, where he dug tunnels. He was saved by a German commander, who gave him kitchen duty instead of the exhausting outdoors work, where "people were dying all around." With Allied planes overhead, he was taken from Mauthausen to a camp where they had virtually nothing to eat. "People were eating people."

While Henry was fighting to survive, so too was Arnold Zweig, the man he had worked with in Lodz. Arnold had seen his father beaten to death on the streets in Lodz. Later he was to be separated from his mother when they were taken to Auschwitz on the last transport to leave the ghetto in September 1944. They had been told by the Germans that they were going to a village to work, the same village he had been taken to three weeks before to deceive them (he realized later), so that there would be no resistance to this final deportation. From Auschwitz, where there was no room for them in these final months, he wound up in Gross Rosen, and then in the Friedland camp in the Sudentenland. He was spared a death march because the German commander of the camp had a girlfriend in the village and simply did not want to leave her. He dallied so long that the Soviets were able to overrun the camp, and Arnold was saved.

In the Lodz ghetto, Morris Manela had opened a small shop to make leather knapsacks. He was able to supplement the starvation rations of his family by stealing some potatoes every night from a field in the ghetto belonging to Chaim Rumkowski, the head of the *Judenrat,* or Jewish Council. "If I had been caught, I'd be dead, but who cared? The ones who were scared, they're dead already a long time." In April 1943 his mother, father, four brothers, and five of his six sisters were taken away, never to be seen again. In 1944 he was taken to Auschwitz, where he lost his only remaining sister. "If you sit here for a million years and write what I tell you, there will not be enough time or ink to write what the Germans did to us."

Morris was soon sent to Dachau and in the beginning of 1945 was forced on a death march with ten to fifteen thousand others. Their destination was the Tyrol Mountains where according to Morris, "they were supposed to shoot us all." While walking, he sneaked out of line and ran to a German home. The family threatened to call the police, but he counterthreatened, telling them that "if the Americans come first, I'll get you." His argument prevailed, and he survived to tell the story. (He died in 1986.)

Nazi Europe had been blanketed by a vast network of concentration camps and their dozens of subsidiaries. Many of these camps beggared description. Some were more notorious than others. One such camp was Plaszow, outside of Crakow. Arriving there along different paths, all strewn with human wreckage, were seven of the refugees interviewed in Pittsburgh, six Jews and one Christian.

Estelle Forstenzer came from a very wealthy Jewish family in Poland. Her father had owned a big flour- and sawmill outside Rzeszow. Before the war she had hoped to be a pharmacist, but her plans were to change dramatically with the German invasion. The Germans took over her parents' estate and forced the family into the ghetto at Rzeszow. In 1941 her mother, father, and two older sisters were sent on a train out of the ghetto (she learned later it was a death train) and she was sent to the Plaszow slave labor camp. She worked in a stable and slept in a barracks. She recalled how the favorite sport of the camp commander was to ride his horse and shoot people as he passed by. For one year she survived in the camp before being transported to work at an ammunition factory in Skarzysko-Kamienna, where continued explosions took many lives. Finally liberated at a subsidiary of the Buchenwald camp she was "just barely alive."

Norman Infeld's father owned a big liquor distillery in Crakow. When the German came in, the Infelds were forced to become employees of a Polish Christian salesman of German descent, whom the Germans made head of the factory. In 1942 this arrangement came to an end when Norman was forced into the designated ghetto area of the city. He was able to get a "good" job cleaning the streets, but when the ghetto was liquidated, he too was taken to Plaszow. He was there one year, making brushes. From there he went to Mielec, to Flossenberg, and finally to Dachau. On a death march from Dachau he was able to escape. "How I survived, I have no idea. There were tanks shooting at me. I ran with two other guys. I don't know what happened to them."

Mark Stern was also touched by the concentration camp of Plaszow, as was Moshe Taube, who as fate would have it was to wind up working in Pittsburgh in the same establishment as Mark. Moshe, who had fled to the Soviet-occupied side when the war broke out, had returned to Crakow five months later in a fateful move. In October 1942 his mother and sister were taken to the death camp at Belzec, and in March 1943 he and his father were transported to Plaszow. His work consisted of "schlepping boards and stones." Moshe was to be one of those Jews on "Schindler's list." Schindler was a German business-man who saved 1,200 Jews by insisting that they were needed in his factory. With the Russian advance, he was able to move his factory to Brunnlitz in the Sudentenland and was permitted to take "his Jews" with him rather than liquidate them, as the Nazis were doing elsewhere.[3]

While the worst camps and the worst conditions in those camps were generally reserved for the Jews as a group, individ-ual Christians like John D. were inmates and victims of some of the infamous concentration camps, as well. John was an inmate at Plaszow. He had been arrested in the winter of 1942 because of his underground activities. He was first taken to a small prison near Gestapo headquarters "where they beat the hell out of me for a week," and then he was sent to Plaszow. His job was to collect the bodies of the people who had died during the night. He too recalled the feared commander of the camp, who shot people for sport. John was there six months before being trans-ferred to a camp near Stuttgart, where he drove a truck. Because of his knowledge of the terrain, he was able to escape during an Allied bombing raid and cross the border into Switzerland, where he contacted some Jewish businessmen to help him and his two friends get tickets to Zurich. From there they were smuggled by the French underground to Marseilles and then

onto a small fishing vessel to Italy. He joined the Second Corps
of the Polish army under General Wladyslaw Anders and was in
training to fight the Germans when the war ended.

Maria S. was arrested on September 24, 1940, for helping
Polish prisoners of war escape to Hungary from her town of
Gorlice in southern Poland. At the time she was a twenty-six-
year-old grade school teacher. For a number of months she was
kept in solitary confinement at Jaslo and then taken to Tarnow.
In 1941 she was transferred to Ravensbruck, a woman's camp in
Germany. Maria recalled how in the beginning it was "all right"
for her but that later it was to get "worse and worse and worse
and worse." She had to help build a road. "If you rested, you
were attacked by dogs." She frequently saw Hermione Braunsteiner Ryan, the first naturalized American deported for sus-
pected war crimes. Stealing extra food was never called stealing;
it was called "organizing." She and some others had been able to
receive food packages from Polish families and shared them with
some Jewish girls who were kept in a separate block and "who
were really in bad shape." They also started an underground
school for the teenagers in the camp.

Maria was used in a medical experiment. The Nazi doctors
injected some bacteria into her arm that caused a swelling in the
back of her head. At one point, she was placed in solitary
confinement for weeks with just water, cabbage soup, and one
piece of bread a week. When she was released, she was so sick
that she felt she would have died had it not been for the efforts of
a Polish doctor. When she recovered, she was taken to Bergen
Belsen.

Night and day I saw processions of people dragging bodies, bodies
that often didn't have any more big rear muscle on them, because it
had been put in the fire and eaten. . . . Everything smelled. . . . I
had to help dig the graves. If you fell in, you stayed there. I never
gave up hope or lost my faith in God and the future. I never lost my
belief that there was a spirit among Poles, that I was part of, for

God first and then country. Each generation has its own struggle—
to make freedom, to make our own country. We survived because
we never said "me." We tried to help one another.

Helena B. also was sent to Ravensbruck but did not come to
know Maria until after the war in Pittsburgh. She had been part
of the Polish intellegentsia before the war and had survived the
Nazi scourge against the Polish elite by escaping to Rumania.
Along with her child, she lived with wives of Polish officials on
the Adriatic coast of Yugoslavia and under Italian protection
until the Germans invaded the area in 1944. She was separated
from her son and then taken by cattle car to a prison at
Klagenfurt and then to the Ravensbruck concentration camp for
fifteen months.

I was determined to go out through the gate and not through the
chimney. I ran from one block to another to escape selections. I
knew what I had to do. I worked outside leveling ground for houses
for the SS. I smeared my eyes with salt to show that I had to go to
the doctor. After that I was sent to peel potatoes for twelve hours a
day in a cellar filled with water. I got rheumatism in my hands and
knees and had crusts on my hands, which were double their size.

On May 1, 1945, Helena, along with an estimated 4,000 other
Polish women, was taken to Sweden as part of an agreement
worked out by the Red Cross. After the war she was reunited
with her child and her husband, who had been a prisoner of war.

Father Marcel P. was one of the thousands of Polish priests
who was arrested by the Nazis, but he was not arrested until
August 1944. As a chaplain in the Polish underground army, he
had managed to shelter two Jews in his Franciscan monastery
until 1943, when the Germans occupied the monastery and the
Jews had to hide elsewhere. When he was finally seized, he was
kept one month in a Crakow prison and then sent to a camp at
Flossenberg in eastern Bavaria, near Czechoslovakia. "The youn-

ger guards were the worst, because they had been taught to hate any other group. The older ones were still influenced by a Christian education."

He was the only priest there and worked digging stones and carrying them to help build a road. "Our treatment was as bad as the Jews'. There were only some Hungarian Jews left; all the others had died already." Through the efforts of a Polish foreman, Father Marcel was transferred indoors, out of the bone-chilling cold, to do record keeping. On Christmas Eve he was transferred to Dachau and, because of a typhus epidemic, was again able to stay indoors, this time as a tailor. He was liberated in April 1945 only a few hours before he and others fully expected to be executed on orders from Berlin.

On September 17, 1939, less than three weeks after the Germans invaded Poland, the Russians marched in for their share of the Polish spoils, according to the secret clauses of the Molotov-Ribbentrop Pact which had been concluded in August. The Soviets claimed they were coming as "liberators," but their real mission soon became apparent enough. For Polish army personnel desperately trying to avoid falling into German hands as the front collapsed around them, capture by the Russians was as perilous, if not even more perilous, than being taken prisoner by the Germans.

Marion K., who now lives in Springfield, Pennsylvania, outside of Pittsburgh, was in the Polish army in 1939. His unit was overrun by German tanks in the vicinity of Przemysl, and he was captured on September 8. He escaped from the Germans by jumping from a freight car, but only a week later, after fleeing to Lvov, he was captured by the Russians.

As usual, the Russians were sneaky and lousy. They shook hands with us and told us they were going to take care of Germany; that we should lay our weapons down. What could we do? I thought maybe they would help us, but my buddy knew them better and warned me that we will never see our home again. They loaded us into freight cars so we were packed like sardines. As soon as we were loaded, their attitude changed and they started to curse us. The locomotive was turned from west to east, and there was nothing we could do.

In May 1940 Marion was packed into a boxcar for three weeks en route to Siberia. He passed through the town of Kotlas and on to Vorkuta, the notorious slave labor camp above the Artic Circle. There he labored building a railroad, while all around him people were "dying like flies."

Stanyslaw P., who at age nineteen had formed a student infantry batallion against the Germans, escaped into the forest around Lvov in order to become a partisan. But instead of the Germans, he met up with the Russians and was taken prisoner on November 19, 1939. He was put into an old army prison in Lvov and tortured over a ten-month period. "It's amazing how much the human body can take." He continued:

We were mixed with hardened criminals, as was the Russian practice, and given salted herrings to eat with no water. I developed dysentery. Finally, I was given a mock trial and sentenced to death. For six weeks I was there all by myself. I heard executions going on daily. The way I kept my sanity was to play with a mouse and give it some crumbs. I don't know why they wanted to execute me. I was only a platoon leader, but maybe because I was one of the oldest in our group. When the door opened and they came for me, I felt a sense of relief. At least the waiting was over. But they wanted me only to sign a paper to thank Stalin for coming to Poland's aid and ask forgiveness for our sins. When I refused, I was taken back to my cell, beaten again, but not too badly this time. Two days later my sentence was changed to ten years at hard labor.

In a few weeks we were loaded onto cattle cars and taken close to the Chinese border in Manchuria. Many died, because you could suffocate on the trains. Sometimes we had no water for four to five days. The youngest and the oldest went first. Then we were sent back through the Ural Mountains through Kharkov and then north to Onega Lake in Archangelsk Province in September 1940. Only 10 percent of the 2,500 prisoners or so were Polish. There were people from all over Russia. We went on barges across the lake and then marched another 350 kilometers north across the tundra. We had to build our own shelter. Soup was made of fish heads. We ate floating fish eyes like candy. Our labor camp was seven miles from the White Sea in the direction of Murmansk. For over a year we lived there, laying rail lines. In September 1941 I was released with a loaf of bread and told to go. When I finally was able to get near Kuibyshev where the Polish units were being formed and saw some guys in Polish uniforms, I had tears in my eyes. We were crying and kissing one another like idiots.

In 1939 Janusz K. was nineteen years old and going to architectural school in Lvov. When the war started, he joined the Polish underground army, like many other high school and university students. Their purpose was to try to get people out of Poland to join the army in France. In November 1939 Janusz himself was ordered to get through Hungary to France, but he was caught by the Russians when he stayed behind with a buddy who was wounded near the border. Like Stanyslaw P., he was taken to prison in Lvov. His family learned of his whereabouts only when his father discovered their family dog sitting outside the prison. When Janusz was taken further into the Ukraine, his faithful dog disappeared. Janusz was given a sentence of eight years in labor camps for his "anti-State, counterrevolutionary activity," according to the fifty-eighth paragraph of the Communist criminal code. In September 1940, after his request for a trial had been denied, he was shipped to Ubieska Province to work as a lumberjack. He was released a year later because of the amnesty for all Poles in Russia after the Germans violated the nonaggression pact and Poland and Russia found themselves fighting the common Nazi enemy. At the time, he weighed just ninety-six pounds; he learned that he had lost his father and grandmother from starvation after they had been deported to Uzbekistan in Russia.

Joseph P. had retreated under Polish army orders in a private car to eastern Poland in order to regroup against the Germans. When the Soviets advanced, he was still in his uniform as a second lieutenant.

When they came on the seventeenth, they came in like locusts. Everybody was on their own. I threw away my uniform and got into civilian dress. Instead of trying to get to Warsaw, we decided to head south to Lvov and then across to Hungary. We were a quarter mile from the Hungarian border when the Russians yelled halt. We ran. There were bullets all around. The dogs caught me, and we were beaten with pistols. They thought I was the biggest spy because nobody runs away from machine guns like I did!

Like the others, Joseph was interrogated in Lvov, sent into the Ukraine, and in September 1940 was shipped to Kotlas, a huge transit camp in Siberia holding some 15,000 to 25,000 people. From there he was taken to the Dvina River, transported on barges, then in trucks, and finally on foot, until he was unloaded in a field. "They stuck some poles in the ground and told us, 'You will work here and you will die here.' My job was to lay railroad bedding on swamps. In two months, out of 420, only 180 were left alive." Joseph was later taken to Vorkuta where he, like Marion K., was eventually released to join the Polish armed forces after the amnesty in 1941.

Like the Germans, the Soviets embarked on policies of expropriation and deportation during their occupation of Poland in the first year and a half of the war. Walter W. worked on the railroad in the small eastern Polish village of Karolwka.

When the Russians came in, they 'liberated' us from everything. We lost our rights. They took all kinds of property. We had to depend on whatever they gave us or whatever they said. You didn't even have the right to ask for anything. We had to wait before they would give us anything. I stayed on the farm with my parents. We were forced to go to a school organized by the Russians on Sunday. Every weekend, one person from the family had to be there. They used to say how good they were and how they were protecting us from the capitalists. I couldn't work on the railroad any more because they hired Asiatic people instead. We did have food from our farm—they took some, but not all. We couldn't slaughter an animal until we got permission. If you killed three pigs, you had to give one or two to the government. They controlled everything.

Viktor H. was one of the Polish professional people whom the Soviets (like the Germans) had targeted, but the Russian manner was to deport them into the vast expanses of the country rather than execute them immediately. Viktor was only twenty-three years old and had worked for just six months as a grade school teacher when the Russians invaded eastern Poland. He was jailed in November 1939 and then was sentenced, in the familiar pattern, to hard labor in Siberia for being a "dangerous element." He wound up in the Ural Mountains, where he estimated there were at least thirty labor camps. He worked as an electrician until his release in November 1941. On his way to join the Polish army, which was being formed, he searched for his parents, who had been deported in February 1940 to Siberia. After he found them, he traveled with them south to Uzbekistan. "Nobody knew where they were orginizing the Polish army. It was terrible, because in the transports people had typhoid and were dying. There were whole boxcars of dead people. My parents died in 1942 of typhoid and I was sick too. There was no medicine, nothing. I finally met a Russian who knew where the Polish camp was, and I arrived just in time in August 1942 to move out with them across the Caspian Sea to Pahlevi in Iran."

Marina, who was to marry Viktor H., was also caught under Soviet occupation. She was nineteen years old in 1939 and lived in the small town of Busk, in eastern Poland. Her father, who had worked as an intelligence agent for the Polish government in Russia and realized the danger he was in, still did not want to flee and leave his ailing wife behind. On April 11th he was arrested, and two days later, Marina and her mother were awakened by knocking at the door in the middle of the night. They were taken not to the north, but to Kustani Province in south central Russia to work on a collective farm. After the amnesty in 1941, her father found them, and they were able to follow the Polish army to Pahlevi, Iran. Marina later became a nurses's aid in the army and met her further husband in Italy. "He was the only one who was not fresh!" she laughed. They were married in July 1946 and five years later came to Pittsburgh.

Stanislawa S. and her father were arrested in the middle of the night. They both had been involved with the Polish underground, reporting on Russian movements and supplies near their home in Kosow, just ten miles from the Russian border. In the fall of 1940, they were sentenced to hard labor. Stanislawa was sent first to prison in Stanislawow and then transported to Karaganda, the slave labor camp in Kazakhstan, which—along with Vorkuta in the north—was notorious. Years later she remembered the fish eyes staring at her from the fish soup. She too was to suffer from a whole host of ills in Karaganda, including lice and open sores. After the amnesty in 1941, she traveled on her own to Tashkent to find the Polish army. She reported (as did all the other refugees) on the typhoid that was raging in this refugee area, with "people dying like flies." She acted as a nurse; at the end of the war she was with the Polish army in Italy. Her father had died in Russia of disease after being deported, and her mother, left alone at home, had been killed and multilated by the family's Ukrainian neighbors.

Fabian B. had been too old at age twenty-six to be drafted into the Polish army in 1939. He had dropped out of grade school after only four years in order to help his father on the farm and to earn money hauling logs for a lumber factory. He was living in a small village in eastern Poland under Russian occupation when, during the week between Christmas and New Year's in 1939, the Russians forced their way into his home at 1:30 in the morning and charged him with being a spy for the Nazis. His protest that he did not know how to either read or write was ignored, and he was taken to jail in Grodno. He stayed for seven months in a cell that was so crowded that "everybody had to turn together. There was no place to lie down." During his "routine questionings," his eardrum was broken. After seven months, he was forced to sign a statement and was given a five-year jail sentence. In October 1940 he too was loaded onto a boxcar traveling to the Archangelsk Province and to the Rusa River. From there he was sent to a labor camp. He volunteered to work in the kitchen (pretending to have been a chef in the Polish army for two years) in order to avoid laboring on a road to Alaska. They had been told that the USSR was planning to get back that territory from the United States as soon as the war was over. In September 1941 Fabian was released to join the large Polish army camp at Buzuluk. Unlike many other men who were given no provisions for the arduous journey south to join the Polish army being constituted under General Wladyslaw Anders, he was given a train ticket and a seven-day supply of food.

His wife-to-be Frances B., was at that time married to another man and had two children. Her husband, who was a police chief and feared for his life, had been smuggled across the Hungarian border along with some other army and police officers. He was eventually able to get through to Yugoslavia and on to France. He was killed, however, in January 1941 when his plane was shot down after he joined the British Air Force. Frances, who was alone with the children, was arrested on February 10 (the same day many others in the Pittsburgh group were arrested). After midnight, the Russians knocked with their rifles on the door to tell them they were being taken to Siberia. "The entire village was evacuated in twenty minutes. It was so cold, stormy. I'll never forget this moment. I didn't cry, because my husband told me when he left not to cry because 'the enemy wouldn't enjoy your tears.' The animals started to follow the wagons like it was a funeral and the dogs howled. The Communists couldn't take all the noise, so they shot the dogs. When I crossed myself, a Russian said 'there is no God, because he wouldn't let this happen.' "

The Jewish refugees had a somewhat different pattern than the non-Jews in the group. Many of the Jews had deliberately chosen to flee to Soviet-occupied territory when Germany and the USSR had initially divided the country in 1939. Based on some sixth sense or some first-hand experience with the Nazis, Jews often fled—alone or with a small group of friends—believing that life under the Russians would somehow be better for them than under the Germans. The experience of Wolf Friede is typical. He was living in Pabianice, a small city near Lodz about thirty miles from the German border. When his father, along with other Poles, was taken away by the Nazis with only his prayer shawl, or *tallit*, the younger Friede decided to escape to Russian-occupied territory. For two weeks he survived in the fields outside of Bialystok, until he was allowed into the city by the Russians. Friede registed for labor, as all refugees were compelled to do if they wanted to remain in the area, and was sent to a town near Moscow. "We organized a strike to protest the working conditions. Other nationalities were there too. They thought we were crazy and begged us not to strike for fear we would all be killed. But somehow we got away with it. 'God takes care of fools,' it says in Psalms." Friede was sent to work in a textile factory and then in 1941 headed for Tashkent. The Russians wanted him to go into the Russian army, but he ran away. At the end of the war, Friede was able to take his Russian wife and return briefly to Poland before moving on.

Sally Melmed lived in Krasnik in central Poland. After one month of German occupation, her grandfather decided that she should try to get to Soviet-occupied territory with a group of young people who were planning to leave. Her father's comb factory had already been confiscated, and he had been taken away. People were afraid to go out on the street. Sally's grandfather believed that she, at age nineteen, might be the only one to survive the war.

(His premonition was to prove correct, as the entire family was to perish in Treblinka in 1942.) Sally made her way to Kowel, in Russia, where her father had some business associates. When the Soviets in late November 1939 declared their intention to have refugees register as Soviet citizens or return to German-occupied Poland, Sally registered and was sent to the forest of Archangelsk. She persuaded her boss that she could not be a lumberjack and was sent to school to learn Russian. After five months, she got an office job and was able to organize a group of twenty Poles to escape to Moscow. They were arrested, but escaped again. Sally told an incredible story of writing a letter to Stalin asking for payment of her tuition to medical school at Kharkov. For some reason (perhaps Stalin wanted to show Russia as the true "liberator" of the Polish people or to make a special gesture to a Jew to gain their acceptance), she not only got a response from Stalin but got the scholarship as well. When the Germans attacked, the university was evacuated to Olmsk, where she lived until 1945. "I was not singled out as Jew. We lived among the Russians. It was bad for everybody." With the cold, the hunger, and the suspicion abut the fate of her family trapped under the Nazis, she could not continue. But she did marry, have a child, and was later evacuated to Poland after the war, weighing just ninety-five pounds.

Isaac Greenberg was a young tailor living in Warsaw in September 1939. In October he escaped to the Russian side, along with tens of thousands of other Jewish men who left Warsaw and Lodz. However, he went back to Warsaw to get his family to come with him. He brought out seventeen people, but his own kin refused to leave, fearing life in Russia. He was to make yet another trip across the Bug River, which divided the German and Russian zones, saving the lives of two young Jewish boys who were about to be shot at the border for having lied about the money they were carrying. Today, those boys and the others he saved are still alive, while Greenberg's own family perished at Treblinka.

While hundreds of thousands crossed back and forth over

the border separating the German and Russian forces in Poland in the frantic opening weeks of the war, by October 30, 1939, the borders were officially closed. After that time, border crossing meant risking one's life, although Jews continued to attempt to cross into Russian territory right down to the outbreak of the German offensive against Russia in June 1941. The story of David Guss illustrates the danger. David was working in a barber shop near the Bug River in Chelm. A friend of his brother's with an SS uniform on came in to warn him to escape to Soviet territory because "all Jews would be shot. We thought he was joking, but he knew what he was talking about. When Jews were rounded up and shot at random in October, I escaped and hid for a week in the basement of a Polish friend. When the SS came looking for me, my friend's mother said that I was her son. But after she learned that she would be killed if the Germans found out she was hiding a Jew, she asked me to leave."

Another Polish friend helped David and his brother cross the border. As they were climbing out of the freezing cold river, they were caught by the Russians. The Gusses were taken to jail, accused of spying, given prison sentences of ten and twenty years, respectively, and sent to the Ural Mountains 2,000 miles north of Sverdlovsk, probably around the area of Vorkuta, where other Poles had been sent. A Russian girl befriended David, and he was able to change his job from cutting wood outdoors to cutting hair indoors. "She saved my life, because nobody survived there. The most you could take outdoors was six or seven weeks." He was released to join Ander's army in 1941 but found that

they were just taking older Polish Jews. If a Jew hadn't been in the army before, they didn't need you. I traveled from Tchkalow near Buzuluk to Tashkent and was caught trying to escape over the Iranian border at Ashkhabad. I was taken back eventually to Frunze, the capital of the Kirghiz Republic, where my luck still held because I met another woman who got me a job. I told her I would marry her, but when it was announced that every Polish citizen could return to Poland after the war, I changed my mind, even though I promised to bring her to Poland to get her to sign the papers to release me. If she had said no, they never would have let me go. She was a good woman, but when I left Russia in May 1946, that was the last time I saw her.

For Jews who had fled into Russian-occupied territory without provoking the Soviet authorities, the question that soon faced them was whether to accept Russian citizenship. In so doing they were being asked to read the future. What would happen to them if they accepted? What would happen if they said no? For those who refused to accept Russian citizenship, the consequences were both severe and immediate. Helen Birnbaum was one of the majority who said no to Russian citizenship. As a result, she was sent to Siberia, traveling for seven days to Archangelsk to the Bisholovitch camp. She worked there for fourteen months, until September 1941, when she was released along with other Poles. She and her brother were able to travel four weeks to Tashkent in the south central Asian republic of Uzbekistan, where many Poles were gathering . "The city was unbelievable. The crime was terrible. People would walk over to you in broad daylight and take whatever you had away and there was nothing you could do. . . . It was just open season for kids with knives." Helen did not move out with the Polish army evacuation and was to wind up on a collective farm, or *kolhoz*, near Chimkent, in Kazakhstan, where she along with the Russians starved until April 1946, when her mostly Jewish transport was sent back to Poland.

Mieczyslaw Borkowski (now known as Michell Borke) had attempted to join the Polish army in September 1939, but when the Russians entered Poland on the seventeenth, he gave up and decided to try to continue his medical studies. He went first to Bialystok and then to Lvov, which were both in Russian hands. Since his father was a prominent surgeon,[4] the Soviets refused to let him register, on the grounds that his father was a capitalist. He worked digging trenches in Lvov until he made what he thought was the decision to go back to German-occupied Poland rather than become a Russian citizen. However, instead of allowing him to return as they had indicated they would, the Russians sent Michell to Siberia in one of the great deportations in June 1940. He was sent to camp with both Jews and non-Jews at Yashkar Ola, east of the Volga River, between Gorky and Kazan.

After Michell's release in September 1941, he decided to join the Polish army, but was dissuaded because of the illness of his cousin who was with him. In the summer of 1942, his uncle was asked to run one of the Polish orphanages at a village near Ulyanovsk. The orphanage was set up in the aftermath of the Sikorski Agreement of 1941 between Poland and Russia, after the German invasion. He stayed with his uncle until the end of April 1943. It was at that time that the graves of 5,000 Polish officers in the Katyn Forest near Smolensk were discovered by the Germans, and charges and counterchanges flew back and forth between the Soviets and the Poles. The Poles claimed that the murders had been carried out by the Russians under their occupation and not by the Germans. The Russians broke off diplomatic relations; the Polish ambassador in Russia was declared persona non grata; the Polish orphanage as well as other Polish facilities were closed by the Russians, and Michell and his uncle were relieved of their positions. His uncle was arrested in November 1943 and executed on trumped-up spy charges. Michell, his aunt, and his cousin were repatriated in March 1946.

Bernard Gelman, who lived in the town of Mezrich, 100 kilometers east of Warsaw, had also decided to cast his lot with the Russians. When the Soviet army withdrew behind the Bug River according to the terms of the Molotov-Ribbentrop Pact, he left with them. However, he—like the great majority of Jews— refused to accept Russian citizenship, believing that the war would not last long and not wanting to be stranded in Russia when it ended. Consequently, he was arrested, packed into a cattle car, and shipped north past Murmansk to the Komi River. From there, he was taken farther north on buggies into the woods, to cut 100 trees a day. "There were mostly Jews there, and most didn't make it." While Bernard was officially released in the winter of 1941, he was unable to leave the tundra until the summer of 1943. In 1944 he was informed by the Russian authorities that he would have to join the Russian army. Ironicially, he was stationed at Maidanek, a major Nazi death facility for Jews, including Michell Borke's father. Bernard remained there throughout August 1944, wondering why his Russian unit was not called up to assist the Poles in the Warsaw uprising against the Nazis in August 1944.

For the minority of Polish Jews who chose to register with the Soviets, life was somewhat easier. At least they were not to face the rigors of deportation to Siberia or the Ural Mountains in 1940 and 1941. Marcia Scheingross accepted Russian citizenship after fleeing from Warsaw. She was sent to a city in the Ukraine, where she and her husband both secured good jobs. When the Germans invaded the Ukraine, the Scheingrosses were shipped to safety, along with many other Russians, over the Volga River to Kazan and then 400 miles to the east of Kazan. Marcia's husband decided that they should try to get to Tashkent, like hundreds of thousands of others. There they slept in the park for three weeks in November 1941 until the city government sent them to a small town near Fergana in Uzbekistan. "I had only one dress; we worked very hard for four years; we didn't have enough food or clothing, but we survived and nobody wanted to kill us because we were Jewish."

Under the terms of the agreement worked out between the Polish government in exile by General Wladyslaw Sikorski and the Soviets, all Polish civilians deported to the USSR were to be released. The Russians had deported an estimated 1.5 million

under their occupation in eastern Poland, but as many as half
that number had already perished in the wastelands of the Soviet
Union. With the amnesty, people traveled from wherever they
had been incarcerated in the northern and eastern reaches of
Russia to Polish staging areas, which were under the charge of
General Anders: in the Ukraine, in the south of Russia, and in
the central Asian republics of Uzbekistan, Kazakhstan, and
Kirghizia. Many went through Tashkent, or the legendary Sa-
markand (where Scheherazade is supposed to have spent her
thousand and one nights), or Frunze. It was because of this
agreement that all of the Christian refugees interviewed were
able to get out of Russia. Of the sixteen Christians who found
themselves in Russia, fifteen were evacuated with Ander's army
through Iran in the summer of 1942, including two women who
worked as army nurses and went through the Middle East to
Italy, where they arrived in time to participate in the battle of
Monte Cassino. The other women civilians wound up in Polish
orphanages and facilities in India or East Africa after being
evacuated along with Anders's army personnel. One Pole got out
of Russia by the northern route, by ship from Murmansk to
Glasgow. No Jews among the Pittsburgh refugees were evacuated with Anders.[5]

The impact of Soviet policies and occupation on the Polish
nation was profound. Yet that impact differed between Christians and Jews. Because Jews were not deliberately singled out
for murderous treatment, they considered the Russians saviors
in comparison to the Germans. Jews were offered Soviet citizenship, which, if they accepted, meant they could live like everybody else, however miserably that might be. If they chose not to
accept citizenship, then they faced the same Siberian deportations and *gulags* as those millions of others who had incurred the
disfavor of the totalitarian regime. Thus when Jews compared
life under the Russians to life under the Germans, there was no
hesitation as to which regime they preferred.

Furthermore, the stories of those Jews who survived under

the Soviets simply do not reflect the same level of desperation as those who survived under the Nazis. People did not live in daily fear for their very lives, nor did they feel that their ordeal was specifically occasioned by the fact that they were Jewish. This is not to say that Jews did not die in the Soviet Union as a result of the slave labor policies and executions, but more Jews survived in the Soviet Union than in Poland under the Germans. It is estimated that 100,000 Jews perished along with some 700,000 non-Jews in Russia as a result of forced deportations. The exact figure will never be known.[6] On the other hand, it is estimated that approximately 300,000 Polish Jews survived in Russia, constituting the bulk of the Polish Jewish survivors.

In contrast to the Jews, the bitterness expressed by Polish Christians toward the Russians was very deep. For many subjected to the Russian occupation or deportation, the Soviets were worse than the Germans. Polish hatred for Russia was fueled when Russia seized a large chunk of Poland. But even after Poland and the USSR both became combatants against the German aggressor, relations were still strained and, ultimately, severed. The discovery of the murdered Polish officers in the Katyn Forest in Russia was the coup de grace to relations between the two.

A year later, during the Warsaw uprising of August 1944, when the Polish underground army called for the assistance of the Russians encamped just on the other side of the Vistula River outside Warsaw, the Soviets refused the plea. The uprising was defeated, Warsaw was leveled, its million inhabitants were deported from the city, the military force of the Home army was destroyed, and the political authority of the Polish government in exile, which backed the Home army, was dangerously weakened. The Soviets were able to establish their puppets in Poland and lay the groundwork for the Communist takeover of the country on the heels of the defeat of the Nazis.

Thus at the end of World War II, the Soviet presence remained in Poland. After all the sacrifice and struggle of the

Polish people, a brutal totalitarian regime still stalked their homeland. It was actually this Communist takeover rather than the destruction wrought by the Nazis that motivated the Christian refugees to leave their country. The antipathy of these refugees today toward the USSR is predicated on what they witnessed of its treachery from 1939 on.

3

Point of No Return

▶▶▶ THE POLISH PEOPLE SUFFERED terribly during World War II. The statistics of wartime deaths are the best indication of the ferocity of the attack upon the nation. Six million Poles died—three million Jews and three million Christians, or nearly one-fifth of the total prewar population of the country. Beyond the deaths, an enormous number of Poles had been uprooted, more than nationals of any other country except Russia. Refugees from Poland numbered more than 4.5 million people. This number included 2.1 million forced to move as a result of German expulsion and forced labor within Poland, 2.2 million forced outside of their country as a result of both the Germans and Russians, and an additional 200,000 or so who voluntarily fled German- or Soviet-controlled territory.[1]

The following table shows where the Pittsburgh refugees were at war's end:

	Christians	Jews
Germany-Austria	31	21
Poland	2	11
Russia	0	14
Italy	14	0
Africa	2	0
England	3	0
Czechoslovakia	0	13

Liberated Europe	5	1
India	1	0
Sweden	1	0

Polish Christians had been scattered not only throughout Europe, but throughout the world. Some civilians, particularly women and young children, were transported to Polish facilities in Africa or India after their evacuation from Russia in 1942. Men and women who had been able to link up with Allied fighting forces were in Italy, Britain, France, the Low Countries, or Germany at war's end. Some of them were part of the First Army Corps that General Wladyslaw Sikorski, head of a new Polish government in Paris, had raised in June 1940 after the surrender of Poland. For example, Stefan G. had gone through Rumania, to Greece, Marseilles, and then to Polish headquarters in Paris before the fall of France in June 1940. He had been rescued in the Allied evacuation at Dunkirk and taken to England in June 1940. As a professional engineer attached to the Polish Squadron 307 (the Night Fighters), he was in the Battle of Britain. He was later transferred to command headquarters as a major under the British in the Polish air force reserve and helped in the preparation of the Allied invasion of Normandy. At war's end, Stefan was attached to Allied headquarters in Brussels.

The majority of army personnel, however, were under the command of General Wladyslaw Anders in the Polish Second Army Corps. They had traveled from prison camps in Siberia, to Buzuluk on the Volga, to Tashkent in the south of Russia, to Pahlevi in Iran, to Baghdad, Jerusalem, Cairo, Tobruk, Monte Cassino, and Bologna. Other men had been drafted into Polish units under Russian command after March 1944. Many of the Christian refugees, particularly the women, were in Germany at the end of the war, taken there for forced labor or deported there after the unsuccessful Warsaw uprising in August 1944.

The Jewish refugees, on the other hand, were fairly concentrated in only a few places at the conclusion of the war. Some had survived the camps in Poland, Czechoslovakia, or Germany; others had come out of hiding in Poland, were partisans, or were part of the estimated 300,000 Jews who had survived in Russian territory. One man had been drafted into the Russian army. Another had been a prisoner of war with the Polish army.[2] Wherever they had been, both Christians and Jews had been away from familiar surroundings, sometimes for the entire duration of the six-year war. This displacement was the first factor in an ultimate decision to emigrate.

There was also a tremendous sense of loss. Among the Jewish refugees it was particularly overwhelming. The statistics on family deaths are staggering for this group. Although many of the Christians lost at least one close family member—a spouse, parent, sibling, or child—the Jews usually lost their entire immediate as well as extended families. The following table shows the numbers of the refugees in Pittsburgh who lost zero through nine numbers of their immediate families:

Deaths in Family	Christians	Jews
0	37	2
1	17	8
2	4	6
3	0	9
4	1	7
5	0	9
6	0	11
7	0	4
8	0	1
9	0	1

Although Jewish and Christian family size was comparable, thirty-seven Christians and only two Jews indicated that their immediate family members had all survived. Forty-three Jews but only one Christian lost three or more immediate family members. David Guss, the ebullient barber who was repatriated from the USSR after the war, was one of only 8 surviving members out of an extended family numbering 280 persons. Abe Salem, who also had escaped to the east, was the only one left out of a family of 170. Morton Cieply was the only one of 200 left alive, and Melvin and Aron Goldman were the sole survivors from a family of 65. The personal loneliness from the loss of loved ones and the destruction of the Jewish way of life and community was added to the trauma of being wrenched from one world to another.

In addition to these psychological traumas, the physical condition of many survivors at the end of the war was not good. The refugees' descriptions of their health at liberation is shown below:

	Christians	*Jews*
Good health	32	10
Fair health	20	18
Bad health	7	32

The contrast between Jews and Christians is evident. Fifty-two Christians were in fair to good health, about equal the number of Jews (fifty) who described themselves in fair to bad health. Of the ten Jews who indicated they were in good health, six had survived in the Soviet Union, two had lived in Poland as Christians, one had been in hiding as a Jew, and another had worked in a factory in Czechoslovakia. Many of the Jews who were liberated believed that they had literally only hours left of life. Abraham Enzel weighed just seventy-eight pounds and Sam Shear, barely eighty-five pounds. Sam remarked that he was full of lice and had not had a bath in three years. He certainly was not alone. Sarah Joskowitz described herself as a "walking dead person" when she was liberated from the Ravensbruck concentration camp. Others were suffering from a variety of diseases and deficiencies. Of the seven Christians in the Pittsburgh group who described their condition as bad at the end of the war, three had been in concentration camps, one had been put into a camp after the Warsaw uprising, and the other three had been engaged in forced labor.

After the war, both the Christian and Jewish refugees had to restructure their lives. They had been physically uprooted, had lost family members, and had their health weakened. Their reasons for leaving Poland or not returning to Poland varied.

For the Christians, the Communist appropriation of the country, including the ceding of large areas of eastern Poland to Soviet Russia as the boundaries were moved westward, was the most compelling factor. Fully two-thirds of the Christians asserted the Communist takeover was the primary reason they did not go back. Some were actually afraid to return because of stories they had heard from relatives and friends about those who had gone back who were never heard from again. The prospect of resettling in a Poland under Communist domination was simply not acceptable. Communist rule not only meant the snuffing out of economic opportunity and personal freedom, but it also conjured up memories of the repressive Soviet occupation from September 1939 to June 1941. Moreover, even though the Soviets sent representatives to persuade Poles remaining in the West to return to their homeland and the United Nations Relief and Rehabilitation Agency was encouraging repatriation (people were given sixty-days' rations in what was known as Operation Carrot), representatives of the non-Communist Polish government in London made it very clear over the BBC what might await soldiers should they decide to go back.

The situation and views of the Jews were somewhat different. The crucial factor in their decision to emigrate was the devastation wrought not by the Soviets but by the Nazis. Poland was a graveyard, the place where Jews had lost virtually every person who had been near and dear to them. To return to such a place was unthinkable. Furthermore, the persistence of anti-Semitism in Poland was crucial. Survivors felt that their very lives were endangered if they remained in the country. They had real cause for their fears. Polish government figures indicate that at least

351 Jews were murdered between November 1944 (when the Germans were pushed back into Germany) and October 1945, and many other Jews were attacked, robbed, and wounded.[3] The worst pogrom of all occurred in the city of Kielce on July 4, 1946, a full year after the Nazis had been defeated. Forty-two Jews were murdered after the crowd had been incited by the age-old libel that Jews killed Christians and used their blood for ritual purposes.

Bernard Gelman was one of those who decided shortly after the war not to stay in Poland. He had escaped to the Soviet Union and had been sent to Siberia when he refused to become a Soviet citizen. He had joined the Polish army under General Zygmunt Berling in Russia and was stationed in Maidanek, where hundreds of thousands had died under the Nazis. After the war ended, while he was still in the army, he revealed to his compatriots that he was Jewish. One day shortly thereafter, some Polish soldiers opened fire on him. He was not struck—but that was enough for Bernard. He left Poland shortly thereafter.

Other Jews who had been released from the USSR and had returned to Poland reported harrowing experiences. The train that Wolf Friede was on stopped near the death camp of Belzec. He recounted seeing bodies and parts of bodies lying on the ground. "The A. K. (Home army of the free Polish government in exile) surrounded the train, which held about 1,000 people, all Jews. They threw stones at us, yelled that they did not want us here, and scared us to death."

When Irwin Lewenstein arrived in Crakow on board one of the trains filled with repatriates from the USSR, "Poles at the station complained how many Jews were still left alive and made signs indicating they wanted to cut our throats." Sally Melmed, whose family had died at Maidanek, went back to Poland after the war, but never returned to her home in Krasnik, a small town in central Poland. The day before her planned visit, the massacre of Jews at nearby Kielce occurred. She joined the mass exodus of surviving Jews who fled Poland to the safety of the displaced persons camps under Allied control in western Europe. Another Jew, Arnold Zweig, had survived Auschwitz and planned to go back to his hometown of Lodz to put a stone on the grave of his father, who had been killed by the Nazis. He dragged a piece of marble all the way from Friedland in Czechoslovakia to Lodz. But when he arrived in the city, he found his house had just been ransacked. In fear for his life, he barricaded himself inside his home and then left two days later, never to return.

Many Jewish survivors who left Poland and ultimately arrived in Pittsburgh insisted that the climate of hate in the country was merely a continuation of what they had witnessed prior to the war and even during the war. Others felt that postwar anti-Semitism was at an even higher pitch than it was before the war. Amid the charges and countercharges between the Soviets and the remaining Home army supporters in Poland, who were anti-Communist, Jews were often the scapegoats. They were accused of conspiring to bring about the Communist takeover of the country. This identification of Jews with communism had been alleged even before the war, despite the fact that the majority of Jews were religious and considered atheistic communism anathema and its political system oppressive. Those Jews who had turned to communism as a solution to the problem of anti-Semitism in Poland were a small minority of the Jewish population, as were those who registered as Soviet citizens after their escape from the Nazis to Soviet territory during the war.

Over half of the Jewish refugees, including fourteen who were repatriated directly from the Soviet Union, had returned to Poland. Most were searching for surviving family members. In contrast, only two of the fifty-eight Christian refugees who were already outside the country chose to go back to Poland. Five out of six of the Jewish refugees did not stay in Poland for fear anti-Semitic violence. Most gave this as the primary reason for leaving Poland after the war.

By the end of 1945 the Communist government had closed Poland's borders. After that time, leaving the country became infinitely more difficult. It is estimated that out of the 120,000 Jews who left Poland after the war, only 15,000 did so as regular emigrants; the rest immigrated illegally to Western Germany, Austria, and Italy, usually with the help of the clandestine arm of the Jewish defense forces of Palestine known as the *Brichah*.[4] For many of the Jews in eastern Europe, including those interviewed in Pittsburgh, the assistance of the *Brichah* agents in helping survivors get over the Polish border was crucial. Of the thirty-three Jewish refugees who were in Poland at some point after the war looking to leave, at least eighteen specifically indicated that they were assisted by the *Brichah*.

Even after the refugees arrived in displaced persons camps, their travail was not over. Some had it worse than others, but all faced difficulties. Both the United Nations Relief and Rehabilitation Agency and the U.S. army were clearly unprepared for the large numbers of persons seeking to enter the displaced persons camps under their auspices. The camps were crowded and lacked proper supplies. Yet the Americans who initially greeted the survivors earned high marks for their warmth and understanding. To the U.S. soldiers, who knew virtually nothing about the Nazi concentration camps, the shock of their discovery was overwhelming. Survivors were showered with gifts of whatever the soldier could give them. In some instances the candy bars and rich foods proved fatal to survivors whose digestive systems after years of starvation could not function properly. William Friedman, who was liberated while he was on a death march between Dachau and the Tyrol Mountains in Austria, reported how the Americans literally "threw chocolate at them. They killed people out of the goodness of their hearts because of the rich food."

Irene Szulman, who also was on a death march in Germany, remembered that "the Americans didn't know what to do first for us. Some GIs even offered us guns to go after the Nazis. I was offered one, but I didn't take it. The moment had passed; I was already human, even though I had dreamed about killing German children the way they had killed ours." Mordechai Glatstein also was told that he could do with the Nazis as he wished. "A few Jews did take revenge, but I had my freedom, and that was enough."

The sympathy of the Americans was to fade after the first flush of liberation.[5] One major factor accounting for the change was the replacement of the fighting soldier with new recruits who had no understanding of what many of the survivors had gone through. Thus they did not have that extra measure of compassion to deal with persons, particularly the Jews, still in shock from wartime traumas.

The early policy of the United States in its administration of the camps was not properly considered. Jewish displaced persons were often in camps with anti-Semitic non-Jews. It was no secret that many persons seeking asylum in the camps were not victims of the Nazis. Many, particularly from the Baltic countries, had fled to the West to escape the advancing Russian armies. Some had been Nazi sympathizers, or worse. These people were accepted into the camps as bona fide displaced persons, who were subsequently entitled to come to America. In fact, U.S. displaced persons legislation in 1948 was deliberately drafted to give Balts priority over the victims of Nazism, particularly Jews.[6] A number of the Jewish refugees testified that on the boats taking them to America were numbers of people who openly expressed their pro-Nazi sentiments.

The conditions of the camps were such that, in response to public pressure, President Harry S. Truman in July 1945 sent the dean of the University of Pennsylvania Law School, Earl Harrison, on a fact-finding mission. His report became political dynamite when he charged that "as matters now stand, we appear to be treating the Jews as the Nazis treated them except that we do not exterminate them."[7] His plea to improve conditions in the camps was heeded by Truman, who communicated

his orders to a sympathetic General Dwight Eisenhower, su-
preme allied commander in Europe.

But the Jews were not the only ones to protest conditions in
the camps. Polish groups, including the Polish American Congress (PAC), also complained. After Harrison's publicized tour
of the camps, the PAC appealed to President Truman to alleviate
the plight of Polish refugees in Germany. In a letter dated
October 8, 1945, the PAC wrote

in hastening to commend you for your quick action in taking reso-
lute steps to alleviate the pitiful physical and spiritual conditions to
which Jewish refugees have been subjected, we consider it also our
moral duty to inform you that we are gravely disturbed by the omi-
nous silence to the tortured cry from the depths of the hearts of
approximately one million Polish refugees in the same American
area of occupation. The status of these Polish exiles is pathetic. . . .
Above all, these Polish refugees do not want to be forced to return
to their homeland.[8]

Like Jewish groups, the PAC urged a revision in the U.S.
immigration law in order to admit displaced persons into this
country.

Only a few of the refugees in Pittsburgh, all Jews, criticized
poor conditions in the camps. One of these was Albert Levenreich, who recalled joining a protest directed against the American authorities at a camp in Linz. He claimed that Jews had
been treated as "prisoners" rather than as refugees. The protest
elicited a satisfactory response from the Americans, as local
Germans were apparently evicted from available housing so that
the refugees could be housed better. Bernard Gelman described
the protest at Linz as a "little riot." Abe Kohane was far more
critical. He talked about "the Holocaust after the Holocaust,"
because of the inadequate attention he received after his release
from Buchenwald. "We were totally neglected." Victims were
not given the psychological help they so desperately needed.

Conditions did improve for Abe, however, after he was transferred to the camp at Landsberg, the major camp for Jewish
displaced persons. At least ten of the Jewish refugees were there
for some period of time after the war. The camp, which was in
Bavaria west of Munich, held no less than 23,000 persons
between 1945 and 1951. Life at Landsberg was highly organized. In addition to a Jewish police force, the camp had a full
structure of social and educational programs. The Jewish Organization for Rehabilitation and Training, known as ORT, had
important training schools in a number of camps, including
Landsberg. These facilities gave people the opportunity to learn
or relearn various skills and trades.

There was another large camp at Felderfing, southwest of
Munich along the highway to Garmisch Partenkirchen and Inns-
bruck. Mordechai Glatstein wrote for a newspaper in the camp,
and Sam Shear, who had weighed eighty-five pounds when
liberated on a death march in Bavaria, organized a soccer team
and played along with his brother.

Yet while some Jews worked in the camps in various capaci-
ties, the majority of camp residents were not permitted to do
anything. Irwin Lewenstein, who had escaped from German-
occupied Poland, been drafted into the Russian army, and then
escaped again from Poland after the war with the aid of the
Brichah, summed up the situation this way: "We were not
allowed to work. Our life was not to live, not to die, just to
survive. We got food from UNRRA weekly, and my wife used to
knit sweaters for American GIs, so we got extra food." Many
others described this time after the war as a "waiting period," as
the refugees waited for the go-ahead to relocate and establish
new homes for themselves. Until an ultimate destination could
be determined for them, the policy of the occupation authorities
was to have these civilians sit it out. Aside from the training run
by ORT, there was virtually no opportunity for camp residents to
be trained or employed outside the camps unless they chose to
go off on their own. Some Jews, particularly those living outside

the camps, did make extra income and in some instances substantial sums on what was the black market in Germany. Although this kind of activity was illegal, there was little the
authorities could do about it.

The overriding goal of these displaced persons was to get out
of Germany. Morris Manela, never one to mince words, put it
this way: "I could have been filthy rich in Germany. I had a big
store in Munich after I left the camp at Felderfing, but when I
got my entry papers from the United States, I sold it [the store]
for pennies. I didn't want to be with those German bastards."
Morris was certainly not unique. To Jews who had lost virtually
everything at the hands of the Germans, the prospect of remaining in Germany was anathema. They wanted to get out, and the
most favored destination was Palestine. This overwhelming desire was noted by Earl Harrison in his report to Truman in 1945
and by many other observers at the time.

At least half of the Jewish refugees indicated that their first
choice at the end of the war for a future homeland had been
Palestine. Many displaced persons had heard David Ben Gurion, the future first prime minister of the State of Israel, when
he had made a tour of the displaced persons camps around the
Munich area in October 1945 and urged the Jews to go to
Palestine and fight for the future Jewish state. Yet with the
exception of only two persons, all of those in the Pittsburgh
group came directly to the United States and never did get to
Palestine. The reasons for the change in direction varied. For
some, when the time came for them to go to Palestine, they or
their spouses were not fit enough to make the illegal entry
attempt. Since immigration to Palestine was still restricted by
the British and was often a matter of running the British gaunt-
let, only those Jews who were in good physical condition were
accepted by the Jewish authorities to try to break the blockade.
William Friedman and his wife were scheduled to go to Palestine
on the famous ship *Exodus*, but his wife was pregnant and they
had to cancel. Dora Iwler, too, was supposed to be on that ship,

but because of her pregnancy, could not go. Janina Winkler also wanted to go to Palestine, but she could not because of the malaria she had contracted while in Uzbekistan during the war. The Zimmetts were not allowed to go because of Thelma's deformed foot caused by the amputation of her frostbitten toes during the war.

Other Jewish refugees who had originally intended to resettle in Palestine were warned by relatives and friends who had recently immigated there not to come. They cautioned about the hard life in the country or the fighting. Morris Manela's cousins wrote him not to come because "there was no work, no housing, no food." Rose Perlmutter's sister wrote her that she would only wind up in Cyprus if she tried to go to Palestine because of British immigration restrictions. Frances Greenberg did sail on the *Exodus*, but the British forced her return to Lubeck, Germany, and the displaced persons camp at Leipheim. After that experience, she waited for a visa to the United States. Sally Melmed also did some "rethinking" after she heard about what happened to her friends on the Exodus.

Other survivors admitted that they simply were too weary, too emotionally drained, to become pioneers in Israel and face yet another struggle, this time against the Arabs. They felt they had been through enough and did not want to deal with any more deprivation and hardship if it could be avoided. "I went through seven hells, and I couldn't take any more," concluded Harry Feldman.

For the remainder of the Jewish refugees, their first choice all along was the United States. For anyone who had family in America, the hope was to join them. As Nathan Forstenzer commented, "After so much death and destruction, whatever family was left was very important." For the others, the United States was the best place to start to rebuild their lives, something they were desperately anxious to do.

For the Christian refugees, the situation was considerably different. While mention has been made of the protest by Polish groups against conditions in the displaced persons camps, the fact is that a significant minority of those who refused to go back to Poland were not even living in the camps. They were able to get jobs with the American military as service personnel or were in military units under the English. Those persons affiliated with the English military were not even considered displaced persons. While forty-two of the Jewish refugees indicated they had lived in displaced persons camps after the war, only sixteen of the Christians said they had done so.

According to U.S. government figures, approximately 154,000 persons of Polish nationality came to the United States under the Displaced Persons Act passed by Congress in June 1948 (amended June 1950). A memo of the Veterans of the Polish Armed Forces in Exile paints a more complete picture of those Poles who were admitted to the United States after the war, but there is some confusion in the numbers. In contrast to the U.S. government record, the Veterans confirm a total number of only 100,000 Poles who arrived between 1945 and 1952. The Veterans included arrivals over a longer period of time, from the end of the war in 1945 up to and including the emigration under the Displaced Persons Acts of 1948. The lower totals, however, reflect the fact that the Veterans were not including Polish Jews in their tally.[9]

The Veteran's memo listed four different Polish groups who entered the country. The first was Polish exservicemen who had been prisoners of war in Germany, including the insurgents from the Warsaw uprising (20,000); the second was Polish exservicemen in Great Britain (20,000); the third was the families of exservicemen (25,000); and finally "Displaced Persons from Western Germany" (35,000). Thus it is clear that large numbers of Polish Christians were in England before immigrating and connected in some manner with the Allied forces. This is reflected among the Pittsburgh refugees. While forty-five Jews emigrated to the United States from Germany, only eighteen Christians came from there. In contrast, half the Pittsburgh

Christian group had gone to England at some point after the war and most were there immediately prior to their immigration to the United States.

The high number of Poles in England had to do with the fact that the British took over responsibility for many persons (about 114,000) of Polish nationality after the war, since Poland had officially been an ally of Britain. They organized what became known as the Polish Resettlement Corps. The Corps was organized by the British government in the fall of 1946 in order to help disband and ultimately resettle Polish military personnel and their dependents. As part of this effort, other Polish nationals were brought to England as well.

For individuals in the Corps, including many who are now living in Pittsburgh, the experience and program in England meant the opportunity to work or get an education or trade. Janusz K. was able to get started in his own remodeling business after learning some skills. John D., who had served with General Anders in Italy, went to electronics school and then got a job. Viktor H., who also had been with Anders, worked first as a policeman, took a course in shoemaking, but wound up at a factory job. Alina J., who joined the Polish army in Italy, went to a school of social work and got her degree in England through the Corps. Bernice N. took a course in nursing and became a private nurse.

However, despite the efforts of the English, not everybody who was part of this resettlement program appreciated that effort—or the English for that matter. Marion K. recalled being "fed up with everything; we were fighting to go back to Poland, not to England. We go there and they put us to work digging potatoes; they didn't care about the Polacks." Rudolf M., who was able to go to school and earn a degree in chemistry, felt that despite his degree he still was limited in his choice of jobs because he was Polish. He compared his life in England to that of a black man in the United States. "There was a real prejudice against us." Lidia M. liked the English, but her husband did not. "He thought they were very superior and insular—like we were exotic animals. They used to ask us a lot of questions as if to study us as strange creatures." And Stefan G., who had been a Polish major in the British Royal Air Force, noted that "the British were very suspicious of me from the beginning because they never had experience with a better-educated Pole." Janusz K., who also was an officer attached to the RAF, was blunt: "I hated England. England is a country where you are always a bloody foreigner. The more successful you are, the more bloody you are, the more I was pushed out."

Whether it was the attitude of the British themselves, the difficulty of exile, or the perception that better opportunities awaited them elsewhere, in the first five years after the war some 10,000 Poles left England for Canada, South America, the United States, or Australia.[10] Whatever their attitude, the experience of the Corps in England was part of the legacy of a significant number of Poles who came to this country following the war. For many, important skills—including English language proficiency—were gained during this association.

For those Polish Christians who were to come to the United States, this country was not necessarily their first choice, except for those who had some connection. At least six of the Christian refugees had relatives working and living in the greater Pittsburgh area prior to World War I. Often their male relatives had worked in the mines or mills of western Pennsylvania and had returned to Poland, as many were wont to do in the years prior to World War I and the imposition of immigration restrictions in 1921 and 1924. The ties to the United States and Pittsburgh were felt by these Poles' children and grandchildren. For example, every Sunday in prewar Poland Maria S.'s mother, who had been born in Harrisburg, would read to her young daughter about America. Thus it was no surprise that Maria headed for the United States after the war.

For many refugees, however, the United States was never really a serious possibility initially, because they had no relatives to ease them past U.S. immigration restrictions and limitations. The Displaced Persons Act, which initially allowed 200,000 refugees to enter the United States, was not passed until June 1948, more than three years after the end of the war in Europe. Bernice N. remarked, "You didn't decide. They decided for you. Whatever country came through with a visa, that was the country you went to."

Some persons were actually afraid to come to America. "I didn't want to come to the United States, because I had read about the cowboys and how the Indians scalped you," Bernice confessed. Edmund W. was afraid of "all the gangsters." But he came to this country after an American pilot assured him that the notion that America was infested by gangsters was pure "bull." Louise S.'s decision to immigrate to America was even more accidental. She was all set to move to Australia, but when she went to a fortune teller the day before she was supposed to sail, the fortune teller warned her about what awaited her "down under." She reversed gears and headed for America.

There is irony in both American and British efforts to resettle Poles after the war, since so many Poles were bitter about wartime and immediate postwar policies of England and the United States. Their feelings ranged from disappointment and resignation to anger and bitterness. "We were sold like pigs in a slaughterhouse," said Mieczyslaw G., referring to the Yalta Agreement. "It was the worst sell-out in modern history," Stanley W. asserted. Many felt "abandoned," "betrayed." Stanley K. and others in the Polish armed forces fighting in Italy had expected to continue their fight for freedom aganist the Soviets. They had hoped that, since the Poles had made such a contribution to the fighting forces to help save the Western democracies, that these same democracies would in turn continue the struggle until Poland itself was free.

The blame for what they saw as the Allied giveaway of Poland rested, in the opinion of the refugees, on the shoulders of either Franklin Roosevelt, Winston Churchill, or both. To Stanislawa S., Allied policy was "like a bone in my throat. . . . It really is an irony how World War II started in defense of Poland and ended with its giveaway by Churchill and Roosevelt. I guess they were just weary of five years of war." Viktor H. felt that "America didn't understand how much we love our country; it's like they played cards and we lost. They gave it to the Soviets." Helena B., whose husband had been in the Polish armed forces under the British, was bitter. "Polish soldiers took Monte Cassino, and then Roosevelt gave everything away at Yalta." Joseph P. remarked that "in 1939 FDR said that Poland is the inspiration of the free world, but in 1945 the same Roosevelt did not want to receive the prime minister of the free Polish government in London. He was sick, but he also didn't understand the Russians. He thought he could trust them, but they only understood power." Stanyslaw P. argued "we could have been a moral voice even if we could not do much short of a major confrontation. We should have at least said no. Perhaps it was expediency, perhaps naivety." Lidia M. put it this way, "Roosevelt was a child who went into the lion's den. He thought he could trust 'Uncle Joe,' but he couldn't."

The brunt of the refugees' anger, however, was saved for Churchill. Many Poles believed that he was the real culprit. "Churchill brainwashed Roosevelt," asserted Stefan R. "He used us, but then never helped us or gave us anything." Jan P. was even more blunt. "Churchill was a dirty dog. He promised Poland a free country and then for some reason, they just forgot about us." Some, like Janusz K., excused FDR. "He was sick at Yalta, but Churchill sold us out in clear conscience." Adam S. concurred. "Churchill was worse than Roosevelt, because England had a greater obligation to Poland than the United States did."

The bitterness and suspicion of many Poles toward the British was evident in their view of the wartime death of General Wladyslaw Sikorski, the esteemed leader of the Polish government in exile. His untimely death in a helicopter accident in

1943 was a mortal blow to the power and prestige of the Polish government in London, for no other Polish leader could command such respect. His loss left the Poles bereft of strong leadership at a crucial time in their relations with the Soviet Union. Some of the refugees discounted the official explanation that the crash was an accident. Some accused the Russians of sabotaging the plane, and an equal number blamed the British for his death, pointing out that, since the British were intent on maintaining friendly relations with Russia, getting rid of Sikorski with whom the Russians were openly feuding was very expedient. Janusz K., who had arrived in England in 1942 after his release from Russia, was in training to become a fighter pilot at the time of Sikorski's death. He was convinced "the British did it." He was very suspicious of the way the plane went right into the sea. "It is impossible for all four engines to have stopped suddenly, the way the British said. And after the crash, the British forbade Polish forces from recovering papers and sending in their own divers." Stefan G., one of two Polish majors among the refugees who was with the British, also believed the death of Sikorski was no accident. "He had many connections and contacts and was very much in the way of an agreement with the Russians. Moreover, from a technical point of view, the explanation given does not convince me. I've seen too many crashes to take the British explanation."

The Christian refugees were especially intense in their feelings toward Britain. No matter what the British might have done in sponsoring the Polish Resettlement Corps, it was clear that that did not counterbalance or atone for what was perceived as a real failure of Allied foreign policy. On the other hand, the Jewish refugees were totally unconcerned with the question of Allied policy. It was clear that their hearts and minds were on other concerns and issues. The following table shows the number of refugees and their opinions on British and American policy toward Poland.

	Christians	Jews
Allies sold Poland out; I feel bitter	41	3
I feel critical but not bitter	6	4
I have no opinion	3	3
Poland deserved what it got	0	12
I did not care what happened to Poland	0	24

The apathy, or even satisfaction, at the postwar fate of Poland on the part of the Jewish refugees is clearly related to the anti-Semitism they experienced in Poland before the war, during the war, after the war, or throughout. Jews were often bitter at what they felt was a rejection of them by Polish Christians and therefore could not bring themselves to feel sympathy or concern for a people and a nation that had so turned on them in their hour of need. Indeed, this feeling of betrayal was their emotional legacy from Europe, the intensity of which has certainly not abated over time and distance.

While not always appreciated or effective, British efforts to help Christian Poles develop skills nevertheless gave them the opportunity to return more quickly to normal life and in a number of cases allowed them to advance to positions they might not have been able to attain without such help. This contrasted sharply with the experience of the majority of the Jewish refugees, who in these same years were in limbo. While the British through the Polish Resettlement Corps deliberately set out to smoothe that transition, the Jews had no such sponsor. They were not officially considered allies and generally had no opportunity to reorient themselves in a normal work environment. Whether they wanted to or not, they were forced to stand still. This prolonged period of uncertainty and frustration certainly did not make their adjustment to life and work in the United States any easier.

Yet there was one thing both Jews and Christians could do, even stuck in a displaced persons camp—they could start a family. Indeed, married persons comprised 62.6 percent of the immigrants who came to America under the Displaced Persons Act.[11] Three out of every five people admitted came as a family group. Many of these marriages, not surprisingly, took place in the years immediately following the war. This is certainly reflected among the Pittsburgh refugees. Out of a total of 104 marriages contracted by the 120 persons interviewed (only three men remained bachelors—one Jew and two Christians, one of whom was a priest), more than half of them (56) took place in the four years after the war, from 1945 to 1949 (30 among the Jews and 26 among the Christians). During the war there had been only five marriages, four between Jews living in the relative security of the Soviet Union and one by a Christian.

The Pittsburgh refugees testified to the veritable explosion of postwar marriages in Europe. One woman who had determined not to settle down immediately recalled how she had gone to twenty-seven weddings in Europe after the war. "Every week, it seemed, I was a bridesmaid!" After the war, interest in the opposite sex revived and so did the opportunities to meet men and women in displaced persons camps, army facilities, or elsewhere. Yet it often appeared that the motivation behind the marriages was far more complex than just boy meets girl and they fall in love. For some, particularly the Jews, the rush to wed was the result of a heartfelt need to find companionship in a world devoid of loved ones; for others, it had to do with security. Dora Iwler, who married after knowing her future husband only one month, admitted that she "liked him," but did not love him at that time. "There was such hurt then; I wanted to get married." Dora Zimmerman's future husband offered to marry her at the Landsberg camp. Her uncle who had been helping her was dying and told her to marry the young man. "Who will take care of you?" he had argued. She was married within two weeks and many years later recalled that "everybody got married out of loneliness."

Along with the propensity for marriage after the war, there

was also a desire for children. By the end of 1946 nearly 1,000 Jewish children were being born per month in the displaced persons camps.[12] Between 1945 and 1952, thirty-three children were born in Europe and twenty-four in United States to the Jewish refugees interviewed in Pittsburgh. This represented 47 percent of all the children that were to be born to this group over the span of their child-bearing years. Among the Christians interviewed, twenty-one children were born in Europe and seven more in the United States, which represented 30 percent of the total number of children born to them.

Psychologists have referred to a "refugee state."[13] This psychological phenomenon—brought on by loss of homeland, threat to survival, physical suffering, and social degradation—can threaten the stability and security of the individual. Both the Jewish and Christian refugees suffered from some sort of "refugee state," however one chooses to define it. Their experiences, attitudes, and trauma were part of the European legacy they carried with them across the Atlantic to their new lives in America.

4

"I Lift My Lamp"

▶▶▶ FOR THE WAVE OF POSTWAR IMMI-
grants, like all those who had preceded them, the
voyage to America marked a beginning in a new world far away
from the heartaches of Europe. At least 400,000 people were to
reach these shores in the aftermath of World War II, from 1946
to 1952. That journey had taken some by way of Russia, Iran,
the Middle East, Europe, Africa, Asia, South America. For
others, it had been a nonstop trip direct from Germany. They
were generally young—in their twenties and thirties,[1] and some
were very young—like Henry Mangurten, who was just sixteen,
alone, and a survivor of the Lodz ghetto and of Auschwitz. Jessie
K., aged thirteen, was also orphaned as a result of the war. Her
father had been lost in action with the Polish army; her mother
and baby brother had succumbed in the wastes of Siberia. She
and hundreds of other Polish orphaned children had been taken
out of Russia to India as a result of the Sikorski Agreement in
1941, and then to Mexico after the war to await admission into
the United States. In July 1946 she came to this country with
about forty other Polish children; they were sent to the Holy
Family Institute in Elmsworth, just outside Pittsburgh.

Just as orphaned children were able to get into the United
States within a year or so after the war, so too were those, like
Raymond C., who had been born in this country. Raymond
arrived on January 1, 1946, aboard the *Ernie Pyle* (a ship named
for the famed war correspondent who was killed in the south

Pacific in 1945). But most Polish refugees faced an endless round of delays and problems in entering the country; the 1924 law limiting immigration and setting a quota of approximately 6,000 on Polish immigrants was still in effect.

In December 1945 President Truman issued an executive order directing American consular officials to give priority on quota lists to European refugees languishing in displaced persons camps. The hope was that some 39,000 refugees from the American zones of occupation in Germany, Austria, and Italy would be able to enter the country each year under existing quota regulations. "This is the opportunity for America to set an example for the rest of the world in cooperation toward alleviating human misery," declared the president.[2] However, in the thirty-month period from January 1, 1946, to June 30, 1948, when the Displaced Persons Act went into effect, only about 40,000 came to these shores despite Truman's intentions. Indeed, the bulk of the migration that was to come to Pittsburgh did not arrive in the United States during these months but came in the late 1940s and early 1950s under the act.

The Truman directive, while not having a dramatic impact on the numbers entering the country, nevertheless established an important procedure. Prospective immigrants could now be sponsored by accredited nonprofit voluntary agencies, which were allowed to sponsor individuals on a so-called community assurance or affidavit. Heretofore, persons seeking visas to the United States had to have the sponsorship of an individual who was able and willing to swear to support the newcomer. The new provision was to allow many persons to be admitted who might otherwise never have been able to come here, provided of course that they fell within the rigid quota limitations. Some of the agencies given accreditation under the directive included the United Service to New Americans (Jewish), the Hebrew Immigrant Aid Society, the National Catholic Committee for Refugees, the Polish Immigration Committee, and the United States Committee for the Care of European Children. Their activity is reflected in the fact that of the 28,789 displaced persons admitted into this country by the end of November 1947, 36 percent had been sponsored by voluntary agencies and 64 percent by individuals.[3]

The United Service to New Americans (USNA) (formed in 1946 by the merger of the National Refugee Service and the National Council of Jewish Women's Service to the Foreign Born Department) handled the bulk of the community assurances (affidavits) for the Jewish community. In turn, the New York City–based USNA depended upon the cooperation of Jewish community agencies throughout the country to back up the assurances given by the national agency. That meant that local communities with the collaboration of the local Jewish agency were to finance and handle the resettlement of persons as directed by the national office. Thus there was continuing communication between New York and professional staff workers of Jewish community institutions in cities around the country, including the Jewish Social Service Bureau of Pittsburgh. Next to the American Red Cross, USNA was the largest voluntary social service agency in the country at the time. At the height of its operation in 1948—before a separate agency was established to handle immigrant resettlement just in the New York area—it employed nearly 800 persons and spent $10.5 million. In fact, between 1946 and 1951 USNA spent over $34 million primarily for relief service.[4]

The USNA was assisted in Europe by two other Jewish agencies. The Joint Distribution Committee, which was supported by funds from the annual United Jewish Appeal, helped channel displaced Jews into the USNA pipleline. The Joint, as it was called, was the largest social welfare agency in Europe and provided a considerable amount of relief supplies to Jews in the displaced persons camps. The Hebrew Immigrant Aid Society (HIAS) was also authorized to provide assurances to prospective Jewish immigrants to America. It also helped Jewish refugees immigrate to Palestine.[5]

Advocates for Catholic displaced persons were led by the Vatican. Monsignor William Carroll, a priest from the Diocese of Pittsburgh who served as an aide for years in the Papal Secretariat of State in Rome and who was the Vatican's delegate at a meeting of the International Refugee Organization in Geneva in early 1947, indicated that "the Vatican recognized in the plight of the displaced Poles in Europe, a sad condition that merits special sympathy and assistance."[6] Generally, Catholics in displaced persons camps relied upon the assistance of the War Relief Services of the National Catholic Welfare Conference. This agency, which had distributed from December 1943 to June 1946 more than $2.5 million in aid to Polish refugees in the Middle East and Europe, was called upon to provide additional services to displaced Catholics seeking to emigrate from Europe.

A second agency, which specifically assisted Catholics seeking to immigrate to the United States and provided corporate assurances when necessary, was the Catholic Committee for Refugees (CCR). This committee had been founded in 1936 to assist German and Austrian refugees from Nazism to settle in New York. Since 1940 it had operated under the leadership of Reverend Emil N. Komora. When newcomers came to this country under the aegis of the CCR, they were met at the dock in New York by representatives of the Bureau of Immigration of the National Catholic Welfare Conference (NCWC), the umbrella Catholic social service agency. Thomas Mulholland was the port director who had handled matters in New York since the inception of the service in 1921. Bruce Mohler, who was his boss, had also been on hand from the beginning. He was director of the Bureau of Immigration of the NCWC in Washington. The collaboration between these two was vital to the work of the CCR.

While both Christians and Jews had their accredited agencies to assist in their care and resettlement, there clearly was a difference in the effectiveness of the various organizations; the bulk of the agency assurances issued under the Truman direc-

tive were from Jewish agencies.[7] It is reported that between
March 31, 1946, and June 30, 1948, 25,594 out of 35,515 new
arrivals were Jewish.[8] This was true despite the fact that less
than 20 percent of the displaced persons population in Europe
was Jewish.

This poor showing on the part of the Catholic agency was
viewed with considerable consternation by Catholics and other
interested parties. In the files of the NCWC there is much
correspondence on the situation of Catholic displaced persons in
Europe. In a letter from Bruce Mohler to Father Swanstrom of
the War Relief Services, Mohler writes that "we definitely seem
to have lost out to the Jews, at least in the early stages."[9] A Miss
Buckley of the NCWC sent a memo to Mohler about a meeting
she attended on August 29, 1946, with people from the U.S.
visa service.[10] She wrote that at the meeting the CCR was asked
to report on its activities but was not able to even indicate the
number of its overseas personnel, nor the number of people
admitted under its corporate affidavit to date. In contrast, she
said, Miss Petluck of the USNA "knew her work thoroughly and
spoke with authority." Furthermore, the assistant to the commissioner of the U.S. Immigration and Naturalization Service at the
meeting "complimented the Jewish agencies on their efficient
organization and said that the Catholic and Protestant societies
ought to do better." The assistant said she had never been able
to find anything out about Catholic overseas personnel, and the
only one she had ever heard of as the Catholic representative
was a Father Flynn, whom she had not succeeded in locating.
She reported that many non-Jewish people in various camps had
no opportunity to file for visas.

This observation was corroborated in a letter written by a
Catholic layman to Mulholland, who "was very much incensed
because he could not locate a Catholic representative all over
Germany, nor did he meet up with any one over there who had
been in contact with one."[11] "He had also been told to look for a
Father Flynn, but could not find anyone who had even heard of

him. In contrast he noted that "the Jews are entrenched in every little town and hamlet and are giving excellent service to their people."

With reports like these, the CCR finally improved their services. By October 1946 the elusive Father Flynn had been removed from his post, and there were Catholic agency personnel listed in Frankfort, Munich, Stuttgart, Bremen, and Berlin. These representatives overseas were soon urging the CCR to grant more corporate affidavits. "Unless we get an extension of our corporate affidavits, our position next month will be as embarrassing as it has been three months ago."[12] Still trying to improve its image in the fall of 1947, the NCWC ran five articles in its bulletin about the fine work of the CCR. When Mulholland suggested to Bruce Mohler that perhaps the articles on the CCR should be followed by similar laudatory pieces about the NCWC Bureau of Immigration, Mohler wrote back that that was not necessary. The news stories about the CCR "were very appropriate at this time by virtue of recent adverse propaganda against the ability of the CCR to carry out the work for displaced persons satisfactorily."[13] Apparently Mohler didn't think such image building was needed for the NCWC Immigration Bureau in New York.

Leonard Dinnerstein, in reviewing the role and activity of voluntary agencies assisting displaced persons after the war, concluded that "the Jewish agencies were on the scene first, they had the largest resources in terms of money and personnel, and the greatest interest in helping the survivors of the Holocaust."[14] For the 400,000 Catholic displaced persons in the American zone in Germany and Austria, the Catholic War Relief Service had a staff of only five persons in April 1946. Catholic personnel themselves recognized the paucity of their efforts and the disparity between themselves and the Jewish organization.

It should be noted that for the approximately 117,000 Jewish Displaced Persons in the same area, there is a staff of 117 persons, or

one staff person for every 1,000 displaced persons. . . . Without
meaning to appear critical, and yet considering the question objec-
tively, it must be said that because of insufficient personnel and
inadequate funds, this Committee [CCR] has been unable in the
past eight months to do the work it was called upon to do.[15]

Bruce Mohler, in a confidential letter to the public relations
director of the Catholic Daughters of America in Cleveland,
complained about the situation. He felt he had all he could do to
keep up with those Catholic displaced persons who had already
come to the United States.

Of course you know that we are up to our necks in bringing over
Catholic DP's and while only a few have come, it has taken all that
war relief services (handling visas overseas), the CCR (reception on
arrival, placement, guarantee of support), and our bureau (serving
affidavit documents of relatives and friends) can do. You say why
not do more? Well, the Jews are after 170 million dollars this year
(100 million last year) and they will get it. We in the Sunday collection last year got less than 2 million and anticipate 5 million from
the current effort. . . . If Catholics comprise 75% of the DP's, we
would get 350,000 DP's. . . . Let's get down to brass tacks. Who
will foot the enormous bill of transportation and support!?[16]

Mohler went on to point out that, when he first learned of the
Truman directive from the commissioner on immigration, "Jews
were then organized to function with no end of workers in
Germany, plenty of money and were actually responsible for the
Directive".[17]

Mrs. Sarah McCarthy of Cleveland, public relations director
of the Catholic Daughters of America in her city, for her part felt
that she had to have some kind of background from Mohler
because of the pressure her organization was under by Jewish
women to support legislation liberalizing immigration into the
country. "My own feelings are that they [the Jewish women] have
exhausted the patience of everyone in hammering away, and now

with quotas exhausted, they are out for more."[18] She opposed a revision of immigration laws because of "the economic situation," but concluded that "if our Catholic people should have the same amount of persistence and fervor for their cause as these gals do (I think the women in these meetings are more persistent than the men), then we would not be worried about raising the 5 million nor would the NCWC headquarters be disturbed about having sufficient budget to do the big job that has been cut out for them."[19]

The disproportionate number of Jews entering the country in the early phases of the Truman directive was of growing concern not only to Catholic authorities, but to American officials both in the State Department and Congress. In April 1946 there was a plea from Howard Travers, chief of the Visa Divison of the Department of State, for Catholics to grant more assurances. He wrote that the low numbers of Catholics on the early refugee ships "has caused us some embarrassment since the President wanted a fair distribution of refugees."[20] Mohler responded that he had no idea of what was happening until early January and that the Jewish organizations had been at work on the project for a long time. When Travers was replaced, Mohler wrote to Father Komora of the CCR that Hoering, his replacment, had given him the word that Catholics would have priority over Jews on the waiting list if individual or corporate affidavits were available for the Catholics. Mohler considered Traver's successor to be "practical, understanding and quite concerned about the Catholic displaced person, especially the Poles."[21]

Despite the relative proportions of Jews and Christians, the fact of the matter was that the total number of immigrants arriving under the Truman directive was not going to put much of a dent in the numbers of displaced persons trying to find a new home. The problem was recognized by a group of prominent Jews of the American Jewish Committee (AJC), who sought to bring at least 100,000 Jewish survivors to the United States. Accordingly, sparked by members of the important AJC, a

Citizens Committee for Displaced Persons (CCDP) was organized under the official leadership of Earl Harrison in the fall of
1946. This committee was a nonpartisan, multiethnic, and religious group working to create broad-based support for proposed
displaced persons legislation and to bring pressure to bear on
Congress. They indeed had undertaken a formidable task.

The fight in Congress had already begun between those who
argued America should do its "fair share" to ease the plight of
displaced persons and an influential group who argued that we
had done enough and that we should not allow any more "unde-
sirables" into the country. There is no question that the "undesir-
ables" they were referring to were the Jewish survivors of the
Holocaust. Evidence of the extent of prejudice against Jews in
the Congress of the United States has been amply documented.[22]
A document marked "personal" and "confidential" that was sent
to all the Catholic dioceses, including the diocese in Pittsburgh,
commented on the proposed Stratton bill of 1947, which called
for the admission of 400,000 displaced persons into this country
over a two-year period. The memo is particularly illuminating. It
noted that the Stratton bill appeared headed for defeat for a few
reasons. One was because there was considerable opposition to
tampering with the immigration legislation, legislation that had
prevailed since 1924. However, a second and related reason was
the disproportionate percentage of Jews who would presumably
enter under its provisions. Penned into the margin of the memo
was the note that "the real reason was the fact that too many Jews
had come in up to the time the bill had been introduced."[23] The
memo went on to state that the biggest obstacle in Congress
appeared to be the feeling that if any legislation was passed,
Christian groups in the United States were not prepared to take
their full share of the people admitted under the bill. The line of
reasoning that followed was that, since only the Jewish organizations were adequately prepared to handle the matter, the vast
majority of those who would enter the United States under any
displaced persons legislation would thus be Jews. As diocesan

directors were cautioned by the NCWC, "this opposition is not out in the open and is subterfuged by using opposition on other points. We are convinced however, that this single factor looms large in the minds of a great number of the members of Congress."[24] To emphasize this further, in the margin next to this statement it was marked "deciding factor." The memo went on to urge that every effort should be made through local diocesar resettlement committees to make it known to local congressmen and senators that Catholics were preparing in a definite way to resettle displaced persons and that the overwhelming majority of them were Christian.[25]

The CCR supported the Stratton bill, since it anticipated rectifying the imbalance in numbers of Catholics entering the country. Charles Rozmarek of the Polish American Congress (PAC) and other spokesmen for Catholics, Lutherans, and the Federal Council of Churches followed in endorsing the measure, which had long since secured the support of the CCDP under Earl Harrison. Local CCDPs were organized around the country, including one in Allegheny County (Pittsburgh area).

The first organizational meeting of the Allegheny County CCDP was on January 23, 1947, shortly after the national CCDP had been launched. The Allegheny CCDP was actually an expanded version of a committee on immigration and displaced persons which had just been set up by the American Service Institute (ASI) in Pittsburgh. The ASI was a social service agency supported entirely by the Community Chest. Established in 1941 as a result of the recommendations of a social study of Pittsburgh taken in 1937, its purpose as originally stated was

to assist in the ethnic, cultural and economic assimilation into the community of new Americans residing in Allegheny County; to encourage their participation in community life, as individuals or as groups; to cooperate with individual and with nationality organizations in relating themselves to public and private social and civic agencies; and to give technical assistance to residents of Allegheny

County who desire to become naturalized citizens of the United States."[26]

The ASI was considered by its founders to be unique in the country. It was to provide assistance in immigration and naturalization matters; provide information on ethnic, racial, and religious groups; secure interpreters, translators, and speakers for interested individuals and organizations; compile and publish materials on intercultural relations; and promote a program of intercultural education in schools, churches, and so on.[27]

In December 1946, when the national CCDP was formed, the ASI in Pittsburgh appointed a committee to work on the problem of immigration policy and displaced persons, because it felt that nobody was adequately dealing with this problem.[28] The committee designated by the ASI board included Dr. John C. Smith, chairman of ASI, Mrs. Alex Lowenthal, an active member of the Jewish community, Father Charles Owen Rice (Catholic), the Very Reverend Peter M. Kreta, a Russian Orthodox, and Ms. Helen Green, who was on the staff.

The formation of this ASI committee was also sparked by the American Jewish Committee in New York, with which Mrs. Lillian Friedberg, an activist in the local Jewish community, was in touch. There was correspondence between the national CCDP, which the American Jewish Committee was quietly spearheading, and the local ASI displaced persons committee. On January 23, 1947, the ASI committee along with other invited community leaders met with Dr. William S. Bernard, executive secretary of the national CCDP, to learn about what was happening on the national level so that the local group could provide the proper information to the public. There were eighteen persons, including Bernard and representatives of various religious groups, the ASI, organized labor, and the city government. Invited but not attending were twenty-one other persons representing the spectrum of the local Pittsburgh community.[29]

After this meeting with Bernard it was decided to organize an

Allegheny County CCDP, whose objective would be to stimulate the passage of legislation to admit displaced persons, educate the community on their problems, broaden the base of interested persons, and raise funds. One of the first actions of the local CCDP was to meet with the Pittsburgh section of the National Council of Jewish Women to coordinate efforts. The NCJW through its Service to the Foreign Born Department had long been active both nationally and locally in assisting refugees and resettling them in the United States. The NCJW was enlisted in the lobbying effort in behalf of displaced persons, to duplicate material sent by the national CCDP and mail it to more than 2,000 of its members. The Council of Churches of Christ was also prevailed upon to send information to their mailing list of 5,000 persons. A Speakers Bureau was set up under the direction of Mrs. Alex Lowenthal (although it apparently received few requests), and publicity and membership subcommittees were also designated.[30]

Operating on a budget of only a few hundred dollars raised by local contributions, the Allegheny County CCDP did appear to initiate a communitywide effort to educate people about the displaced persons problem. While the local CCDP initially favored no specific legislation, by May 1947, when Earl Harrison appeared in Pittsburgh to address the twenty-fifth anniversary meeting of the Federation of Social Agencies, it supported the Stratton bill, following the lead of the national CCDP which Harrison chaired. In the files of the Allegheny County CCDP are various letters to newspapers, civic and religious organizations, and television and radio stations urging them to support the legislation or to show the movie *Passport to Nowhere*, which portrayed the plight of the displaced person. People were urged to write their congressmen.

When the Stratton bill failed to come out of House committee, it appeared to take the wind out of the sails of the Allegheny County CCDP—at least there is no record of continued lobbying and educational effort, although the committee still existed on paper. A further blow came in February 1948 when the ASI had to cut staff support to the CCDP because the Community Chest failed to meet its quota and the ASI itself was financially squeezed. However, the ASI continued its other activities regarding immigration, including sponsorship of a Visitors Bureau for New Arrivals, which had been organized early in 1946. The ASI recruited and trained volunteers to tell new Americans about educational opportunities and to refer them to social agencies where necessary. Generally, volunteers were garnered from an assortment of women's clubs and numbered between twenty to thirty at any one time. In a report in April 1951, the Visitors Bureau claimed to have visited over 1,600 new arrivals in the Pittsburgh area since its inception in 1946.[31]

After the failure of the Stratton bill, the legislation that finally emerged from the Eightieth Congress was far less liberal than the Stratton measure and was riddled with the prejudices of many congressmen. The Displaced Persons Act of June 1948 allowed 205,000 displaced persons to enter the United States over a two-year period from July 1, 1948, to June 30, 1950. These numbers were to be mortgaged against quotas for each nationality group as stipulated by the legislation of 1924, so that no other persons from various countries in central and eastern Europe would be able to enter the country for years into the future. Moreover, the cutoff date for eligibility for displaced person status was set at December 22, 1945, well before the 150,000 Jews who fled Poland in 1946 after their release from the Soviet Union arrived in the camps of the Allied-occupied zones. Priority was given to immigrants who had been farmers, with 30 percent of the places to go to this group and 40 percent to people from the Baltic countries. Prior assurances were required for both employment and housing.

The act was criticized by President Truman, who called it blatantly "discriminatory," but he signed the measure anyway, operating on the theory that half a loaf was better than none. The drive to amend the act began almost with its passage. The chairman of the Allegheny County CCDP was among those who urged revision of the law. However, various delaying tactics were taken by key senators, and it was not until two years later that an amended bill was finally adopted. The new law extended the life of the original act for one year and raised the number of eligible displaced persons to 341,000. The cutoff date of December 22, 1945, was changed to January 1, 1949, and the various priorities to farmers and Balts were dropped. Furthermore, refugees who had gone to France, Belgium, Sweden, Switzerland, Holland (in addition to Germany, Austria, and Italy) after the war were now included. Polish exservicemen and their families who had gone to England were also made eligible for admission to the United States. A final extension of the law was granted to run through June 1952 to ensure the utilization of all the visas that had been authorized.

When the act finally expired in 1952, the United States had accepted 380,000 people under its provisions, or approximately 40 percent of the displaced persons registered in Europe. Despite the initial disproportionate share of Jewish immigrants, by 1952 the ratio clearly reflected the proportions of each religious group in Europe. All told, under the Truman directive and the Displaced Persons Act, 45 percent of immigrants accepted by the United States were Catholic, 20 percent were Jewish, and 34 percent were either Protestant or Greek Orthodox.

While the CCDP had achieved its goal in terms of the numbers of immigrants admitted into the United States, there had been concern about the backgrounds of some of the people accepted. In a memo submitted by the AJC on behalf of thirty-three Jewish organizations (including the Community Relations Council of Pittsburgh), a test was advocated for all persons applying under the act. Under the proposal, a person would be excluded if they in any way had lent support to the Nazis. The nature of that support was clearly spelled out.[32] This provision was not acted upon by the Congress, much to the consternation of the AJC.

The NCWC had geared up to better meet the needs of the displaced persons when it appeared that legislation was likely. By the end of 1947 there were reorganizational plans afoot to set up a new far-reaching program to assist in the processing and relocating of displaced persons throughout the country. It was recognized that this was necessary in order to bring over the numbers of Catholics waiting to be resettled. What resulted from the reorganization was the establishment of the National Resettlement Council authorized by the Board of Bishops in November 1947. This new advisory body under Father Swanstrom (formerly of the CCR) was linked with and backed up by Catholic resettlement committees that were set up in 120 dioceses, covering 19,000 parishes throughout the country. These local committees were to educate their parishioners on the displaced persons problem, secure proper legislation, identify potential sponsors, raise funds, and follow up with assistance once the displaced persons arrived.[33]

The National Resettlement Council was composed of, among others, representatives from the War Relief Services of the NCWC in Europe, the NCWC Bureau of Immigration out of Washington and New York, the CCR, representatives of local dioceses, and eleven nationality groups who had been actively working on immigration matters on behalf of their compatriots. It was recognized that not only was it vital to establish a nationwide structure backed by local communities, but that better coordination with various nationality groups was also necessary. The NCWC reported that the lack of coordination among such organizations "has resulted in a dissipation of Catholic effort and in a failure of Catholic efforts to collectively bring an adequate number of DP's and refugees to the United States."[34]

Two nationality groups with which the NCWC was trying to work more closely and which were put on the National Resettlement Council were the Polish Immigration Committee and the American Relief for Poland. Both of these groups had been working to bring displaced persons to America, and it was felt by all concerned that linking efforts would be more productive. The Polish Immigration Committee (PIC) had opened its office in New York City on February 2, 1947. The idea behind its formation had come from the Right Reverend Monsignor Felix Burant, who had served as a chaplain in the U.S. armed forces during World War II. After the war he had been assigned to the predominantly Polish church of St. Marks in New York City and found himself in a community into which many Polish immigrants were arriving.[35] Monsignor Burant was to serve as the inspiration and guiding light of the PIC for many years. The PIC acted as a liason between relatives in this country and prospective immigrants who needed affidavits of support. It also made sure that displaced persons were greeted at the piers and arranged for temporary housing for them when there was no individual sponsor to meet the boat.

In the files of the NCWC are references to the work of Father Burant's group in May and June of 1947, when Bruce Mohler of the NCWC Bureau of Immigration and Burant of the PIC were in touch for the first time. Burant in May indicated that he had "plenty of money at his disposal" and that he could "promptly lay down with Father Komora of the Catholic Committee on Refugees any funds that he might need for visa fees, inland transportation expenses and future support in the U.S." He said he had also "taken off Father Komora's hands for placement quite a number of Polish DP's who were already here from Germany."[36] Mohler apparently did not appear too excited about this overture from the Poles and other nationality groups. He wrote Mulholland that "you are well able to handle the nationality groups, who, suddenly inspired with a desire to show some activity for their countrymen, can be expected to be rather demanding."[37] Mulholland, whose letter to Mohler crossed in the mail, complained that Father Burant had indicated he was ready to give all assistance to the Poles, including meeting them on the piers in New York.[38] For Mulholland, this appeared to pose a problem because "I want only to have sufficient workers on the pier to do efficient work and of course do not mind having a reserve, but I am not going to be told by the representatives of various organizations whom I am to select nor am I going to have people going on the piers with our arm bands just to dance attendance on some one individual."[39] By June 1947, Mohler wrote Mulholland that "judging from the facts now on hand, this group is floundering more or less and the only benefit we can see is that they do take a little work off the shoulders of the Catholic Committee by virtue of guaranteeing expenses and future support."[40]

Floundering or not, the PIC affiliated with the NCWC was recognized by the newly constituted National Resettlement Council on November 30, 1948. From the vantage point of the NCWC, the hope in linking up with the PIC was to speed the efforts to bring more Catholics into the country. From the standpoint of the PIC, such a tie to the NCWC meant that it was able to take advantage of services the NCWC offered. The Polish group felt that the clearing and processing of Polish assurances would be expedited by NCWC with the proper government agencies both in this country and in Europe.

The Displaced Persons Act of 1948 was to greatly increase the activity of the PIC. A small staff was established under the direction of Walter Zachariasiewicz at the end of 1948. Zachariasiewicz was himself a Polish emigré who had been imprisoned in the Soviet Union, released to join General Wladyslaw Anders, and had arrived in America after working for the Polish government in exile as general secretary of the Social Welfare Ministry.[41] The staff of the PIC devoted itself to securing as many of the required job and house guarantees as possible; providing jobs and homes for those displaced persons who had lost their sponsors; giving medical, legal, and material assistance to those in need; and rendering whatever other services were necessary. Under the direction of Zachariasiewicz, the organization grew in size and scope.

Zachariasiewicz himself was the first to admit that the work of the PIC, while patterned after the model of the HIAS, could never match the activity of that seasoned organization. Unlike the HIAS, the PIC had to work through the NCWC for corporate affidavits because it was not recognized as a corporate sponsor by the Displaced Persons Commission until July 1951. In addition, the funding for its operation was small. Zachariasiewicz indicated his relief budget was never more than $20,000. The remainder of his funds went to support office personnel (from three to six persons in the early 1950s). He claimed that approximately 20,000 persons supported their appeal for funds, although a membership report in 1954 indicated there were only 600 to 800 supporting members. People who had been helped by the PIC were asked to repay the loan extended to them, usually amounting to $100 to $150, and to make small contributions to continue the work of the PIC. During the first two years of its existence, the PIC received a subsidy from the American Relief for Poland to the tune of $4,000 a month. From October 1950 to December 1951, the Polish American Congress also contributed $1,000 a month, and an annual ball held by the PIC raised an additional $10,000 a year. The average monthly expenses of the PIC from August 1952 to March 1953 amounted to $2,000 to $3,000.[42] Father Burant traveled a good deal to solicit funds and obtain individual assurances. Only $20 a week was spent on publicity, but two or three releases a week about the displaced persons' situation were sent to forty Polish newspapers in the country, including one in Pittsburgh, and to thirty-five Polish radio programs.[43]

Much of the work of the PIC was carried on by a core of dedicated volunteers in New York City as well as in Buffalo, Detroit, Chicago, Cleveland, and Hartford. (There was no committee in Pittsburgh, despite its large Polish community.) Mulholland, who was not one to lavish praise, finally acknowledged that the PIC was the only affiliated organization that had consistently met the commercial ships carrying newcomers to America. The other affiliated organizations sent workers only for specific appointments.[44] William S. Bernard, who was the dynamic force behind the CCDP and who was the AJC person responsible for these matters, asserted that 40,000 Polish nationals were resettled in the United States or elsewhere directly or indirectly through the services of the PIC.[45] The authorized history of the PIC shows that between 1947 when the committee began its operation to September 1952 the PIC was able to obtain assurances for 17,893 from Germany, Italy, and Austria; 4,592 from Great Britain; and 1,065 out-of-zone refugees from other countries—for a total of 23,550 during those years.[46] Given the fact that the PIC was continually plagued with financial difficulties and had a small staff, it was able to accomplish a great deal.

Two other Polish groups were involved with Polish displaced persons. The American Relief for Poland (ARP) was organized during the war with headquarters in Chicago. It provided help for Polish prisoners of war in Germany and assisted Poles scattered throughout Europe, including various individuals who were to settle in Pittsburgh. When the war was over, the organization began concerning itself with resettlement and had two or three representatives in Europe. According to Zachariasiewicz, even though ARP was in place before the PIC, Father Burant felt the need for a new immigrant aid agency that would be more effective and help all immigrants and not just those heading for the Chicago area.

The American Committee for the Resettlement of Polish DPs was another organization interested in Polish displaced persons, particularly in the Chicago area, and brought in a few thousand displaced persons. This group was formed in 1948 by the Polish American Congress. It had its Pittsburgh connection through Judge Blair Gunther, a resident of Pittsburgh who became chairman of the national organization. Its aims paralleled the aims of the PIC: "To assist in the selection of those displaced persons of Polish ethnic origin from European DP camps who are eligible for entry into the United States, to secure employment for them and a place to live, . . . to secure funds to successfully accomplish the above mentioned resettlement program."[47] Between June 1, 1948, and May 20, 1952, 360 telegrams, 6,240 letters, 210 memorandum to senators and congressman, and 430 pieces of correspondence on the subject of displaced persons were sent out by this organization.[48] By December 31, 1951, the American Committee for the Resettlement of Polish DPs had obtained 35,000 affidavits, mostly from the Chicago area.[49]

Organizational activities on behalf of Polish displaced persons after 1948 thus involved a number of loosely connected groups, each pursuing its own course with a minimum of resources and some measure of success. An inability or unwillingness to link efforts hurt the cause of these displaced persons. But the problems in the Polish Catholic community ran deeper. There was not widespread support either financially or in other ways from the larger Polish American community of six million in the United States. Walter Zachariasiewicz and many others have pointed out that the Poles who had come to America a generation before were simply not concerned about this latest round of Polish immigrants. There was little sense of comraderie. Thaddeus Krysiewicz, who compiled a history of the Polish Immigration Committee, wrote this stinging commentary:

The assistance rendered by the Polish-American community appears to be only lip service and not an actual interest in the welfare and happiness of their blood brothers. They cannot see the benefits that would accrue from an active interest and participation in the work of the Committee, perhaps, because of a blindness built upon jealousy, indifference concerning the masses of Polish people, or complacency. They reason they had no one to help them with their troubles and problems so why can't these new Polish Americans do the same.[50]

Another Polish historian wrote that the disappointment of Polish organizations in not being able to obtain more assurances or affidavits for the Polish displaced persons "might be due more to increased Americanization." There simply was not the same interest in Poland. She concluded, "it is hard to determine which of the reasons—increased Americanization, lack of funds, unwillingness to take responsibility for strangers, or the Committee's deficiencies played the most important role."[51]

In Pittsburgh, whatever involvement there was on the part of the Polish community in the displaced persons' issued was obtained by appeals through various lay organizations, such as the Central Council of Polish Organizations and the Polish National Alliance, through the Polish-American press, and through local Polish churches. Judge Blair Gunther, a noted lawyer in the city and prominent in the Polish American Congress, was invited to the Allegheny County CCDP but he did not attend.[52] Although there was a plethora of other Polish organizations in the city, there were no representatives on the Allegheny County CCDP from any of these groups. Since the CCDP was looking to reach out into the broad community to those organizations they felt might be active, it appears the Polish community was not ready or willing to be part of a larger effort.

The only local organized effort to aid Polish displaced persons was established in 1948 by the Catholic diocese and the National Catholic Resettlement Council. Bishop Boyle of the Pittsburgh diocese appointed Reverend Thomas Lappan to head the Pittsburgh Diocesan Resettlement Council. Previously, he had headed the War Relief Services in Pittsburgh. Lappan appealed to priests, asking them to find homes and jobs for displaced persons in their parishes and to make appeals from their pulpits.

While documentary evidence is scant, we do have a report dated January 3, 1952, from Father Lappan to the Most Reverend John F. Dearden, bishop of Pittsburgh, indicating that, as of December 1, 1951, 300,664 displaced persons had entered the United States. Of these, 107,954 were brought into the country with the assistance of the NCWC; and out of these, 2,133 had come to the diocese of Pittsburgh through the Resettlement Council. Of these 2,133 persons, 1,476 had come to relatives and friends who had filed affidavits for them, while the remaining 657 persons had come under the blanket assurance program of the Resettlement Council.[53] There was no breakdown of how many of this number arriving were Polish nor how many of the blanket assurances received and used were from Polish sources. In a separate report on resettlement by institutions or organizations, it was noted that the Central Council of Polish Organizations in 1951 sponsored two families, for a total of seven persons, and that one family of five persons was sponsored by the Polish National Alliance. No other Polish organizations were listed.[54]

The individual parish that sponsored the most families in the Pittsburgh area was the parish of Father A. M. Twardy of St. Leocadia, in Wilmerding. He and his parish gave affidavits for seven families. Indeed, a few of the refugees interviewed were listed in the 1952 report and during their interviews referred to the goodness of Father Twardy. No other churches were specifically cited by written reports or by the refugees. While individuals might come forth in response to appeals made through churches, Polish organizations, national agencies, or the local Polish press, there was no agency, ad hoc group, or committee in the Polish community to spearhead a citywide effort in behalf of displaced persons legislation or to aid in Polish resettlement in Pittsburgh.

The lack of a local network outside the limited efforts of the NCWC Resettlement Council in Pittsburgh was in sharp contrast to the very organized, very active, and very expensive efforts that were undertaken by the Jewish community in Pittsburgh from the time the war ended to the expiration of the Displaced Persons Act. There were a process and a structure of aid and relief operating not only in Europe but in U.S. communities in which displaced persons were settled.

The years from 1945 through 1948 were of profound significance for Jews around the world. It was during those three years that the struggle for the state of Israel was most actively waged. Holocaust survivors in Europe played a significant role in that crusade both through their active efforts to reach Palestine illegally to fight the British and through the pressure and support generated by their plight in the displaced persons centers of Europe. They helped create the ground swell that resolved itself in the United Nations' vote for the partition of Palestine and the establishment of a Jewish state. The Pittsburgh Jewish community, like Jewish communities throughout the nation, was caught up in the turmoil of the times. An energetic effort was being made to bring survivors out of camps to America at the same time that American Jews were being asked to support the movement for a Jewish homeland and, later, its struggle against the invading Arab legions. The drama of Jewish community activity against a backdrop of momentous world events is the focus of the next chapter.

5

A Jewish Community Faces the Refugees

▶▶▶ THE JEWISH COMMUNITY OF PITTS-
burgh, like other Jewish communities throughout the
country in 1946, was caught in a whirlwind of international
events. While the Nazi slaughter had finally ended, the postwar
ordeal of the survivors was just beginning. About one million
European Jews, exclusive of those in the Soviet Union, had
survived the war, many of them in desperate circumstances.
This number included 80,000 Jews in Poland, out of prewar
Jewish population of 3.3 million. By 1946 these Jews were
joined by at least 140,000 Polish Jews who had survived under
the Russians and had just been repatriated. As a result of
conditions in Poland and propelled by the Kielce pogrom in July
1946, more than half of these 220,000 Polish Jews fled to
displaced persons camps in central Europe. By the summer of
1947 nearly 250,000 European Jews, all told, were in the
western zones of Germany and in Austria and Italy.[1] Their
overwhelming desire to go to Palestine was being thwarted by the
policies of the British government, which controlled the country
under a United Nations mandate.

The Jewish press in Pittsburgh ran continual stories about
the plight of the refugees in Europe, about conditions in the
camps, about the Nuremberg War Trials and their revelations
concerning the Holocaust, about the effort to open Palestine to
Jewish immigration, and about the responsibility of American
Jewry to help their less fortunate coreligionists abroad. Pitts-

burghers were made well aware of the fact that the United Jewish Appeal (UJA) in response to the unprecedented needs overseas had upped its nationwide goal from $50 million in 1945 to $100 million in 1946. The United Jewish Fund (UJF), the Pittsburgh arm of the UJA, in accordance with this escalation, had doubled its fund-raising target to $1.5 million.[2] This made the UJF effort the most ambitious private philanthropic campaign in the history of the city.[3] The week of May 5th was proclaimed by Mayor David Lawrence as UJF Week in the city of Pittsburgh.

With large-scale legal immigration to Palestine blocked, an effort began in the United States to allow more immigrants to come to this country. The Citizens Committee for Displaced Persons (CCDP), spearheaded by the American Jewish Committee, was formed when it became clear that the Truman directive would not prove very effective in bringing large numbers of displaced persons to this country. While efforts were launched by many groups, including the Allegheny County CCDP, to liberalize the immigration law, the Jewish immigrant aid organizations shifted into full gear to help surviving Jews in Europe. This included the Hebrew Immigrant Aid Society (HIAS) and what by 1946 became known as the United Service to New Americans (USNA).

While these organizations had large staffs abroad and worked very well, they needed to rely upon the good auspices of Jewish communities across the nation in order to resettle the immigrants they were trying to get out of the camps in Europe. Pittsburgh was one of 100 towns and cities throughout the United States linked to a national and international network to bring over and resettle Jewish displaced persons. In the years immediately following the war, communications between national and local offices flew back and forth as people on each level wrestled with the problem of displaced persons. American Jews had viewed with horror the news of their coreligionists in Europe. Now they had their opportunity to welcome the survivors. How would they respond?

Immediately after the Truman directive was announced in

December 1945, a new coordinating body known as the Joint
Committee on Service to New Immigrants was established in
Pittsburgh to involve all those Jewish organizations and agencies
that had theretofore devoted time or resources to servicing immigrants. This included the United Jewish Fund, the Federation of
Jewish Philanthropies (the coordinating body for local Jewish
health and welfare agencies), the Hebrew Free Loan Association,
the Jewish Social Service Bureau, the National Council of Jewish
Women, Montefiore Hospital, the Ladies Hospital Aid Society of
Montefiore, the Young Men and Women's Hebrew Association,
the Irene Kaufmann Settlement, and the United Vocational and
Employment Service. All these organizations and agencies had
been serving the social, medical, recreational, financial, and
vocational needs of immigrants as well as of the community at
large. Their representatives were invited to sit on the newly
established Joint Committee, which was to disseminate information and give direction to the shape of Pittsburgh's displaced
persons program. The fact that such a committee was set up
testified to the network of social service institutions already in
existence and the willingness and need to coordinate them in light
of the expected arrival of a wave of Jewish immigrants.

The Jewish Social Service Bureau (JSSB) (the family and
child welfare agency in Pittsburgh) sat on the Joint Committee
and assumed responsibility for the local refugee program. This
was the professional body that communicated directly with the
USNA in New York City for information and assistance. The
JSSB was notified by the USNA when immigrants were en route
to Pittsburgh so that they could alert relatives or volunteers to
meet them. An appointment for the new arrival was usually
arranged at the JSSB on Fernando Street for the following day.
Temporary housing was procured (too often at the run-down
Steel City Hotel, which one social worker admitted was a "flop
house"). A social worker from the JSSB would take the newcomers to a local store, arrange a budget, and talk to them about
learning English and about the free medical services offered to

them at Montefiore Hospital. Aside from the department of the
JSSB that handled relief and casework service, there was the
Committee on Service to the Foreign Born under the direction of
Zena Saul. Its responsibility was to offer assistance in the search
for relatives, the processing of papers, naturalization and citizen-
ship procedures, and other legal matters.

The second major agency in the city that worked with Jewish
immigrants was the Jewish vocational agency known as the
United Vocational and Employment Service (UVES). Leonard
Weitzman (who is currently director of the agency, which has
since been renamed the Vocational Rehabilitation Center), was
a young worker at the agency in 1947. He explained how the
refugees came to him after being referred by the JSSB.

Essentially, anybody who needed a job and wanted to work was
referred to us; the only ones who did not come were those who were
sick or hospitalized. Recent arrivals were interviewed and tested in
a special diagnostic program. Their skill was translated into whatever job openings we had available. A sheltered workshop, as it was
called, was offered to those people in need of special training, to
learn to cope with a work schedule, work with other people, or take
responsibility and account to a boss. The agency looked to find jobs
for applicants and acted as the intermediary between worker and
employer when we were called upon.

In its activity, UVES paralleled other agencies of its kind in
cities throughout the country.

The YM&WHA (today, the Jewish Community Center) was a
very important institution in the Pittsburgh community in the
1940s and 1950s. Its membership in 1949 stood at a record
6,223 members and its annual budget was $215,000. It boasted
a wide variety of programs, including fifty-four clubs, a physical
education program, a summer camp, a health facility, and an
educational center, which reached into the non-Jewish community. It was estimated by the director, Herman Passamaneck,
that the wide range of courses brought approximately 500 men

and women into the building on South Bellefield Avenue every night.[4] Its paid staff consisted of about seventy persons, including two dozen social workers.[5] The game room and lounge of the Y building were open to all and were used by a large number of newcomers. Newly arrived immigrants were given a one-year free membership, and many of them frequented the Y dances, held on Sunday nights.

In December 1949 Mr. Passamaneck reported that the fifty new Americans who came to the Y every Saturday night had formed a Blue and White, or New Americans Club. It originally included both married and single men, but the married men gradually dropped out. In addition to affording an opportunity for casual conversation, there was pingpong, social dancing, and games such as checkers, chess, and card playing. Passamaneck was very pleased with the club, remarking that "one has to see these new Americans enjoying their new found contacts in order to realize how much happiness they derive from them. . . . The desire of newcomers to join and participate in 'Y' activities is wholeheartedly supported by the staff and board of the Agency."[6] The appreciation was apparently reciprocated, because in a note sent to Passamaneck the members of the newcomers club thanked the board and the staff of the Y for the "hospitality which had been extended to us. We appreciate the help and guidance which the 'Y' has offered to us as new Americans."[7]

In addition to the help provided by professionals at the JSSB, the UVES, the Y, and Montefiore Hospital (which provided free medical care when needed), a large number of volunteers assisted in the resettlement process. Their contribution was as important, if not more important, as that of the paid staff. Volunteers were often called upon to supplement the services of the professionals, and in the smaller communities in the country with little or no professional staff, the task of integrating the newcomer into the community fell almost entirely upon the shoulders of volunteers. Volunteer leaders also were responsible for raising and allocating the funds from the local fund-raising

campaign. In fact, without the involvement of volunteers throughout the country, the magnitude of the Jewish community's response and indeed the response of the entire country to the
plight of the displaced persons of Europe would have been
greatly diminished.

Two volunteer organizations in Pittsburgh were very active in
the resettlement of Holocaust survivors. One was the Friendship
Club, an informal group formed in the 1930s in Pittsburgh.
According to two of its founders, it began as a casual gathering
of several young German Jews who had fled Nazism. The club
eventually approached the Y and Zena Saul, who before 1937
and the establishment of the JSSB, still worked in the Service to
the Foreign Born department of the National Council of Jewish
Women (NCJW) in Pittsburgh. By 1936 the club was meeting at
the Y so that newcomers could get together and help each other
adjust to a new environment. A deliberate decision was made to
conduct the affairs of the group in English. Speakers were asked
to talk about current events and opportunities on the local scene.

After World War II the Friendship Club decided to reach out
to the Jews who began arriving in the Pittsburgh area from
Poland and other Eastern European countries. The success of
this effort is debatable, but there is no question that a sincere
effort was made. Lotte Markus, the wife of one of the Friendship
Club old-timers, felt that the non-German survivors "just didn't
feel right" in the club, which was composed predominantly of
German and Austrian Jews. People would be invited to meetings
but, after coming once or twice, would drop out. She was
disappointed with this failure to gain sustained participation on
the part of Holocaust survivors. Ernest Nachman—who had
arrived in Pittsburgh in 1939 on a voyage of the famous ship, the
St. Louis—was president of the club between 1943 and 1953.
He had a little more positive feeling about the response of
Holocaust survivors to Friendship Club overtures, but admitted
being buffeted by two competing factions within the club. While
efforts were made to reach out to postwar newcomers through a

Chanukah party, picnics, and free one-year memberships, "there was a minority of club members who didn't welcome them, who wanted just a German club and rejected Jews from Poland." Nachman saw himself as a mediator between those who were ready to extend hospitality and those who resented the newcomers. He estimated that about 100 Holocaust survivors did join for some period of time.

To outside observers like Myrtle Fisher, actively involved with the Women's Division of the UJF and with the NCJW, the Friendship Club women did a "terrific job." They were "extremely conscientious" and "served a terrific purpose in taking people into their homes and making sure they were happy socially." To Dorothy Mallett who headed up the NCJW project to provide clothing and furniture to refugees, it was the Friendship Club women who "were the loyal ones, who came everyday and sorted clothes and helped, because they knew the language and were able to get along better than we were."

Many members of the NCJW Service to the Foreign Born Department were also members of the Friendship Club. Generally however, it was the NCJW that got the recognition for such hospitality —not only because of overlapping membership but, perhaps more importantly, because the Friendship Club had an "image problem," in the words of Ernest Nachman. With the exception of Nachman, most of the members of the club were not involved in other organizations in the Jewish community and wanted to keep the club small and nonestablishment. Thus it was not surprising that there was no reference to the activities of the Friendship Club between 1946 and 1951 in the pages of the *Jewish Criterion*, a weekly Pittsburgh newspaper. Perhaps because the Friendship Club was generally perceived in the community as a fledgling organization very much under the wing of the NCJW, it was not represented with all the other agencies and organizations in the city on the Joint Committee.[8]

The NCJW was the other volunteer organization vitally concerned with refugee matters. It certainly was not surprising that the NCJW played such as active role in the resettlement of newcomers: as early as 1903, at the request of the federal government, the NCJW had undertaken to meet, protect, and give service to unaccompanied women and children at the piers of New York City. In 1906 in Pittsburgh an Immigrant Aid Committee was formed "to extend the hand of good fellowship to our newly arrived sisters, to endeavor to convey to them our knowledge of conditions and give advice and assistance."[9] In the 1920s, the Pittsburgh NCJW hired Zena Saul as a professional in charge of immigrant matters, and in the 1930s it set up a committee of women responsible for "service to the foreign born." There were auxiliary committees on immigrant employment, English classes, furniture and household goods, housing, naturalization, recreation, visiting, and typing.

The Committee on Service to the Foreign Born numbered seven persons in 1946, but its numbers were to expand significantly within a few years, and so were its projects. A popular English class was offered once a week and so was an American government class. An employment bureau assisted in getting sitters and nurses for newcomers, and a locations index was established to help immigrants find friends and relatives overseas. Beyond this, the committee set up a speakers bureau to inform other organizations about immigrant concerns and did some interviewing and clerical work to assist the JSSB.[10]

Housing very quickly became the major problem facing immigrants after the war. Three thousand veterans were returning to Pittsburgh and finding it all but impossible to find a home.[11] For newcomers the prospect was even worse. The Joint Committee asked the NCJW to lead the effort to find suitable housing for new arrivals in Pittsburgh. Accordingly, articles began appearing in the *Monthly Bulletin* of the NCJW asking the 2,200 members to be "on the lookout for any living space, furnished or unfurnished anywhere in the city,"[12] NCJW members took the lead in ferreting out available housing.

By 1948 the NCJW was in high gear as the arrival of

newcomers into the Pittsburgh community accelerated. Its Committee on Service to the Foreign Born now numbered some sixty women, and various subcommittees focused on employment, vocational training, visiting, transportation, and conversational English. The effort to do visiting however, was running into snags. There were problems of communication between NCJW members and Holocaust survivors. Those problems were not spelled out, but it was felt that training sessions were needed so that NCJW volunteers should not go in "cold" to avoid "any bad psychological reactions."[13] However, the training sessions were poorly attended, and only eight families ever requested the NCJW's visiting service.

NCJW members were much more successful in arm's-length transactions in which they did not necessarily come in contact with the survivors themselves. In October 1948 the Commitee on Service to the Foreign Born reported that members had been finding both temporary and permanent housing for at least ten and usually twelve immigrant families a month. They also made follow-up calls to see how people were managing. English classes had been organized at the homes of the various committee members, and fourteen immigrant women had been trained to serve at dinner parties so they could augment their incomes. The NCJW furnished their uniforms.

In December 1949 a harried Joint Committee called upon the NCJW to undertake a relief project to provide clothing, linens, household items, and furniture to new immigrants. This was proposed as a means of saving the JSSB some expenditure at a time when the financial strain on the Jewish community was most severe. (More will be said about this later.) The project continued for twenty-three months, until February 1952, when the budget picture for the JSSB improved considerably. During that time it was estimated by the Jewish Family and Children's Service (the old Jewish Social Service Bureau) that $14,000 to $15,000 was saved by the NCJW's volunteer efforts.[14]

In January 1950 the NCJW prepared to launch a major

collection undertaking. It was advertised in the *Jewish Criterion* as "an emergency clothing drive." People were called by members to contribute "clean, wearable and warm clothing of every description," as well as dishes, linens, blankets, and so on. Items were to be delivered to the NCJW lounge on Forbes Street or to any of the stations throughout the city in synagogues, community centers, and the Jewish Home for the Aged. A motor corps of NCJW volunteers was available to travel to every part of the city to pick up items people wanted to donate.

The result of this undertaking "was so tremendous that it required 5 weeks to process all the items. The phone just kept ringing with people who wanted to make contributions." A thousand dresses and suits, at least 150 overcoats, and many thousands of pounds of other clothes and household items were collected.[15] Jewish cleaning establishments cleaned and mothproofed many of the items, so that in March the project was ready to open to new Americans in the basement of the JSSB at 15 Fernando Street.

Just one week after the conclusion of the collection drive, the NCJW held a linen shower as another way of collecting goods. The public was invited to a musical program, and the price of admission was some new linen object or the cash for one. The NCJW held at least one other linen shower when supplies ran low.

Dorothy Mallett, a housewife who had been a social worker before starting a family, was placed in charge of the NCJW clothing effort by president Pauline Oseroff. She worked two or three mornings a week picking up donated clothes. She viewed the project as an outmoded relief system but recognized that the community "was absolutely in dire straits" and did not have enough money to adequately fund immigrant relief services. But there were other professional social workers at the JSSB who were uncompromising in their opposition to this relief project and quit their jobs as a result. They believed that the project would demean and possibly undermine the independence of their immigrant clients.

Dorothy never had a problem getting people to help. She called upon women who were not necessarily active in the NCJW but who had department store experience and who knew clothing. "They set everything up just like a store, with racks and displays." The Friendship Club women were in the store every day to be on hand when the social workers brought the new Americans in. The shop was open six days a week, and it was estimated that about six to ten people came in daily, about thirty to forty over the course of the week. Other NCJW women, including Marjorie Balter (jokingly known as Margie Vendome, for the high-priced boutique for ladies at Kaufmann's), worked in the basement at Fernando Street sorting and sizing clothes.

Gertrude Silverblatt was another NCJW volunteer very involved with the clothing project. She had just quit her job in retailing at Gimbel's when she was called upon to help out. She went to the forty or fifty Jewish wholesalers on Penn Avenue and on Fifth Avenue asking for merchandise. "We got such a good response. I went also to department stores. Even Hornes, which was not Jewish, contributed! Men helped out, too. A group used to borrow trucks and pick up heavy loads for the clothing store on Sunday mornings beginning at eight o'clock." By June 1951, 318 orders for clothing had been filled and the homes of twenty-one families had been furnished in full or in part. Indeed, when the operation was closed in February 1952, two years after it had started, a total of 500 orders had been filled for 175 families.[16]

By 1952 ninety women served on the Committee on Service to the Foreign Born, but the number was to drop sharply with the expiration of the Displaced Persons Act. In terms of costs, when peak numbers of immigrants were arriving in Pittsburgh in 1949 and 1950, the NCJW was budgeting between $1,200 and $1,500 annually for immigrant needs, mostly for English classes at Peabody and Allderdice high schools, when public schools were not operating English classes.[17]

The activities of the NCJW cut across a broad spectrum of concerns, from greeting newcomers to finding jobs for people, from housing to education, from clothing to recreation. Its volunteers gave to the local refugee program a dimension and a boost beyond the resources of what other agencies could provide. Outsiders might consider the scale of the effort awesome, as indeed it was in comparison to the efforts made by other local religious or ethnic groups. Bruce Mohler of the Bureau of Immigration of the National Catholic Welfare Conference and many others were not a little jealous and resentful of the Jewish ability to raise funds and to field an extensive network of professional and volunteer agencies and organizations.

Yet there were serious concerns also within the Jewish community, where a cacophony of multiple appeals jeopardized its ability to meet the ambitious needs of the displaced persons program.[18] The years when the displaced persons were arriving in this country were also the years when Israel was being established and was fighting for her life. American Jews were deeply committed to the Jewish state, and this was played out in terms of both emotional preoccupation and financial support. In addition to their weighty international concerns, local Jewish agencies had gone begging during the war years and were now clamoring for larger pieces of the pie that was being collected by the United Jewish Fund (UJF). This was the backdrop against which the commitment to the resettlement of Jewish displaced persons in America was made. The struggle of those who had to raise funds and then assign priorities in their allocation was formidable.

The budget committee of the UJF in Pittsburgh was charged with the responsibility of setting the goal for the campaign and determining the allocation of funds. It had to not only determine which of its thirty-five beneficiary agencies would get what, but to decide how much money would be sent to the United Jewish Appeal to aid Jews around the world and the United Palestinean Appeal to help the Jews in Palestine. In 1946 when the international situation began heating heating up in Palestine and displaced persons were streaming into camps in Europe, the budget committee decided that, despite the demand for assorted increases in Pittsburgh, they would keep levels the same to all the local recipients with two exceptions. They were the Jewish Social Service Bureau (JSSB), the professional agency in charge of refugee needs, and the United Vocational Employment Service (UVES), which offered vocational counseling and job placement. By so doing, the committee pledged the Jewish community to local refugee needs. This commitment was further underscored in Pittsburgh with the formation of the coordinating committee mentioned earlier—the Joint Committee on Service to New Immigrants. Donald Steinfirst, the executive of the JSSB, was named chairman of the Joint Committee.

Despite the institutional buildup and President Truman's directive, only 5,610 displaced persons came to the United States in 1946—and only ten "units" of either single persons or couples came in up to September 1946 through the community assurance program of Pittsburgh's Jewish community. By mid-1947 the JSSB was providing assistance to only sixteen units, constituting twenty-four persons. However, the expectation remained for a considerable increase in the numbers arriving in the United States. Accordingly, the United Service to New Americans (USNA) asked Pittsburgh to support a quota of ten units per month plus fifteen orphaned children between June 1947 and January 1948. To accommodate this "threatened" influx (in the words of a JSSB spokesmen), the JSSB went to the board of directors of the Pittsburgh United Jewish Fund for $150,000 in relief monies, nearly $10,000 in salaries for additional personnel, and $4,000 for extra office costs.[19] The board in response to this request passed a motion recognizing in principle the obligation to care for as many refugee families and individuals as possible. However, rather than authorizing a blanket allocation, they determined to have the Budget Committee of the UJF review the situation monthly and take out of the monies allocated to the United Jewish Appeal overseas those funds necessary for the resettlement of refugees in Pittsburgh.

The Joint Committee accepted the number urged on it by the USNA in New York while recognizing the serious financial and housing problems such a commitment would entail.

While more persons came into Pittsburgh during 1947 than during 1946, the pipeline was not open and flowing. As things turned out, instead of the sixty-plus units that the USNA in New York had asked Pittsburgh to take, only twenty-eight units came to the city between July and November 1947—twenty from southern France and Shanghai, seven from New York, and one intercity transfer.[20] In addition to these units, Pittsburgh was sent seven orphaned youths, so that the total number of orphaned youth being cared for by the JSSB at the time was fourteen.[21] Instead of the nearly $165,000 the JSSB anticipated for refugee needs, the real expenditure was $75,000, a significant sum but not nearly as high as what the Joint Committee on Service to New Immigrants had thought would be required.

Yet the problem of housing began to grow more difficult during the second half of 1947. Most immigrants were in family units rather than by themselves, and they needed more space. The old Gusky Orphanage, originally a temporary housing facility, was no longer deemed suitable. New arrivals were being sheltered in an assortment of living arrangements, including two temporary hotels, one in East Liberty and one on the North Side. The JSSB actually approached the UJF to consider purchasing an apartment building for the new arrivals. However, the purchase plan was killed when Louis Falk, Jr., president of the UJF, counseled against such a long-term investment. Moreover, UJA officials in New York were very concerned that local monies would be taken from the UJA allocation and applied to refugee needs in the local community, and they advised that as little money as possible be tied up with housing.[22] They had every right to be concerned, because this is exactly what happened in Pittsburgh. Out of the $75,000 spent in fiscal 1947 by the JSSB, $45,000 did come out of funds earmarked for the UJA. More would have been taken from the UJA allocation if there had been the expected influx of displaced persons.[23] This tug of war between the needs of Jews throughout the world, including the displaced persons waiting in Europe and those persons who had been able to get out and were en route to America, was only to worsen.

In 1947 Palestine was in turmoil and Jews were suffering in camps in Europe. The headline of a feature article in the *Jewish Criterion* read: "Plight of European Jews Indescribable, Says Eisenhower." The story went on at length to tell how General Dwight Eisenhower at the formal opening of the 1947 UJA appeal (whose goal was $170 million, up $70 million from the preceding year) declared that "the needs of the 1.5 million Jewish survivors in Europe are so great that only one who has seen, as I have, the mental and physical effect of savagery, repression and bigotry upon the persecuted of Europe can realize the full need of the material help and encouragement you propose to give."[24] To give even more weight to the appeal, in the editor's column was a reprint of an invitation that had been sent by a Jewish father to the friends of his child on the occasion of his child's birthday. It went:

> A tiny token gift please bring along,
> To add to the birthday fun and song.
> A dime or a quarter at the most
> Any little thing will please this host,
> As something toward a gift to send,
> In honor of———to her friend
> A child in a camp far away,
> Whose only mother is the UJA.[25]

In response to the national campaign effort, a citywide quota committee was organized in Pittsburgh by the UJF to determine the community's contribution to the total UJA effort. Milton Susman, editor of the *Criterion*, applauded this organizational move as a step toward better fund-raising in the city. "The money is there," he wrote, but it just has to be "loosened from its mooring."[26]

A goal of $2.26 million was accepted by the quota committee, with $1.7 directed to the UJA. There was real concern about meeting this goal. The *Criterion* editorialized that "this city will be the testing ground for the national drive."[27] UJA headquarters in New York said that "as Pittsburgh goes, so will the nation go."[28] Within a few weeks of the start of the campaign in April, the $1.4 million that had been pledged in 1946 was topped, as the Pittsburgh Jewish community went on to raise about $2.17 million from 20,000 contributors out of a total Jewish population of some 50,000.[29]

The plea for funds became even more dramatic in 1948, the "Year of Destiny," as it was labeled by UJA leaders. "The Price of Freedom Comes High" blared a full page ad in the *Criterion*. "Sure you gave last year, and the years before that, but this is the crisis. 1949 will tell the tale whether Hitler's work will be finished for him, or whether the land of Israel will rise as a new nation for those who wish it. It's entirely up to you—and you have to live with your conscience. Give now and give as never before."[30]

This was the challenge that confronted the Pittsburgh Jewish community in 1948. Nearly 250,000 Jews were still behind bars either in displaced persons camps in Europe or in camps in Cyprus under British guard. The armed struggle for Israel was under way; the murder of hospital personnel on the way to Hadassah Hospital on Mount Scopus was just one of the news stories that shocked the public. In light of the emergency, the national UJA goal was set at a mind-boggling $250 million, up $150 million in just two short years. The UJA borrowed $50 million in advance of the start of the campaign in order to send immediate cash for weapons and supplies to the Jews fighting in Israel. The local Pittsburgh goal was set at $3,515,000, with $2.5 million earmarked for the UJA and local refugee aid, which were now lumped together despite the concern of the national

UJA.[31] While this goal was a half million less than that requested of Pittsburgh by the UJA in New York, it was $800,000
more than UJA received in 1947 from Pittsburgh. Milton
Susman wrote that "the enormity [of the goal] has many a head
throbbing. . . . It is an unparalleled responsibility, but it is an
unparalleled time."[32]

Despite the fact that the UJF drive was not the only money-
raising campaign in town, a reality that continued to cause UJF
leaders much consternation, Pittsburgh raised $2.9 million, an
unprecedented amount for the community, but still $600,000
short of the goal set by the UJF board in 1948.[33] In light of this
shortfall, the UJF had to drastically cut allocations to beneficiary agencies with the exception of the JSSB and UVES. Obviously, the JSSB and UVES were in a class by themselves, for
they continued to command the funds they needed to carry on
the refugee program. The total cost for relief was $105,314 out
of $112,000 allocated for the year, with seventy-eight units (132
persons) arriving.[34] About one out of every two immigrants came
under the assurance of the JSSB. Expenditures were not cut,
because immigrant relief funds were already seen to be at
minimum levels. Moreover, beginning in 1947 the escalating
costs of the refugee program was taken from the funds set aside
for the UJA overseas.

In 1949 the Jewish communty in Pittsburgh was to face its
greatest crisis regarding the local refugee program. The snags in
the processing machinery under the Displaced Persons Act of
1948 had been worked out, and Jewish agencies such as the
HIAS and the USNA were able to get the people out of Europe to
this country. The total of Jews arriving during the year amounted
to some 38,000, with an estimated 31,000 coming in under the
Displaced Persons Act.

The heavy movement in 1949 of displaced persons is reflected
among the Pittsburgh Jewish refugees interviewed. While only
three families arrived between June and December 1948, in the
first six months of 1949 twelve units arrived, including families

and individuals. During the second half of 1949, a full twenty units arrived. Even though fewer units arrived than were actually expected, nevertheless, the refugee load of the JSSB went from 115 in December 1948 to a staggering 199, up 73 percent, in just one year. The cost of relief for just December 1949 was an unprecedented $24,251.[35]

While Jewish refugees to Pittsburgh were "piling up" (in the words of the JSSB) in the summer of 1949 and costs were escalating rapidly, the monies collected by the Pittsburgh UJF were actually declining. A total of $2,395,000 was raised in 1949, but it was $1.3 million short of the local goal and a half million dollars less than the amount raised by the UJF the year before. This caused great dismay among those struggling with budget allocations. At the October UJF Budget Committee meeting, there was much discussion about refugee costs. While the board had authorized $150,000 for the care of newcomers, no ceiling had been imposed, and the JSSB had been given the right to reappear before the committee any time to make additional requests.

The ability of the Pittsburgh Jewish community to continue to support large refugee expenditures in light of other pressing needs was seriously questioned at the Budget Committee meeting. One person felt that if local expenses continued to rise and if the money to support the refugee program continued to be taken from the UJA allocation, then "our assistance to the UJA would be seriously impaired." Other committee members believed that it was just as important to take care of the refugees coming into Pittsburgh as it was to take care of them in Europe. Still others felt that aid to new arrivals in Pittsburgh was actually aid to Israel, for it meant relieving the young state of a burden which it would have trouble bearing if all the displaced persons had gone there. The suggestion of a ceiling on aid to local refugees was opposed on the grounds that it would cut off refugees already in Pittsburgh and that this would be unjust and harsh. It was also pointed out that the Joint Committee had already made a commitment to take on prospective immigrants in the pipeline to Pittsburgh.

The outcome of the discussion was a grant of $183,000 to the JSSB for 1949. This decision was described as a compromise between "what we should have liked to have done if sufficient funds had been available, and the limitation placed upon us by the results of the campaign."[36] The allotment of $183,000—of which $168,000 went for immigrant relief—placed the city sixth behind New York, Chicago, Los Angeles, Philadelphia, and Detroit in total annual financial assistance. But Pittsburgh's average monthly grant of $140 per case was higher than that of any of the cities mentioned. Indeed, the average monthly grant throughout the country was only $118 per case.[37]

By December 1949 the leadership in charge of providing funds for local refugee needs was almost in a panic over anticipated costs and the community's ability to foot the bill. As a result, an appeal was sent to USNA (probably by the Joint Committee) requesting a moratorium on assurances for new immigrants from the Pittsburgh Jewish community, which wanted time to catch up with its current needs. But the telegram from the USNA in reply was firm and to the point. It read:

It is impossible to undertake moratorium such as requested which would have effect of Pittsburgh withdrawal of its assurances. This is a peak period of arrival of community assurance cases with all commitments already made and additional openings urgently needed. Such action by a major and leading Jewish community would be disastrous to entire program. We cannot believe you would recommend action causing cancellation of assurances overseas, directly jeopardizing displaced persons now in Europe being processed against your asssurances and embarrassing relationships of all of us with our government. . . . We fervently hope you will find other solutions to meet your problem.[38]

With such an urgent response, the Pittsburgh Jewish community chose not to cancel out of its commitment, but anxiety over the future continued. The JSSB, now known as the Jewish Family and Children's Service (JFCS), was estimating their 1950 costs at a record $250,000 for local refugee care at the same time that intake from the UJF campaign was expected to decline. With the State of Israel defeating the Arab armies in 1948, there no longer was a sense of crisis in the Jewish community, and fund-raising efforts were meeting with less success. In order to send immediate cash for emergency relief to Israel to help immigrants there, the UJF was forced to borrow from a local bank. On top of this, the other beneficiary agencies of the Jewish community were calling for more monies from the UJF in the face of a shortfall in Community Chest funds.

In view of the desperate financial situation, the JFCS voted to reduce costs. It instituted an 8 percent cut in relief to begin in March 1950. This step was taken with great reluctance, given the fact that the cut would have to come out of the food budget of newcomers, since rent and utility costs were fixed. It was at this time that the National Council of Jewish Women was called upon to take over the clothing and furniture needs of the new arrivals. Marcel Kovarsky, the new executive director of the JFCS who had taken over from Gertrude Glick in May 1949, assured the staff that the NCJW project had been dictated by the monetary crunch, but there was a protest. The entire staff signed a resolution which was sent to the JFCS board calling the NCJW effort "a step backward" and "a serious obstacle" to the client becoming an independent member of the community.[39]

By November 1950 an estimated 60,000 to 65,000 Jews were still displaced persons in Europe, with about 20,000 to 25,000 of these expected to be brought to the United States as a result of the 1950 amendment to the Displaced Persons Act, which liberalized and extended the law. To accommodate the anticipated numbers, Pittsburgh was initially asked to provide assurances for an additional 250 (later reduced to 207) units for late 1950 and 1951. The Joint Committee approved the request on principle but again bemoaned the pressure they were under not to take away from monies allocated for the UJA overseas. When the UJF board met to discuss the commitment, Donald Steinfirst, head of both the Joint Committee and the board of the JFCS urged the UJF board to mortgage part of its 1951 and 1952 expected intake to cover 1950 expenses. The assurances, he insisted, were needed immediately, and it was not expected that the majority of immigrants would actually arrive until November 1950. Thus the bulk of the expenses would actually be incurred during 1951 and not in 1950. After a full discussion, the UJF board passed a resolution supporting the quota commitment to USNA, with fourteen persons indicating their approval and four persons in opposition. [40]

The major concern remained money. However, as had happened before, the actual cost was less than anticipated. Instead of a price tag of $250,000, as feared, the actual cost was $189,000. This was primarily because refugee arrivals were down in the Pittsburgh area. Only thirty-two community assurance cases came to the city in 1950, in contrast to the seventy that had arrived in 1948 and the 101 units in the record-setting year of 1949. [41] This decrease in numbers corresponded to the decline in Jewish immigration to the country at large. That total fell from 39,000 in 1949 to 10,000 in 1950. The lower 1950 figure was attributed not only to declining numbers of Jews still in displaced persons camps in Europe, but also to intensified security investigation overseas of potential immigrants and "an extremely confused" situation in the dawning of the McCarthy Age. [42]

Despite the decrease in numbers in 1950, the pressure continued unabated as a final surge of activity under the expiring Displaced Persons Act was expected. It was estimated that costs in 1951 would amount to a hefty $375,000. This expenditure was projected along with the cost from substantial commitments that had been made to Montefiore Hospital for a mortgage on a new structure and to the YM&WHA for capital payments on its new health club facility. Again, the outcome was not as dire as feared. Jewish immigration remained down. Arriving in Pittsburgh were 67 community assurance cases, 35 more than in 1950 but much lower than the 207 that the USNA had requested of Pittsburgh and still well below the record 1949 figure of 101 cases. Moreover, even with the additional cases, the total annual relief cost for the JFCS did not rise. With a good employment situation, people were off the rolls quicker than in the past, so that the total relief cost actually dropped from $189,000 in 1950 to $108,000 in 1951.[43]

The crisis was over; UJF leaders could juggle their customary allocations without the urgency of international and national events weighing so heavily on them. By 1952 discussion of the local refugee program no longer appeared with any regularity in the meeting reports or files of the UJF, the Federation of Jewish Philanthropies, or the JFCS. The JFCS had weathered the storm.

But what about the community as a whole? What did Pittsburghers—both those involved in the mobilization and those who were not—think of the effort that had been spearheaded by professional and some volunteer agencies? Were individual unaffiliated Jews really concerned about the Holocaust survivors coming into their community? How did they respond to the newcomers? Had they really understood the nature of the events in Europe, events that had made these people refugees—traumatized and displaced from a world which no longer existed?

Before the war many in the community desperately, but unsuccessfully, tried to bring in relatives and other Jews from Germany and Austria. Yet when Fred Bader, returning from a trip to his native Germany in 1936, tried to tell people about what he saw under Hitler, he felt nobody believed him. Bessie and Sidney Heymann, prominent Pittsburghers, remembered well-publicized accounts in the newspapers about German actions against Jews, but acknowledged that "they weren't believed." Myrtle Fisher, a lifelong Zionist who had been born in Russia, was very critical of the Jewish community's lack of response even before the war. When stories were told about the desperate plight of the Jews in Germany, it was "shocking" to her "how few people responded." She recognized a failure to take the situation seriously and to believe that such excesses could occur in a cultured country like Germany. However, she also felt that the lack of action was tied in some measure to an anti-Zionist mood among many Jews, particularly the wealthy German Jewish establishment. She pointed to the anti-Zionist American Council for Judaism, which had been established in 1943 and was led in Pittsburgh by Rabbi Goldenson of Rodef Shalom Congregation. This congregation was the largest and most prominent congregation in the city and the bastion of the wealthy German Jewish community in Pittsburgh. Myrtle believed that the hostility to Zionism of this important segment of the Jewish community was tied to their refusal to acknowledge that assimilation was not working in Europe and that perhaps they in America might be threatened as well. Other Pittsburghers disagreed over the strength of the American Council for Judaism in Pittsburgh,[44] but there was no question that Zionism was not to gain widespread endorsement until after the war when all Jews were forced to confront the reality of anti-Semitism culminating in the Holocaust.

After the war, when the Nuremberg War Trials took place and the news reports revealed the glaring reality of the Holocaust, the Jewish community in Pittsburgh was indeed shocked, grief-stricken, angry, and frustrated. Dororthy Blumenthal recalled that "you saw in movies or heard on the radio, but somehow or other it didn't penetrate. . . . After the war we were horrified at what we saw. . . . We really didn't know." Even Rabbi Baruch Poupko, who in 1979 wrote to the United Jewish Federation of Pittsburgh suggesting a Holocaust memorial center, wondered why it took so long for him to do that. "The news was so gruesome, we did not want to believe. . . . We needed time." He felt that during the war there was not an abundance of information about what was happening regarding Jews and that

"American Jews were also victims of a world conspiracy of silence." When asked about their response during the war, a number of persons asked what they could have done. "I'm not proud of the fact that we didn't know what to do for our Jewish people over there, but I don't know what you could have done in those days," lamented Dorothy Blumenthal. "I don't know where our head was in the early 1940s," exclaimed Marjorie Balter. "It took a long time for us to wake up."

Most Jews in corroborative interviews did not criticize the response of the American Jews, much less express any sense of guilt. "We did what we could," summed up one observer. Milton Susman actually took the offensive by taking the famous survivor, Elie Wiesel, to task for charging that American Jews were indifferent to the fate of their coreligionists in Europe. To Susman, this criticism was totally unfounded, because "there was nothing we could do until the Jews were extricated from Hitler's infernal web."

When the survivors of the Holocaust began arriving in Pittsburgh after the war, there was a great expression of sympathy. Paul Mazerov, who was a youngster at the time, remembered seeing them walking on the street. "They were in their late 20s and 30s, but they looked a thousand. People felt sorry for them." Hannah Sidransky, who was a social worker at the JSSB in charge of orphaned youth, felt that there was a great sympathy for the refugees. "It could have happened to me," people thought. Herman Fineberg, who in 1949 was the UJF chairman, talked about the "tremendous sympathy" for displaced persons and how he "used Pittsburgh survivors to further awaken people's awareness for the need to accelerate the movement of people out of the camps." Gertrude Silverblatt felt that she received the many donations she did for the clothing and furniture project she worked on for the NCJW because people knew their contributions were going to Holocaust survivors. Dorothy Mallett said that when the NCJW project was advertised, there was "a fantastic response," a "total investment by the community," that people were "caught up in this cause." She recalled how her husband was called to hire a refugee (which he did) and that there was widespread involvement by Pittsburghers in finding jobs for the newcomers. Majorie Balter recalled the importance of networking, as people asked each other to be on the lookout for job openings for displaced persons.

Dorothy Binstock, long-time activist in B'nai Brith, remembered how members would respond to appeals for clothing collections and help seek employment for refugees. She indicated that B'nai Brith members gave their time and energy to prepare refugees for citizenship and help bring over relatives from Europe. Milton Susman asserted that while it was not easy to help newcomers "become threads in our local fabric" and that "there is never enough that could be done," nevertheless, American Jews "did a hell of a job not only absorbing, but also integrating refugees into our way of life." Rabbi Baruch Poupko agreed and so did Robert Lesser, executive director of the Hebrew Free Loan Association, an organization that was founded in Pittsburgh in 1887. Myrtle Fisher cited the cooperative attitude on the part of Jewish real estate people who were asked to look for apartments, while Jewish laundries and dry cleaning establishments cleaned clothes for the NCJW clothing project free of charge. Leonard Weitzman, who worked for UVES, was of the opinion that the Jewish community in the late 1940s was more sensitive to Holocaust survivors than it was to Russian Jewish immigrants, who began arriving in the 1970s. He said that most of the new Americans in those days were placed with Jewish employers, while only 5 percent of the Russian Jews who came later found jobs in Jewish establishments.

There was considerable agreeement among Pittsburghers that a real outpouring of sympathy for refugees was evidenced and that the community extended substantial help to them. There was no question that the tradition of caring for fellow Jews and the organizational network to give expression to that commitment was in full play after the war. One has only to review the number of organizations that criss-crossed Jewish life and their myriad fund-raising efforts to understand that reality. Moreover, related to all this was the tradition of volunteering. It was a veritable "way of life"; there were "scads of volunteers . . . people were looking to volunteer," said Dorothy Mallett. And indeed, she never had trouble finding helpers to run the NCJW clothing shop. To be part of the organization and to be active was the "thing to do." It certainly was a far cry from the reality of trying to get volunteers today.

However, while there appeared to be many offers of help, this activity usually did not bring volunteers face-to-face with the survivors themselves. With the exception of the reception and hospitality committees of NCJW and the Friendship Club, most efforts did not involve direct contact, and when they did, there were problems.

Ethel Landerman was a young social worker in 1950—first at the JSSB and then until 1956 at Montefiore Hospital.

The staff called people "displaced persons" then. They were not "Holocaust survivors." We had no sense of the Holocaust as we know now, with a capital H. We really didn't understand what people were telling us. The stories sounded too horrible. We simply did not believe them. They needed help, and we had no idea what they were talking about. We were so incredibly dumb! . . . I saw survivors at Montefiore; they were there endlessly. They were blank-faced people. They were depressed and having trouble adjusting to a new life in Pittsburgh. We thought we saw symptons of neurotic behavior. This was in the heyday of psychotherapy or Freudian theories, but our thinking was totally inappropriate. They were grieving, trying to deal with what they had lived through. There were problems understanding them. There were classes given at the hospital in Yiddish, but it was hard. But beyond that, some of the medical personnel had no patience with the survivors. They complained that the DPs were mourning too long, that they were not becoming Americans fast enough, that the war was over; 'enough already!' And the survivors felt their impatience. . . . They used to tell me.

Despite the commitment to support refugee needs and the involvement of many volunteers in the effort, it would not be accurate to conclude that the care of Holocaust refugees was the major concern of the organized community or even a constant preoccupation. While certain agencies and organizations in the community were concerned with immigrants, one group of institutions was conspicuously not. These were the synagogues. No synagogue member who was interviewed and who belonged to either a reform, conservative, or orthodox congregation (and there was a good cross-section of synagogues represented by people who were interviewed) could recall any involvement on the part of the congregation as a body. There were no social action committees then, for example, as there were in the 1970s for Soviet Jews. Free membership was generally extended to any person, not just survivors, who could not afford the dues. There was no special attention given to Holocaust survivors, as evidenced by the lack of any record of discussion on the refugee program in the minutes of Temple Rodef Shalom or the conservative Tree of Life Congregation. Moreover, no respondent could recall the rabbi at his or her synagogue discussing the refugee situation, let alone the impact of the Holocaust on American Jewry in the postwar period. Interestingly enough, Dr. Solomon Freehof, the spiritual leader of Rodef Shalom Congregation and a nationally recognized religious leader, did not deal with the Holocaust or the responsibility to help the survivors in his sermons after the war. The subject simply was not raised. It appeared—as Ethel Landerman insisted—that people, whether or not they were directly involved with the refugee program—really did not appreciate the scope of what had happened. Moral outrage and some understanding came later, much later.

On a more practical level, Leonard Weitzman was outspoken in his condemnation of the lack of synagogue interest in the local refugee program. He insisted that he never had any cooperation from any synagogue or rabbi with job placement for refugees, even though he had written to them requesting their help.

Leonard also extended his criticism to German Jewish business-men, whom he found to be uncooperative in helping Holocaust survivors. "The old-guard German establishment by and large was self-contained and not really involved in the community." His opinion was shared by other observers as well.

It is interesting that there was so little coverage in the local Jewish press on the refugee program. Only a handful of articles appeared in the *Jewish Criterion* outlining the refugee program to any extent in the six years from 1946 to 1951. The local refugee program was obviously not bathed in the glare of publicity the way a similar program conducted on behalf of the Soviet Jews was in the 1970s. Perhaps the explanation lay in the fact that people were very reluctant to talk about what had happened in Europe and who these people were who were coming to America. There was a silence regarding the Holocaust—both while it was happening and afterward. It was a silence maintained by victims and bystanders, Jew and non-Jew. It would appear that the lack of widespread publicity on the refugee program was connected to the phenomenon that lasted for thirty years after the war, during which time nobody wanted to deal with the reality of the destruc-tion in Europe. The refugees were the grim reminders of the past. Their arrival in America and in Pittsburgh evoked great sympathy but not an understanding or a willingness or perhaps even an ability to come to terms with what had happened.

This was the response of Pittsburgh Jews. But what about the survivors themselves? How did they deal with the reality of their new lives in Pittsburgh? How did both the Jewish and Christian newcomers to the city in the aftermath of World War II view the community that they now were joining and the efforts that were or were not made on their behalf? We turn now to an exploration of the attitudes and responses of these postwar refugees and their perspective on their early experience in Pittsburgh.

6

Into the Pittsburgh Crucible

▶▶▶ ON MAY 20, 1946, 795 DISPLACED
persons arrived on board the S.S. *Marine Flasher* to a
cheering throng at the New York harbor, and four days later, the
S.S. *Marine Perch* brought an additional 566 refugees to America. They were the first immigrants to come to this country from
the displaced persons camps of Europe and the first under the
Truman directive issued in December 1945.

While the newcomers began their new lives in various states
around the country, the northern industrial states claimed the
biggest share. Pennsylvania ranked third in the country, behind
New York and Illinois; and Pittsburgh numbered seventh among
welcoming American cities.[1] By December 1951 approximately
24,200 newcomers had been resettled in Pennsylvania, with
Allegheny County (Pittsburgh area) gaining 2,474 of this number, second only to Philadelphia with 7,671. The surrounding
counties of Butler and Westmoreland had welcomed, respectively, 139 and 345 displaced persons.[2]

Under the Displaced Persons Act, 154,556 Polish citizens
(excluding ethnic Germans in Poland who were given special
status) received visas, representing 45.5 percent of the entire
population admitted under the act.[3] While there is no specific
reference to the number of Polish Jews who were admitted,
53,541 Jews were admitted under the Displaced Persons Act,
representing 19 percent of the incoming arrivals.[4] Because it is
estimated that in 1947 at least 70 percent of the Jews in the

115

displaced persons camps were Polish, if we apply that percentage to the 53,541 figure, we get a total number of about 37,500 Polish Jews coming in under the act, leaving then a number of something under 120,000 Polish Christians admitted.[5] As we have seen, immigration under the act peaked in 1949. It dropped considerably in 1950 but was up again near 1949 totals in 1951. However, this was not true for Jewish immigration. The 1951 immigration under the act was less than half the 1949 total.[6]

The arrival dates of the Pittsburgh Jewish group reflect this larger picture, with thirty-two arrivals in 1949, only two in 1950, and nine in 1951, shown in the following table.

Year	Christians	Jews
1946	2	2
1947	4	2
1948, Jan.–June	0	1
1948, July–Dec.	1	3
1949, Jan.–June	2	12
1949, July–Dec.	7	20
1950, Jan.–June	5	2
1950, July–Dec.	3	0
1951, Jan.–June	8	8
1951, July–Dec.	5	1
1952, Jan.–June	4	0
1952, July–Dec.	2	0
1953	0	3
1954+	10	3

No wonder that 1949 was a time of considerable consternation regarding the community's ability to absorb the newcomers. The surge in 1951 could not compare to the numbers two years before.

For the Christian immigration, the second half of 1949 and first half of 1951 were peak periods, corresponding to the pattern of general migration into the country. However, their arrival was more evenly distributed over the years. There is no question that the impact of the 1950 amendment, which specifically provided for the admission of 18,000 ex-Polish servicemen from England and their families, contributed to the total and was an important component of the Polish immigration to the United States after the war.[7] Those persons in the Pittsburgh group who came to these shores after 1952 had gone to other countries before coming as regular immigrants to this country. They had all, however, chosen to emigrate from Poland immediately after the war.

Now that they had finally arrived in the United States, now that they could at long last contemplate settling down in this country, what would they find? What kinds of problems would they encounter? How would they feel about the community into which they arrived, and how would they adjust to lives in a medium-sized American city?

Sociologists, psychologists, and historians have spelled out the factors affecting immigrant adjustment and adaptation. Variables such as the motivation behind emigration, the conditions of departure, and the length and nature of the period of transition to the new society were all important. So, too, were the particular ethnic and social backgrounds of the individuals, their personalities, their expectations and goals, their skills and attitudes, the so-called baggage they brought with them to a new situation. Beyond these considerations, there was the receptivity of the society into which they were arriving in terms of economic opportunity and socialization. In some respects, the wave of immigrants who were displaced by World War II resembled the generations of immigrants who had preceded them. They came to this country hoping to rebuild their lives and eager to begin. They came into established ethnic and religious communities and into a society that accorded them the right to become contributing members. Yet, in some important ways this group was different. They were not just immigrants; they were refugees from a war-torn Europe.

For Polish Jews there was not only the trauma of personal loss but the shattering of the family. While immigrant generations of Jews before them had also sought refuge from pogroms in Europe, such persecutions were dwarfed in comparison to the Holocaust. For Polish Christians, the pain over the loss of their homeland was profound, a loss not only in terms of territory for those who had homes in eastern Poland (now incorporated into Russia) but also in terms of their freedom and independence. The Jews were happy to have left postwar Poland, while the Christians by and large would never have fled their country if the Communists had not taken over. For both Christians and Jews, there was an extended period of transition. Because of the time it took to get displaced persons legislation enacted, the resettlement period was often four years or more. These circumstances were bound to take their toll.

More often than not, Polish Christians had been gainfully employed during their postwar years in Europe because of an involvement with the Polish armed forced under the British (they were officially allies) or as postwar guards for the Americans. They had continued an education or had received training and job skills and they had learned English. Polish Jews, however, often had nothing to do in the camps as they waited for final refuge. While there were some job training programs, many Jews were not able to become self-sustaining or to learn job skills. As one social worker who dealt with Jewish displaced persons in Cleveland noted, whatever skills the Jews might have possessed were "dulled by years of idleness spent in DP camps. Idleness broke down regular work habits so DP's experienced pressures even on the most simple jobs in this country."[8]

Twelve Jews in the Pittsburgh study felt that, next to the wartime years, the period in Europe immediately after the war was the second most difficult time in their lives. However, nineteen other Jews (nearly one out of three) indicated that the second most difficult time in their lives was actually their early years in the United States. This sentiment prevailed even though the Jews usually came to this country under the auspices and with the help of a complex network of social agencies extending from Europe to Pittsburgh. It was clear that, despite the financial support and commitment of both professional and lay organizations, the Jewish refugees had a hard time getting a handle on their lives both in postwar Europe and in America.

Of the nineteen persons who had such a difficult time after arriving in the United States, half were sponsored by relatives. Thus there appeared to be no direct relation between level of satisfaction and sponsorship. Interestingly enough, sometimes the relatives were part of the problem. When one Jewish woman came initially to Chicago, her aunt "went off and left me and my husband without anything." When she got sick and had a miscarriage, there was no money to pay the bill. She wrote a much poorer aunt in Pittsburgh, who sent them tickets to come to Pittsburgh. Another Jewish woman complained that relatives who had brought her and her family over seemed to have "no feelings" and did not help them. One Jewish man related how his American relative did not want her son to take out his Polish-born sister, explaining that her son "was an American boy!" Even when relatives were helpful, that does not appear to have been a decisive factor in the perception of ease of adjustment.

Among those twenty-five Jews in the study who came in under the aegis of the Jewish Social Service Bureau of Pittsburgh, fifteen made positive references to their experience. Morton Cieply admitted how strange and uncomfortable he felt when he came to Pittsburgh, but "I wasn't scared, because I knew I wouldn't starve because of Federation."[9] Sally Melmed appreciated the financial help she and her family received. So did Rose Turbiner, who got assistance for six weeks until her husband, Bernard, was able to get a job. "They were great!" she exclaimed. "The social worker, a Miss Weinstein, was lovely. She even came to visit me when I was sick." Gabriel Hoffman praised the same woman. For six weeks he went to school, at the social worker's urging. But then he told Miss Weinstein he wanted to look for a job. She cautioned him not to rush. "But I wanted to get off on my own and not take any money from Federation. I got a job myself at Kaufmann's as a tailor." Frances Spiegel also remarked about her understanding social worker. "She was a lifesaver; there were always some people who would not be satisfied, but we were." Bernard Gelman commented favorably on the way "they were trying to make you independent. It was hard, but it was the only way you were going to learn. I didn't want to wait for them to find me a job, so I got a job myself as a janitor at Heinz."

Wolf Friede fondly remembered his social worker, a Mr. Nadler, whom he described as a "very good man. He understood our problems. . . . Federation was terribly important for us. We got money. . . . I was a free man; did things myself. They figured we were people and could make our own decisions." "What Federation did for me, God bless!" exclaimed Harry Feldman. William Friedman gave the Federation a lot of credit for helping him. He, like other survivors, was able to get a loan from the Hebrew Free Loan Association (which was partially funded by the United Jewish Fund) for $745 for tools. To him "the Jewish people are enriched to have organizations like that."

Not everybody, however, had such unequivocal appreciation of the Jewish community agencies. One man commented that he was more frustrated than helped. "They were trying to help, but I had no patience. The social workers had a set of rules, and they didn't fit everybody. They wanted me to wait, and I wanted to get right to work." Abe Kohane appreciated the relief for the few months that he needed it, but he did feel there was a lack of understanding on the part of both professional and lay people with whom he came in contact. Mordechai Glatstein also felt a void. "They gave you furniture if you needed it, but we needed a social worker, a psychiatrist, and there was no one to help in Pittsburgh." His wife, another survivor, was more outspoken in her criticism, actually describing her early years in Pittsburgh as a "second Holocaust." "We needed emotional support and we didn't get it." Others echoed her feeling of not getting enough emotional support. Aron Goldman complained that "when we went to Federation, they didn't have time to talk to us. They didn't understand us. Nobody cared. Nobody asked how we were doing. Federation told me it was up to me to get a job. . . ." Another survivor, Jack Sittsamer, described the social workers as "mean." "They didn't seem to care. There was no feeling of warmth." Melvin Goldman lamented, "They brought me over to help me, but they didn't. They sent you down a cellar to pick an old coat, but we needed to talk to people." Janina Winkler resented having to go to the offices of the Jewish Social Service Bureau (JSSB) weekly for review. "We were proud people."

While most of the complaints revolved around a perceived lack of emotional support or understanding, two people did criticize the level of assistance. Albert Levenreich who came in the crunch of December 1949, remarked: "We got not enough to live, but too much to die! . . . I didn't want to take a handout. The social worker couldn't speak Yiddish. She didn't like me. I waited the whole day before she gave me a check. She wanted me to mop floors in the Jewish Home, but I refused. They did try to help me get a job, but I got one myself." Another woman was gentler. She felt that people who had come before them had gotten a "better deal" than she and her husband. (She too came during the peak months in the fall of 1949.)

What did provoke universal criticism was the housing facility in which most arrivals sponsored by the JSSB were placed. The Steel City Hotel was where many newcomers were housed up to a period of six weeks, until other quarters could be located by either the JSSB or the immigrant. No one had anything nice to say about the place. "Horses should live there, not people," commented Harry Friedman. Samuel Frost remembered the rats; others, the mice and cockroaches. Marcia Scheingross, who came with her husband and two children, believed the hotel was worse than the Landsberg displaced persons camp. Sally Melmed's son wanted to know why so many men kept leaving some women's rooms! But

William Friedman waxed philosophical. "It was a terrible place, but you don't look a gift horse in the mouth!"

Did the Jewish newcomers feel welcomed by the Jewish community and did they feel they had anything in common with the Jews of Pittsburgh? Out of those responding to the first question, twenty-two were enthusiastic and seven were somewhat less so. Twenty-one persons answered they did not feel welcomed. Opinions ranged from an enthusiastic appreciation to a sense of bitter rejection. When the question was asked whether people felt they had had much in common with the Jewish community in Pittsburgh, twenty-five persons felt that they had, but an equal number said no. Sometimes people felt they had been welcomed by the community even though they had not felt much in common with local Jews. Of the nineteen people who had cited their early years in this country as the second hardest time for them, about half felt welcomed, half did not. The same ratio prevailed on the question of having much in common with Pittsburgh Jews. Thus while there was no direct correlation between the early difficulty in the United States and perceptions of welcome or commonality, only four of these nineteen people who recalled great hardship felt that they had both been welcomed and had much in common with the local community.

Complaints varied. Some were directed against fellow Jews; others at Americans in general. A number of newcomers griped that Americans were only interested in money, and that since displaced persons didn't have any, they were ignored or even ridiculed. Others grumbled that there was a certain amount of jealousy, and when they started to earn money or purchase a new car, there was resentment. Abe Salem put it this way: "When you're rich, the Americans are jealous, and when you're poor, they don't want to know you." Others felt they were looked down on because they were immigrants, "greeners." Samuel Frost specifically targeted the Jewish community. "They thought we were ignorant; that we hadn't seen a car or a refrigerator. They made us feel like we had come out of the desert."

The Friendship Club had attempted to reach out socially to Holocaust survivors, and nearly one-third of the families interviewed indicated that they had been involved with the club somewhat, going to Chanukah parties, Passover seders, religious services, dances, and general meetings. As one survivor said, "If there was one organization that had an interest in us, it was the Friendship Club. . . . I have to give them a lot of credit." The newcomers welcomed the conversation and hospitality. Norman Infeld met his wife at a Friendship Club dance. But even with this group, the majority of the refugees felt there was a real difference between them and the German Jews who constituted the Friendship Club, beyond the difference in their ages. As one man commented, "I didn't come to this country to hear German!"

Many survivors like Abe Kohane felt that American Jews had little interest and virtually no understanding of what had happened to the Jews in Europe. Survivors were reluctant to talk about their experiences in the Holocaust, not just because it was so painful for them, but also because they felt that nobody would really understand what they had been through. A group of survivors organized their own annual memorial observance of the Holocaust beginning in 1952. One man expressed his bitterness that the larger community was not interested in participating in these services or even in providing any funds for publicity about the event. Furthermore, no survivor talked about any efforts by the synagogues to reach out to them, although they did attend services. In fact, one survivor remembered how shocked he was when a local rabbi of a major congregation announced that, in his opinion, the Jews who survived were collaborators.

Many other newcomers did not express a feeling one way or the other. As Harry Drucker said, "I'm the type of person who never expects anything from anybody. When you're nice to me, I'm nice to you." Julius Aussenberg also was noncommittal. "I didn't expect anything; I made myself welcomed." William Friedman remarked that "in the beginning the Jewish community didn't know what to expect of us, but when they saw we didn't come out of the Dark Ages, they always invited us."

Some survivors recognized that their less than positive feelings might have been tied to their own insecurities or lack of communication skills. As Samuel Frost mused, "Maybe we couldn't accept the welcome. Maybe it was us; we stood away. Maybe we were afraid." Another woman, who had indicated she felt nothing in common with Pittsburgh Jews, also recognized that perhaps her feelings were tied to the fact that she could not speak the language. Estelle Forstenzer did not feel a real commonality on interest either, but for her "it was like everybody was from a different world. They were better off and it was a gap I felt."

While ego strength is an important factor in the ease of adjusting to a new society, the expectations with which one comes to a new society are also important (and certainly easier for a historian to probe). It would appear from the testimony that most Jewish immigrants had modest expectations and set fairly realistic goals. Many said that they had no expectation or that they just wanted to establish a normal life. Their goal was to get married, or if they were attached already, to raise a family and get a job. Morton Cieply remarked, "My only ambition was to have enough bread to be satisfied; to be productive; to make up for lost time." Abe Cymerman expected only "to take one day at a time." Abraham Enzel felt that "whatever I found, I would do. I just wanted to be able to make a living and be happy." Nathan Forstenzer "just wanted to be free; that's all. That was our dream in the concentration camp—to live as a free person, to change clothes when we wanted and take a shower." William Friedman knew the streets were not paved with gold. All he wanted to do was raise a family and get a job. David Guss exclaimed, "I only wanted enough bread and potatoes. I wanted to kiss the ground, be a slave; just let me in!" Gabriel Hoffman also talked about food and freedom. "I'm going to be a free man. I'm going to sit down at a table with a tablecloth and have a whole bread and cut off as much as I want."

Morris Manela wanted only to see the Statue of Liberty. Izak Mikowski "didn't want to be a big shot." Gusta Relis commented she never thought the world owed her anything. "What I make, that is what will be." Harry Rosen was just happy to be alive. Sally Melmed wanted a good education for her children—that was most important, "because that was all we had." Marcia Scheingross felt the same way. "My husband used to say, that if it was our last penny, the children were going to college." Other immigrants echoed this dedication to their children. Ruth Weitz summed things up this way: "I just figured that I wanted to get away from the other side of the ocean. Whatever happened, happened. . . . Father always taught me that you have to work for what you get. Life is two hills—one is up and another down. You pick the one you want to take. Nothing comes by itself."

Interestingly enough, with few exceptions those persons who had had very modest goals indicated their adjustment to America had not been so very difficult. And of the six persons who appeared to have somewhat unrealistic expectations about what they could anticipate in this country, five indicated that their early years in America were indeed the second hardest time for them. The sixth person complained that her entire life had been hard. For these people, expectations and goals were set beyond their reach. One of the persons who was frustrated was Mark Stern. He had wanted to become an engineer, build houses, and become rich and influential—and none of that happened. It was hard for him early on in America because "I didn't know which way I was going. I was a stranger. I couldn't integrate; I didn't know the language." Aron Goldman thought he was going to have it nice and easy. "Gold pieces were going to lay in the streets and I'm going to pick them up. There were rich Jews in America and they would help, but it didn't happen that way." Abe Kohane expected the Jewish community would be "eager to greet us," but he did not feel it happened that way for him.

When the attitudes and expectations of the Jewish refugees
are compared with those of the Christians, there are interesting
similarities and differences. There were the universal problems
facing the uprooted—of learning a new language and culture, of
finding jobs and housing. And there were the specific problems
of this particular Polish emigration. While nineteen Jews in the
survey felt their early years in the United States were second
only to the wartime period in terms of hardship, six Christians
recalled those early years in the United States as the most
difficult time in their lives, while eight more cited those years as
the second hardest. As with the Jews, the reasons given for their
distress varied. There was not only the crunch of establishing a
viable economic life, but there were attitudinal and emotional
problems, including their reaction to the response and receptivity of their sponsor or the receiving society, particularly the
Polish-American Christian community in Pittsburgh.

Some Christian newcomers had trouble with sponsors, either
personally known to them or not. One Christian who came under
the community affidavit of the National Catholic Welfare Conference (NCWC) cited his early years in the United States as the
worst time for him. He found himself working on a farm in Seven
Springs, fifty miles outside of Pittsburgh. "We were treated
worse than animals." His wife continued, "We got twenty dollars
a month and worked like slave labor. Our food consisted of
leftovers from the restaurant there, sometimes with cigarette
butts in it. We worked from seven o'clock in the morning till
after midnight. I had to clean toilets with a rag." They tried to
get back to Germany, but never heard again from the NCWC.
Another respondent, Stanley K., came to this country as one of
the participants of the Long Island farm plan worked out by Mr.
Zachariasiewicz of the Polish Immigration Committee (PIC) in
conjunction with the NCWC, which brought hundreds of Polish
Christian displaced persons over. Stanley said, "We were all
guys of eighteen to twenty-five; we were taken from New York on
a train to Greenpoint, Long Island. We worked and were put up

with other migrant workers in barracks that were like a concentration camp. After four months, I left the potato farm and moved to New Jersey to work in a bakery with a friend."

Not everyone of course had such trouble with a sponsor, although they still might have considered their early years in America very difficult. Through the help of the PIC, Gertrude J., her parents, sister, and brother-in-law were sponsored by somebody who had a farm in Culpepper, Virginia. To Gertrude, who was just seventeen years old at the time, Culpepper was a "huge nowhere," even though her family had had a small family farm in Poland. She and her family stayed on the farm for seven months with a "nice family" while she worked and learned English.

Two Christian families were sponsored through the NCWC and were helped in the Pittsburgh area by Father Twardy of St. Leocadia in Wilmerding. However, while they both thought Twardy was a nice man, they still indicated that their early years in America were very rough. The priest was able to get one man a job and secured apartments for the two families, but his help could not overcome the impression East Pittsburgh made on Janina W. She had cried, thinking that she would choke from the pollution. "All I wanted was to go back someplace, any place."

Only one Christian, Francinski D., delighted in talking about the help he received when he came to this country. He and his wife were sent to Greensburg under the blanket assurance of an Irish Catholic judge through the NCWC. The judge took Francinski and his wife shopping for clothes. "I couldn't believe it," exclaimed Francinski some thirty-five years later.

The fact of the matter is that most Catholics received very little in outright relief from either a Catholic or a Polish agency. As Edmund W. observed "the NCWC wanted to get as many Catholics over as possible, even though they were unorganized. The point was to get us over and then worry about resettling us." The only monies given outright were for minimal transportation costs.

The same situation prevailed with the PIC and the NCWC. In no case did any Christian refugee mention more than $25 being extended to them. A number of persons were angry that they had not been allowed to borrow from the PIC. Walter W. wanted $200 for transportation out of England but was turned down by the PIC. When Fabian B., who had just arrived from England, asked to borrow $11 for a ticket to Pittsburgh, he was refused on the grounds that the PIC only had money to help displaced persons coming in from Germany. When they told him to call his uncle, who was his sponsor, he was "disappointed and mad."

A few Christians recognized the disparity between the lack of organized help they received and what happened in the Jewish community. Stanley W. was disappointed in the big Polish organizations for not assisting more and envied the "Jewish organizing." Adam S., who felt he received a "so-so" welcome, talked about how the Italians and Jews got more financial and emotional support. "I wanted independence, but a little help would have been nice. I don't know why they didn't help—maybe jealously, not caring."

If relief was not extended through the NCWC directly or through a local agency, there was no other agency geared to assist. There certainly were no voluntary clubs or associations—such as the Friendship Club and the Young Men and Women's Hebrew Association in the Jewish community—to provide either assistance in kind or hospitality. The Polish Women's Alliance claimed that they offered assistance, but no newcomer talked of this. Nor did any newcomer talk about any help extended through the church, with the exception of Father Twardy in Wilmerding, or through any local Polish organization. In one account, a refugee was distraught because his local priest had called the displaced persons Communists and had told his parishioners not to help them. Adam L. recalled asking his priest why he never helped them. He never received an answer. Mieczyslaw G. and his wife remembered how they had gone to a

Polish church, but "there was no real interest in us . . . unless you had money."

What concerned the Christian refugees the most was their economic insecurity. They sorely felt the lack of an economic safety net, a sense that did not come across in interviews with the Jews, perhaps because they knew that if they were desperate, they could go to the Jewish Social Service Bureau. As Stanislawa S. acknowledged, their toughest problem was just "to survive. Sometimes we didn't have money to buy our children milk." She and her husband had come from wealthy landowning families in Poland. Her husband, who had been a law student in Poland, took a job at the American Bridge Company as a welder and learned on the job. "He was unhappy with it, but he was so afraid to change it. He was so afraid that the children wouldn't have anything in a strange country. . . . He never missed a day until he was disabled in 1973." For her part, she learned to weave, which eventually evolved into a small business. "My mother always used to say, if you don't have what you like, you like what you have. If I hadn't been brought up this way, I never would have been able to cope."

Henrietta P. was also in her twenties, married, with a child when she arrived in America. She too said

our toughest problem was to survive. My husband made seventeen dollars a week, so I did everything to help out—like cleaning houses. In England and even in Germany, we were always taken care of. But here we were given twenty dollars and suddenly on our own. It was a shock. For the first time in my life I was thrown into a society—with a daughter and husband who was not physically strong—and left to fight for my survival. It took maybe six months to a year. I felt completely lost. I needed some warm conversation.

One man put his feeling this way: "It was the hardest time for me when I arrived in New York, and I didn't know where to go, and I had a wife and child. It scared the hell out of me. During the war there was only me, and it was an adventure. Now I had no money, and nothing to eat, no help, no relatives, nothing." Adam L. complained that after he lost his first job, "I didn't have enough money for coffee."

Expectations were important in the adjustment process for Christians, as they were for Jews. Various observers have indicated that many displaced persons came to this country with inflated expectations.[10] Yet this assessment did not conform with accounts of the Christian refugees interviewed. Either they never had such high expectations or those expectations had been forgotten over the ensuing years to accord with reality. Only one, a Catholic woman, admitted expecting "everybody to be rich, have beautiful homes, maids." Certainly those Christians who had been in the service and who had gone to England with the Polish Resettlement Corps had a great deal of information and understanding about what to expect about life in America. They had contacts with Americans, and thus had gotten a more realistic picture of circumstances in this country. As Robert A., who had been part of the Polish Resettlement Corps, recalled, "I didn't expect that it would be much different here."

One particular reality for the Christian newcomers was that they were leaving their country, parents, and family behind. The author Joseph Conrad, a famous Polish exile in London of an earlier time, spelled out what became known as the "Lord Jim complex": feelings of guilt and shame about abandoning friends, relatives, and all Poles to their fate. Jacek Adolf in his study of more recent eastern European emigrés, found many people touched by feelings of guilt. They saw themselves "like rats deserting a sinking ship."[11] Joanna G. recalled her early years in the United States and how she cried so much because her family made her feel "like a traitor because I didn't get back to Poland." Yet she was the exception among the Christian refugees. While love of Poland had been and continued to be an emotional reality, others reported no feelings of guilt. Perhaps the guilt feelings had lessened over the years, or perhaps this described the feelings of a Polish intellectual elite who dwelt more characteristically in places like Washington, New York, and London. Such people often were closely tied to the Polish government in exile. Most of the Christian refugees in Pittsburgh indicated that their family had become resigned to their staying in the West and had put no pressure on them to return, as soon as it became clear that the Communists had entrenched themselves in Poland. In fact, by the time they arrived in the United States (the late 1940s and early 1950s), Poles both abroad and in Poland recognized that living conditions were much better in the West. Some families in Poland very quickly began to appreciate having a loved one in the West, so that they could receive additional relief supplies, which virtually all of the Christian refugees sent to their families in Poland.

With guilt or without, the Christian refugees were politically aware and concerned about their homeland. In this way they differed considerably from the earlier waves of Polish immigrants, who had come to this country primarily for economic motives and from a Poland divided among three European powers. In fact, the difference in motivation and background was to create a strain between the two groups.

Polish-American immigration into western Pennsylvania had begun in the 1860s, and in 1875 the first Polish church in Pittsburgh, St. Stanislaus Kostka Church, was founded at Sixteenth Street and Penn Avenue in what became known as the Strip District. By 1900 there were nearly 12,000 Poles in the city, spread out from the Strip District to the northern slopes of Herron Hill and on the south side near the Oliver Iron Works and the Jones Laughlin mill.[12]

By the time of the post-World War II immigration there were fifteen Polish organizations in Allegheny County, including the Central Council of Polish Organizations, which had been founded in 1935 to act as a central agency and clearinghouse for all Polish-American organizations in the district. The Polish Falcons were a real presence, with national headquarters in the city and thirty-nine local lodges as well. [13] There was also the Union of St. Joseph of North America, the Polish National Alliance, the Polish Women's Alliance, and the Polish Roman Catholic Union of America, which was the oldest Polish-American organization in the country. In addition to these civic organizations, there were eight Catholic churches with predominantly Polish congregations, five of which had been founded either before or at the turn of the century. Thus the social and fraternal network among Polish-Americans in Pittsburgh and in other American communities where there were large groups of Poles was quite extensive. While the Jewish community was criss-crossed by even more organizations, including a centralized fund-raising mechanism, the Polish-Americans were more highly organized than most other ethnic groups.

When Polish Christian refugees arrived in Pittsburgh after the war, they found a community structure, which they admired. As Stanley K. put it, "We had to give them a lot of credit. They had everything ready for us—churches, organizations, newspapers, clubs." Yet this appreciation did not forestall a certain tension between the two groups, a tension that was related to differences in culture, education, class, and circumstances.

Most postwar Christian refugees had at least a modest education, continuing beyond grade school either in Poland or, after the war, in army facilities or with the Polish Resettlement Corps. The education of the Polish Christians who had arrived before World War I was much less extensive, both formally and informally, in travel and experience. Moreover, the postwar refugees had been raised in an independent Poland, which had instilled in them a great pride. Those Poles who had emigrated from a Poland divided among three major European powers often did not understand or appreciate the nature of the state that had arisen following World War I, nor had they developed a similar attachment to the Polish nation. Not only did they not have the same patriotism, but they were little interested in preserving Polish culture. Poles coming after the war were "shocked" by Polonia (Polish America).

Certain class differences surfaced when the postwar Christian refugees indicated how appalled they were at what they perceived as a lack of respect on the part of the Polish-American community for education and for educated people. New arrivals were ridiculed; they were called "princes," "barons," or "masters," as if they had all been Polish aristocrats, which was not the case although there were more sons and daughters of middle-class Polish professionals and entrepreneurs in the postwar immigration than before. The Polish press carried repeated exchanges of "insulting words and venemous polemics" between members of earlier immigrations and the new arrivals.[14] Some refugees felt that the Polish-Americans were even less receptive to them than were other Americans.

When the Christian refugees who came to the United States under the Displaced Persons Act were asked whether they felt they had had much in common with the older Polish-American community in Pittsburgh, the response was evenly split. Of those who answered, fourteen felt they had something in common with local Polish-Americans, and thirteen felt they did not or that they were uncomfortable with them. However, the group primarily of professionals who sought refuge in the United States after the termination of the Displaced Persons Act in 1952 with one exception felt they had little in common with the Polish-American community. If this group is added to the tally, more Christian refugees indicated they had less in common with the local Polish-American community than those who felt a commonality of interest.

Stanley W. believed his generation of newcomers was well informed about politics, was better educated, had better command of the English language, and was more intellectual than the previous generation. He felt that he had assimilated more in three months than the earlier generation of Poles had in thirty to forty years. Raymond C. recalled how local people simply did not understand what the newcomers had been through. They said things like, "Didn't your insurance pay for the war damages?" Or, "Why didn't you vote the Communists out!" Joanna G. recalled being called a "dumb DP" when she arrived, and that she was laughed at because of her appearance. Lidia M. concluded,

The old immigrants were the sons and daughters of poor, very simple people. After the Second World War, it was a political emigration, not economic. We simply did not have much in common with the old. It sounds snobbish, but we were shocked by quite a lot of things. What shocked us and is a continuous irritation was the equation of being Polish with the polka and eating kielbasy and pierogi. When we came, we were scandalized because they had such limited notions of Polish culture. We do not blame them, but nevertheless, that's why Polish jokes exist—because these people present Polish culture from A to B and do not know the culture from B to Z. I cannot laugh at Polish jokes. I cannot laugh when somebody presents you as an imbecile.

Bernice N. also found little understanding of Polish life and culture on the part of Polish-Americans. "They think differently than we do. They think badly about Poland. They still think farms don't have electricity. They asked me if we wear underpants! They came here and did not learn English. They cleaned houses; they had no schooling to go higher." Another Christian refugee felt that the Polish-Americans seemed to have "an inferiority complex." Stanyslaw P. felt that his generation of immigrants, unlike the others, "were not shy about being Polish. If somebody doesn't like me being Polish, bloody too bad."

Irena K. explained things this way, "The first immigration was for bread. The second was different. The only thing we had in common was that we were both from Poland. Given the circumstances, there was quite a bit of help and acceptance." Her ex-husband explained,

The first immigrants came from the villages. They were hard-working people, but they were a different class. They were not political emigrants. We consider ourselves that. They were very uninterested in politics and not informed about world affairs. They could not see Poland as a free country. They could not relate to the fact that we had grown up in a free country between the wars. We had nothing in common, no common interests. We achieved in a few years what it took them a lifetime. We were successful because of education, a different perspective. We hoped for better things than they, and so we got it quicker. We didn't belittle ourselves or feel we were any worse than Americans. We had education, English, and ambition to work in more than the mines.

Others talked about how jealousy and ill feeling got in the way of a sense of commmonality and being welcomed. Joseph G., who had married an American woman from East Vandergrift, spoke of the resentment he encountered among Polish-Americans because he made a better living than they did. Like a number of the Jewish refugees, Stanley W. found he was welcomed only "until the envy set in when I got on my feet." Henrietta P. remembered how they used to be called "smart alecs from Europe" because they had wanted more from life than the Polish-Americans, who she felt were "against us." In her opinion, there was definitely an "us" and "them" mentality. Maria H., on the other hand, felt welcomed and did not sense any jealousy or resentment. She felt that the Polish-Americans thought the refugees were helpless and that they tried to help them by telling them where to look for jobs. But while she felt that "we came from the same culture," she also noted the differences. "The older immigrants came for work, and I would never have come to America if Poland was free."

Did the Christian refugees feel welcomed by the Polish-American community after the war? The overwhelming majority said yes, very much (twenty-five) or yes, somewhat (fourteen). Only ten refugees indicated they felt they had not been welcomed at all, or very little. Furthermore, it was entirely possible that a newcomer could feel welcomed but also feel little in common with the people welcoming him. What is instructive is that, as with the Jewish refugees, there was no automatic correlation between the perception about the receptivity of the local ethnic or religious community and the feeling about difficulty adjusting to America. Only one-third of those who indicated that their early years in America were the hardest or second hardest time for them also did not feel welcomed. Clearly, different factors weighed most heavily on different people. Table 1 shows the feelings of both Jewish and Christian refugees vis-à-vis their local groups.

Since many Christian refugees felt they had little in common with the earlier immigrants, the Christian refugees formed their own organizations. As Ursula T. explained it, "We didn't feel we had much in common with local Polish-Americans. They were nice, but we were not invited around. . . . Everyone [the refugees] had parties. Everyone helped one another. We considered

TABLE 1
REFUGEE'S PERCEPTIONS OF WELCOME AND COMMONALITY BY THEIR LOCAL
COMMUNITIES

| | | Christians | |
	Jews	Through 1952	1953 and After
WELCOME			
Strong	22	22	3
Moderate	7	12	2
Weak	14	2	2
None	7	5	1
COMMONALITY			
Yes	25	14	1
No	16	11	7
Uncomfortable	9	2	3

NOTE: Not all respondents answered these questions.

each other as family. My daughter called the children of some other newcomers her cousins. Because we had no other families, we all got together."

The division among Christian war veterans reflects the tension between the postwar generation and the earlier immigrants and the desire of the latter group to separate themselves. In 1952 the Association of Veterans of the Polish Army (SWAP) required its officers to be American citizens, a move apparently provoked by the fear that the new arrivals would take control. As a result, a new organization was formed called the Association of Polish Combatants (SPK) for Polish World War II veterans. In Pittsburgh, virtually all the veterans of World War II joined the local chapter of the SPK, and there was real ill feeling between the two groups.[15]

Displaced persons in the Jewish community also organized their own group; it became known as the Council of New Americans, in the East End, where many of the newcomers had settled. Samuel Frost estimated that more than 200 families were associated with this group. They used to have meetings at the old YM&WHA building, which stood on the corner of Negley and Stanton. Abe Kohane was one of the organizers, along with Abe Salem, Morris Dafner, and Wolf Friede. More than a dozen people recalled the parties and informal get-togethers with families. Many of the women used to meet informally at Highland Park with their children.

Other Jewish refugees gathered at the Blue and White or New Americans Club organized by the YM&HA. A number of young, mostly single, immigrants went to the Y for various social activities, including dances. For at least half of the single male sample the activities of the Blue and White Club and the Y dances became a regular part of their lives. Arnold Zweig recalled the group—all single men. Jack Sittsamer, who was just twenty when he came to Pittsburgh in 1949, used to go, and so did Sam Shear, who was twenty-two. So did Morris Manela and

Abe Cymerman, who remembered going to the club every Saturday night. Morton Cieply described the club as "a very big deal. It was important to us because we used to try to forget about our frustrations. We used to plan shows all on our own, which we liked."

In looking at where the newcomers tended to live, one finds a clear difference between the Jewish and Christian refugees. The first homes purchased by Jews tended to be either in Squirrel Hill or the East End, which have large Jewish concentrations. A smaller number bought in Greenfield, which also has a significant Jewish population. In contrast, the Christians were not concentrated in any one area, even though the majority of Polish-Americans lived in the Strip District, Polish Hill, and the South Side. While six Christians did buy houses in the Strip District, the remainder bought houses throughout the city and especially in the suburbs around Pittsburgh. This, if nothing else, was an indication of their willingess to live apart from the local Polish-American community.

Despite whatever problems Christians and Jews might have had in adjusting to the community around them, both groups were able to get jobs within a few months. The Jewish vocational agency wanted newcomers to go to school to learn English for a month or two before looking for a job. However, a number of respondents sought work on their own instead, to get on with the business of rebuilding their lives. Both groups were helped, whether it was by the Jewish job placement service or by relatives and friends, in their respective communities.

There were certain establishments that were employment beachheads for a number of newcomers. This was somewhat reminiscent of an earlier time when Poles, for example, were able to immigrate and get jobs at the Jones & Laughlin and Oliver mills, Heppenstall's, the Penn Railroad, the Armstrong Cork Company, and H. J. Heinz. Fifty years later, the H. J. Heinz plant was still a first-line employer for incoming Christians and Jews. American Bridge was mentioned a number of times by Christians, and the Hyman Blum Company and Kaufmann's were popular employers for Jews.

The early years in the United States were not easy years for either the Christian or Jewish refugees. Yet it would appear that the Jews, despite the professional and volunteer efforts expended on their behalf, had a harder time adjusting than the Christians. More of them looked back on this period as a very difficult one in their lifetimes. More of them felt unwelcomed and not understood by their cohorts in Pittsburgh. More of them did not have any facility with the English language, a deficiency which only hindered their adjustment and added to their sense of isolation. When asked what their toughest problem had been in their early experience in Pittsburgh, twenty Christians as opposed to only three Jews actually responded that they had had no overwhelming difficulty.

Christians and Jews struggled to establish themselves in a new society. They had to deal not only with hard economic realities, but often with emotional and psychological problems as well. Yet they carried on their common struggle isolated from one another, living apart. While they might not have found the receptivity and communal interests they were anticipating among their compatriots in America, neither did they have it from one another. Each group was on its own.

Both groups had come to America in hopes of starting life anew. What had they found in this country? What did they feel they had achieved and what legacy were they leaving for their American-bred children? It is to this contemporary perspective that we now turn in the final chapter of the immigrant's saga from Poland to Pittsburgh.

7

Displaced No More

▶▶▶ THEY HAD SURVIVED; THEY HAD made it. The Polish immigrants who had left their native land on the heels of World War II had come to this country to make a life for themselves. They have been at that business in most instances for thirty-five years or so. How have they fared and were there differences between Christians and Jews in terms of their achievement, their perspective, their values, their concerns? Like those who had preceded them in the first generation, they had become hyphenated Americans. How did they now see their identity, given the reality of time and place? They responded—some simply, some at length, some wistfully, some troubled, some moved. People answered that they were Polish, Jewish, American, or any combination thereof.

Among the Christian refugees, the majority (twenty-nine, or 49 percent) considered themselves Polish-American; eighteen (31 percent) said they were Americans; and twelve (20 percent) still considered themselves Polish. It would appear on the surface that the twelve who answered they were Polish had not really identified enough with American society to consider themselves part of it. However, their response to this specific question on identity was only part of the picture of how they saw themselves in America. Their comments are instructive as well. Esther L. indicated she was a Pole, but she was thrilled to be in this country and considered it the best place to be. And while she had missed Poland when she was younger, she no longer did. Alphonse R., a poor laborer, answered that he was Polish because he was born there. Stefan G., a successful engineer, also said he was Polish because of his origin. "When it came to loyalty, however, that was a different story." All with one exception were American citizens.[1] Most of those who said they were Polish expressed a real love and appreciation for this country and appeared comfortable and content here.

Concomitant with their feelings about the United States, there were varying degrees of nostalgia for Poland among the Christians, with about half of the "Polish only" group not expressing any nostalgia for their homeland at this point in their lives. Walter W. admitted that "every time I talk about Poland, tears come to my eyes. Every year our church has tours to Poland, but I have not gone. I feel it would be harder to go and then have to leave." Antoni R. felt he had been a good citizen, but "I think about Poland because my flesh and blood are there. My children are American, though." Gertrude J. felt that she would never go back, "but deep down, now my heart bleeds for Poland." And Krystyna M. admitted that "my generation is split. We are strongly attached, and yet we wouldn't go back to live there. Now we are strongly attached to America. This is my second country. Because I was born there, I don't think I can get rid of my feeling—it's impossible. You are what you are."

Nostalgia for Poland really had nothing to do with a response to the question on identity, because such sentiments were expressed by those who considered themselves Polish-Americans or even just Americans. They too felt the dual loyalty that Krystyna had verbalized, and that has been the feeling of many first-generation Americans. Lidia M., a librarian, felt the question of identity was very hard. "When I talk to Poles, I can scratch their eyes because they disparage America, and when I talk to Americans, I could do the same thing to them when they talk about Poland. I am Polish to the marrow of my bone, but I am a rabid American." Stanley K., a machine operator working for the railroad, also struggled with the question of identity. "I'm a Pole among Polish people, but a Polish-American among Americans," he laughed. "I'm an American citizen; I can mingle here and there; this is my home, my future—children, grandchildren. Yet whatever is Polish, I support."

Henry K., a retired metalworker from Braddock, acknowledged that he too was an American and a Pole. "I'd do for this country the same as I would do for Poland." Rudolf M., a chemist, admitted that by nature he is more like a Pole. "I still enjoy better Polish friends, Polish food. When I go to a Polish theater, it really hits me in a soft spot. But I live and work like an American and am very glad to be here." Bernice N., who felt that she was first Polish and then American, confided that she always cried on Polish national holidays, but she once walked out on a relative who criticized America. Joseph P. made a speech when he got his citizenship papers about the virtues of America, but he made it a point to say that he would never shoot a Pole if he were ever ordered to do so in the American military. Stanislawa S. described herself as an American, explaining things this way. "When you are adopted and your adopted parents are good to you, you still remember your mother, but you love the one who brought you up." She had no desire to return to Poland given current conditions and felt "there was no place like America to live." John S., the son of a Polish farmer, was a little more earthy. "I'm an American till I croak," he retorted.

If the Christian respondents answered they were Polish, their love of America and their loyalty were clearly in evidence; and if they considered themselves Americans, they still continued to have a very deep feeling for Poland. Many of them had returned to Poland at least once, sometimes more often, in order to see family.[2] Yet there was no one who looked forward to living permanently in that country in his or her retirement years. It was clear that feelings were colored not only by life in America but also by conditions in Poland. For some, their former homes were under Russian occupation. For others, the fact that the country was now run by Communists and that economic conditions were so poor precluded any interest in a return.

The contrast between the freedom and opportunity in this country with what they knew of life in Communist Poland contributed to their positive identification with America. These immigrants had arrived on American shores as Polish patriots, but in the course of their years in the United States, their patriotism had been extended to include a vigorous support for the United States, which had a tradition consistent with the best of the Polish tradition. Post–World War II Poles saw themselves as fighting for the dignity of man, for political independence, and for freedom from tyranny. To live in the country they considered the world's greatest democracy and the premier defender against their archenemy, the Soviet Union, was entirely consistent with their perception of themselves as Polish emigrés and patriots.[3]

A number of the Christians interviewed remembered arguments they had had over the years with young Americans who were not, in their opinion, patriotic. "They don't teach children to fight and die for America," said Frances B., the daughter of building contractor in Poland. "They don't want to go to the army, but the Commies are like a snake and are coming closer to us. That's what worries me. American children don't want to fight. Once there was a young man at a fruit stand shouting that he was not going to fight for America. He would go to Canada first. I yelled back there is no more Polish army to die for the freedom of the United States and England."

Two of the Christians who considered themselves Polish-Americans got involved with politics. Francinski D., the son of a Polish army sergeant who became a laborer in the United States, ran for town commissioner in North Huntington as a Democrat. Stanley W., a cabinetmaker, also was active in local politics in his community just north of Pittsburgh. This activity contrasts with the traditional avoidance of politics on the part of the generation of Poles who had come to American before World War I.

It is ironic that the postwar Christian refugees, who were reputed to have been highly critical of the Polish-Americans they encountered for wanting to be more American than Americans and not really Polish, should themselves have become such staunch Americans. It is paradoxical that a group who had known and loved the free and independent Poland in which they had grown up should have succeeded in adopting an American identity as enthusiastically as an earlier generation, who knew no such political loyalty.

The Jewish refugees were also asked about their self-identity. Were they Jewish, Polish, American, or all of the above? Twelve persons (22 percent) answered that they were Jewish; thirty-five (64 percent), Jewish and American; four (7 percent), American; one, an American-Polish Jew; two persons, Polish-Americans; and one, a Polish Jew. As with the Christian group, the largest number of respondents considered themselves hyphenated Americans. In contrast to 49 percent of the Christians who considered themselves Polish-Americans, 64 percent of the Jews considered themselves Jewish Americans or American Jews. Only four out of the group identified themselves as partly Polish.

As with the Christians, the responses themselves do not necessarily reveal the full picture. Of the four people who saw themselves as Polish in some way, two had absolutely no nostalgia for Poland and would never go back. A third, Janina Winkler, the daugher of a well-to-do engineer from Bielsko, had been back to Poland nearly a dozen times to visit family and friends. She appreciated the intelligentsia she found there and, while she was very worried about anti-Semitism in the United States, she had not found it among the Poles she knew in Poland. On the other hand, she "could never go back to Germany. There, intelligent Germans were mean and bad, but intelligent Poles were not anti-Semitic."

Most of those who indicated they were Jewish, as opposed to

Jewish and American, were American citizens and had strong feelings for America. The gratitude Jews felt to be able to immigrate here, to live in freedom, and to respond to the opportunities they found in America, made them American patriots. They loved this country and felt they were lucky to have been able to settle here. Yet while the Christians may have continued to feel a strong tie to Poland, it was certainly clear that for the overwhelming number of Jews a Polish identity was something they had long ago rejected. As seen in an earlier chapter, while the Christians had been very agitated about Allied policy toward the end of the war and during the Communist takeover, the Jews were indifferent or actually felt the Polish nation got what it deserved. This repudiation of Poland was further evidenced by their responses on self-identification.

Many felt like Lucy Dafner: "Poland was my country. We had been raised to believe that. But then after the war, I washed my hands of the Polish people and government because they did not want us." Irene Szulman said, "They rejected us. We were Poles, too, but they had never accepted us. During the war they turned on us. How else can we feel about Poland today after what they did to us." Jews felt that not only had they lost everything and everyone in Poland, but that the Poles were in some measure responsible for their losses. When Polish Jews and Polish Christians were faced with a common enemy, suddenly Polish Jews were no longer considered Polish. They were Jews only, stranded, spurned, and even betrayed by their fellow countrymen.

Thus the feeling toward Poland and Poles was more than one of sadness; it was an anger and bitterness arising from what they clearly perceived to be the faithlessness and betrayal of a people who they had felt were their compatriots. While some of the survivors told tales of individual Poles who helped Jews, one after another cited instances in which they saw Polish Christians not just fearful to act to rescue Jews (a response which they might have understood) but actually stepping forth to report Jews to the Nazis for payment or just out of hatred. Thus most Jews had absolutely no interest in going back to Poland. Many were quite outspoken about this, declaring they would never go back after what they had been through there. Only four people out of sixty had gone back to Poland for visits, compared to many times that number of Christians.

But while their Polish identity had been lost in the transit to America, their Jewish identity had not. In response to a question on whether the war affected their identity as a Jew, most Jews responded that it had not; a quarter of the group indicated that they felt even more Jewish as a result of the war. They were determined that the Jewish people should live on, especially in light of the decimation they had suffered.

The question on Jewish identity had to do with their ethnic feelings, a sense of peoplehood. However, a question on religious belief and faith elicited responses that were far less clear-cut. Their doubts, confusion, and questioning were evident:

Religious faith became stronger	5
Religious faith remained the same	27
Religious faith lessened	27

A retreat from faith occurred among both the orthodox and less orthodox. The comments of the twenty-seven who indicated some sort of lessening of their belief are insightful. Morton Cieply, who was from an orthodox family, admitted that his faith had been sorely shaken. In Poland he had always consulted with the rabbi before making any major decision, in order to better understand the will of God and the Jewish tradition. But "when I saw the rabbis killed and the synagogue burned, I lost a little faith." He joined a synagogue when he came to Pittsburgh, but admits he only goes three times a year. Regardless of this, his Jewish identity is very strong. Samuel Frost, who came from an orthodox background in Poland, admitted "something happened to me. I go to synagogue on high holidays and say *yiskor* [prayer for the dead], and that's where it ends. But if you talk about the Jews, watch out, because I'm proud to be Jewish." Aron Goldman confided that he had been affected "a lot. I questioned that when we needed God, where was he, and why didn't he strike the hands and eyes of those who persecuted us. I observe today. I thank God I am alive. I respect rabbis, because they keep on the tradition—that's how we survived. But I'm not kosher; I don't belong to a synagogue. . . . The more I suffered, the more I wanted to be a Jew. I'll be a Jew till my last breath, but religiously speaking, it's a different matter."

Frances Greenberg had not been very religious before the war. After the war, she became even less so. "But there is a little light that remains. We observe tradition and try to teach our kids as much Jewish identity as possible. When my daughter made *aliyah* [moved to Israel] and we asked her why, she responded 'because you taught me.' " Frances's husband, Isaac, put his feelings on religious faith this way: "the war endorsed my disbelief."

Some, like Benjamin Grundman, were bitter. "In Auschwitz they gave us food on Yom Kippur [Jewish day of fasting]. The Nazis used to come in and round up the Jews on Jewish holidays. I saw the selections at the camps, saw naked people, lots of incidents, people being chased into gas chambers. . . . Where was God! I saw Mengele so many times. He looked so beautiful; he smiled as he gave children candy and then sent them to the gas chambers." Morris Manela also had an intense reaction. "When I went to high holiday services at the Felderfing DP camp after the war, I started to choke. I almost died. I felt that they had put me in a gas chamber. I couldn't pray, because in my head I went through it again—that there were six million dead. I felt guilty that I had survived."

"I was not a religious believer even before the war," explained Gabriel Hoffman, "and when I saw how the first ones killed were the religious Jews, I asked why. We were like animals to survive. But I'm a Jew; I'm more Jewish now that I was before." Sarah Joskowitz was very orthodox before the war. "It took me a long time to make peace. When you see children burned alive, you have to break. I am a religious person. I feel the good people always suffer, but only God knows why. . . . People cannot answer." Izak Mikowski, who lost his first wife and child during the war, also asked how can you believe when they took so many children and killed them. He had not been very religious before the war. Now he felt that "if people say they believe, they are lying. They are going to *shul* because of their wife and friends." Abe Kohane admitted that he too had been "deeply shaken" in his faith, but this had nothing to do with his Jewish identity. "I suffered so much; I wanted to continue as a Jew." Dora Lipschitz still believed, still kept kosher, and raised her children Jewish, "but sometimes I think it doesn't pay. Why did it happen to all those religious people? I ask myself why."

Abe Salem remarked that he came from a strong religious background, but "how can you say God loves us after they made soap out of us. I have more questions than answers." Jack Sittsamer, too, was troubled. "When I saw my father being killed, I said there was no God, because my father was such a religious man. When I heard that all the Jews were killed, I said for sure there was no God. When I was in Germany after the war, I never went to any *shul*. But when I came to this country four years after the war, it started coming back. What never did change was my pride in being Jewish." Irene Szulman lost her faith in God, but she nevertheless insisted she became more Jewish after the war. Before the war she recalled telling her mother that she would probably marry a non-Jew. After the war she wouldn't think of it.

Only two Jews out of sixty interviewed seemed to reject their religion. One was a woman who because of her intense search for answers felt she had found them in the faith of the Jehovah Witnesses. She was married to a Jewish man, however, and her son had been raised as a Jew. The other apostate, lonely in his bachelorhood, had been a skeptic and nonobserver before the war. He was against all organized religions because he felt they operated to the disadvantage of all. Furthermore, he tended to blame the "fanatical" Jews for separating themselves from non-Jews. In his opinion, hotly denied by other survivors, "the fanatical Jews brought their bitter fate down on themselves."

While some Jews tended to lose some measure of their belief in and devotion to God, many others either felt the same religiosity they had before the war or in some instances even more. Janina Winkler, who was an assimilated Jew before the war, admitted that "Hitler made a Jew out of me. I'm more religious, but especially I have more of a Jewish identity. Before the war I never proclaimed it; now I try to do whatever I can for Jewish causes." Mark Stern did not let his wartime experiences affect his belief. "We walked in as children; we walked out as adults. The only way to survive was to believe in God—God watching over us. If I lost my faith, I knew I would lose my will to live. I know God doesn't punish you; he just doesn't watch everything." Hyman Federman, who hid for twenty-seven months on a Polish farm and then was able to join the partisans, recalled how the people who came home from the concentration camps said there was no God. "I believed I survived because there was a God. When I was in the fields and one boy said to wait here while he got some food for me, somehow I knew he was going to tell the Nazis and that I should run away. I baked matzoh in 1945, even before the war ended. I can't explain it; even here in this country, one believes and the next one doesn't."

Harry Feldman never lost his faith. "I saw God—saw only his miracles, and I believed in them. I survived." Fela Morgenstern concurred:

I always knew God was here. I can't explain everything, like how the universe works, how you are born. Explain to me why some people are born capable and others are not. You cannot explain everything, and you have to believe in a higher power who is in charge of everything. I learned this in my life. Why was I saved and

my younger sister, who might have been better, was not!? I am very
emotional. I know all the philosophies—all baloney, in my opinion.
It all comes down to the fact you don't know anything. If you are a
believer, you can trust a higher power and accept what it is. You
cannot fight your own destiny. The most important thing is to have
hope and to enjoy God's world.

Moshe Taube, who became a cantor at a synagogue after the
war, felt that the war made him more religious. Prayer was a
source of strength.

Before the war, God was an abstract that I believed in, to follow
after my parents. But during the war when I saw life at its lowest
ebb, I developed a personal relationship with God. God became
more of a reality; not just an idea. . . . How does He let this happen? people ask. I say that God is not a man who has to give
account for himself or be judged. Man can offer insight; not explanation. This is beyond the human realm of understanding. Human
reason and mind cannot be compared to God's universe.

Mordechai Glatstein, the only rabbi among the refugees
interviewed, tried to spell out his thoughts.

I was not angry at my God. I was angry at my world. They were
silent for four years. I hoped America and England would help.
They are people of freedom and peace. . . . I lost hope in mankind,
not in my God. They betrayed us, so I came back closer to my God.
Some, like Elie Wiesel [Nobel Prize-winning Holocaust survivor],
were rebellious. But we know from the prophets and the destruction
of the Temple not to put our trust in the nations of the world. Put
your trust in your own peoplehood and God.

There appeared to be no way of predicting how people would
respond on the religious question. Even within the same family,
one child would lose faith, while the other would not, or would

even become more religious. Lucy Dafner never went back to being an observant Jew, but her sister did. Frances Spiegel never lost her belief in God and in fact insisted that her faith kept her going through her ordeal and that there were questions that people simply could not answer. Her sisters however, lost their faith, continually asking where God was when they needed Him.

When we compare the remarks and feelings of the Jewish refugees with those of the Christians, who with one exception were Catholic, we see a very different picture emerging. For the overwhelming percentage of Christians, their experience and the experience of others simply did not prompt the same kind of soul searching or retreat from of their religious faith or observance. For the majority, the war strengthened their relationship with their God, and this relationship was a source of strength to them during the war years. Frances B., who found herself in the desolate expanse of Siberian Russia, gained more faith as a result of her ordeal. "I can feel the miracles and can feel God taking care of me. In my dreams I was touching the clothes of the mother of Jesus. I never lost my hope or my faith." Raymond C. believed that "God had to be with us. We survived a horrible war." Janusz K., who was in Russia, wound up with greater faith. "If I didn't have my faith, I wouldn't have made it. . . . I saw people give up hope and starve to death." Viktor H. felt stronger about his religion. "When I was in Siberia, there were two of us—a Russian and me. I prayed, but this Russian didn't believe in anything. He asked me why I was praying and to whom. Anyway, I was to be released because of the Sikorski Agreement in 1941. When the Russian heard about that, he came over and asked me how to pray!" Gertrude J. was a young teenager when she was taken to Germany for forced labor. "If it wasn't for my religion, I just would have broken down." Stanis-lawa S. felt the same way. And Marcel P., who as a priest taken to Dachau in 1944, secretly got a prayer book and preached in the camp, fully aware of the consequences if he was caught.

Only a few Christians expressed any doubts about God. Joseph P. challenged God when he saw German pilots shooting women and children in the field for fun. Henry K., who was a prisoner of war in Germany, asked why, if he was God's child, he had to suffer so. But he still remained a believer.

There is no question that Christians did not experience the same anguish as the Jews on this subject. And while a few might have questioned God, none ever questioned the faith and traditions of Christians who committed outrages against Jews.

The reasons for the differences in attitude are complex. For one, the Jews suffered enormous losses both as a people and as a culture. The experiences of the Christians were not on the whole as degrading and dehumanizing as that of the Jews. Then too Jews have historically responded to adversity with self-flagellation and moral inquiry, in contrast to Christian tradition.[4] And with regard to the Holocaust in particular, Jews have responded to the meaning of the events in far greater measure than Christians, although that it changing. The Vatican II council set in motion by Pope John XXIII made history in 1964 when it officially repudiated the teaching of contempt and condemned anti-Semitism in all its manifestations. Other churches have since followed the lead of the Catholics. It should also be pointed out that, for Polish Catholics in particular, Catholicism has always served as a nationalistic rallying cry, uniting the people both during and after the war as they confronted the Soviets. The Jewish religion did not have such a national component.

In any event if we look at the tally of the Christians' response to the war, the picture is considerably different from that of the Jews.

Religious faith became stronger	18
Religious faith remained the same	27
Religious faith lessened	4

Apart from the question of religious faith, the Christians did not come out of the experience the same as they had gone into it. Not only had they seen the overthrow of their country and the loss of freedom, but they had undergone a personal odyssey, which often had significant psychological repercussions. Many recognized the changes in themselves. Like Rita K., they were proud of what they had overcome. The women in particular felt that their war experience had made them stronger, "tougher." "In Russia," said Stanislawa S., "you didn't dare show your softness, your gullibility. I was scared on the inside, but heroic on the outside. When my husband was so sick and died a few years ago, I didn't cry."

Yet while the Christian refugees mentioned their strength and ability to cope, many also talked about their greater appreciation for life and a sensitivity to other living creatures, to injustice and prejudice. Mieczyslaw G., a retired roofer, said you learned "to respect your life more, that you can live. In a war, you can have all the riches and you can have nothing. We appreciate being alive, having whatever we have," Janusz K. commented, "I respect more personal freedom and the right of every human being to a decent life. In Poland I was not interested in poor people. Now I am interested in all people having a decent life." Joseph G., too, had changed. "I used to be a very rough, aggressive person. I told off the Germans and wasn't scared of anything. But I saw so much killing that I can't hit a dog now. I even hate to kill a bug. I get nightmares from war movies."

A number of them spoke about how the war had made them appreciate the necessities of life. "I'm a fanatic about not wasting food. I use every last crumb," admitted Irena K. Others talked about a certain awareness, even cynicism, about other people that they had developed as a result of their wartime experience. Stefan G., a young engineer with the Royal Air Force in England, related how the war had "matured" him. "It opened my eyes on many things, like cruelty."

The Jews interviewed echoed many of the same feelings and perceptions. Michell Borke felt the war had actually made him a stronger person, a more mature person. "I would have remained a mama's baby, but I was forced to become my own man. I appreciate people now; but I'm also more realistic about them. I'm willing to accept people for what they are. . . . It was a broadening experience." Jacob Wolhender felt that as a result of the war he became more cosmopolitan and international. Dora Iwler felt that in addition to being more sensitive to any slurs against Jews, she was more sensitive to any injustice—toward the blacks, for instance.

Harry Drucker and others were more cautious than they had been. Some were fatalistic. "You have to face whatever comes up," remarked Estelle Forstenzer. Aaron Fox lost his trust in people. "Before the war, I believed in people more than I do now. Now I feel people do not mean what they say." Wolf Friede felt he could never again have a sense of security about life; that you never know what can happen. Arnold Zweig's feelings were raw. "The war changed me. Inside I'm bitter. I will never accept what happened during the war. I was left with no family, no relatives. I raised children with Dr. Spock's book. It was my bible, but I really didn't know what to do. I don't blame anybody, but I do blame everybody." Ruth Weitz admitted she was jealous of people who had a family.

Like Stanislawa S., Rose Turbiner also felt the war had made her a stronger person. Other women too felt they had learned how to cope. Marcia Scheingross acknowledged that the war had changed her. "I got more life experience. The harder your life is, the more you learn. When it comes easy, you don't know how to handle things. I learned to protect myself, to take advice from smarter people, to be strong and not give up easily, to fight if it's possible."

Irene Szulman, like Mieczyslaw G., had put money in perspective. "I don't care so much now. I know what it means to lose everything in one minute." Frances Spiegel agreed.

I'm not interested in material things. Family life and Jewish life are
very important to me. We had a robbery when my husband was
sick, but I said, I had lost more in my life. If my husband is well,
that's more important. If they stole our television, so what. How
many times did I have to start over again in my life! Because of the
war, I saw how little material goods mean. They took us away naked. You need money to live, but it doesn't mean much. . . . I am a
tougher person, but I'm not bitter; I'm hurting more than I'm bitter.

And Harry Rosen philosophized: "He is a rich man who is happy
with what he has."

It is impossible to measure just how much the war changed
outlooks and affected the adjustment of emigrants to America.
People learned to fend for themselves, to rely upon their own
ingenuity and skills. On the other hand, when people suffered
emotional disorders or nervous conditions, as a number of survivors admitted to, this certainly did not help their adjustment to a
new society. Undoubtedly some of the early difficulties of the
Holocaust survivors and the problems that social workers faced
can be attributed to the trauma of wartime and the extended
grieving process. We need only recall the comments of a significant minority of persons who felt that what the Jewish community offered them was not really what they needed; that they
needed emotional support and understanding and this they felt
was simply not forthcoming from either most of the professional
people with whom they were in contact or the Jewish community
at large.

To obtain a more complete understanding of all the refugees,
it is instructive to look at some figures about their occupational
status from father to refugee to refugee's sons and daughters.
Table 2 is a compilation of the occupational level of the three
generations for the Christian refugees. The largest number of
their fathers, as discussed in earlier chapters, were farmers.
Another significant percentage were in high- or middle-level

TABLE 2
OCCUPATIONS OF MALE CHRISTIAN REFUGEES, THEIR FATHERS,
AND THEIR CHILDREN

Occupation	Father	Refugee	Sons	Daughters
High-level white-collar worker, aristocrat, professional	5	2	5	0
Middle-level white-collar worker, manager, proprietor	11	5	14	15
Salesperson, technician	1	0	1	5
Clerk	2	1	4	11
Craftsman	10	10	7	0
Machine operative	2	5	0	0
Laborer, miner	4	8	1	0
Farmer	22	0	0	0
Service worker	1	5	1	1
Housewife	—	—	—	10
Unemployed, on welfare	0	1	0	2
Student	0	0	5	3
Peacetime military service	1	0	4	0
Total	59	37	42	47

positions or were craftsmen. The drop in status on the part of the male refugees is clear. Fewer refugees were in middle- or high-level positions than their fathers, and many more were laborers, machine operators, service workers, or the like. Their predominance in semiskilled or unskilled jobs is evident not just in comparison to their fathers, but also in comparison to the national norms for all Polish-American males.[5]

There are dramatic changes with regard to the children of the Christian refugees. Nearly half of the refugees' sons are in middle- to high-level white-collar positions, and one-third of their daughters are. It is clear that these children have achieved considerably higher status than Polish Americans in general and have adapted to the requirements of a more service-oriented, technical society. Their educational levels have reflected their higher status. Of the eighty-nine children produced by the Christian refugees, fifty-four are college educated, with a few more too young to enroll. Of the fifty-four, seven have gone on to graduate school. They have moved up the economic ladder and have left the unskilled, lower paid jobs to others.

Given the upward mobility of so many of their children, it is understandable why so many of the Christian refugees have adopted America as their own and have a sense of achievement about their lives. For them as for most parents, their children's security and prospects are of utmost importance. As Stanislawa S. said, "my children were my crown."

How did the sons and daughters of the Jewish refugees fare? And what was the occupational course for the refugees, themselves? After a brief period of economic relief, often provided by organized Jewish agencies, the survivors were on their own. How did they do and where did they go after the profound dislocations of the Holocaust and their long hiatus as displaced persons?

As we have seen in chapter 1, Jews predominated in trade and small industry in Poland. In the Pittsburgh group, the fathers of the immigrants had been proprietors, dealers, or craftsmen, often with their own shop (see table 3). Having a shop or being a dealer was technically a white-collar position, but it certainly was no indication of level of income—many of those in sales were impoverished. It is not surprising that when the Jews came to this country, they generally got jobs in the same areas that they had some experience with in Europe. The largest number of male refugees became craftsmen, half of whom eventually opened their own shops. In contrast to the Christians, who generally obtained jobs as semi-skilled or unskilled laborers, the Jews maintained traditional roles in handicrafts and commerce. As such, the Jews were much more apt to be self-employed than non-Jews. All in all, twenty-five of the thirty-six male Jewish refugees were self-employed. Only two male Christians out of thirty-seven were.

After the Holocaust

TABLE 3
OCCUPATIONS OF MALE JEWISH REFUGEES, THEIR FATHERS,
AND THEIR CHILDREN

Occupation	Father	Refugee	Sons	Daughters
High-level white-collar worker, professional	2	3	23	10
Middle-level white-collar worker, proprietor, dealer	23	12	22	39
Salesworker, technician	17	3	2	0
Clerk	1	1	3	6
Craftsman	12	15	2	0
Machine operative	0	1	0	0
Laborer, miner	2	0	0	0
Farmer	0	0	0	0
Service worker	0	1	1	0
Housewife	—	—	—	1
Unemployed, on welfare	1	0	1	0
Student	0	0	8	2
Peacetime military service	0	0	1	0
Total	58	36	63	58

This desire to be self-employed on the part of so many Jews propelled many of the Jewish men to establish their own businesses fairly early after their arrival in the country. Nineteen of the men had been self-employed for twenty-five years or more.

Jews also demonstrated a much greater propensity to change both employers and careers.[6] Ten Jews had made major career changes on their own accord, while only two Christians had chosen to do so. Dora Zimmerman's husband quit a job making barrels after only one day. The Jewish Vocational Agency had gotten him the job. "He didn't come to this country to make barrels!" she said. He worked as a plumber, doing odd jobs, and eventually became a real estate owner and builder. Sam Shear started working in a junkyard, became a welder, and then went to school to become an insurance agent. This kind of career jumping was simply not the pattern among the Christians, who followed traditional Polish ways in placing a value on job stability and security over risk-taking. In being willing to take risks with new employers, self-employment, or career change, Jews followed their own traditional patterns.

A look at the occupations of Jewish sons and daughters shows how top heavy this generation has become in professional and middle-level occupations. Seventy-two percent of the sons and an incredible 84 percent of the daughters held such positions. While the earlier generations, including both their fathers and their grandfathers, had tended to be independent entrepreneurs, these young people were usually working for someone else, at least at this point in their careers. With such participation in managerial and professional careers, the movement of Jews out of the crafts and small shops so characteristic of an earlier time and place has all but been completed. In comparison with the sons and daughters of Christian refugees, who themselves were also showing a great increase in professionalization, the Jews clearly outstripped them.

This is also reflected in educational levels. Of the 121 children in the Jewish group, 103 completed or were in the process of completing college (85 percent). Thirty-five, or 29 percent, went on to graduate school. In comparison, 61 percent of the Christian children went to college, while 13 percent attended graduate school. These results reflect Jewish national norms. A recent survey indicated that 34 percent of the Jewish population had a college degree. When the data is separated by age, as many as 90 percent of those in the twenty-five-through-forty-year range have at least a college degree.[7]

It is also instructive to note that only one Jewish daughter was described by her parent as a housewife, whereas ten Christian daughters were. This reflects today's pattern of the working woman who either marries later or has children and works. It would appear that the Jewish community is more committed to that reality than the Christian community is. The movement of

Jewish women into high-level white-collar positions is also evident from the data.

In light of the accomplishments of their children, how do the refugees feel about their life in America? Do they feel they have been successful in what they set out to do in life? Do they have a sense of achievement? The answers are shown below:

	Christians	*Jews*
Most definitely	28	23
Yes	18	15
Somewhat	3	7
Not really	8	8
No	1	5

As can be seen, both Christians and Jews felt they had made tremendous strides in this country. They felt they had established themselves and laid the groundwork for their children's success, and this made them proud. When asked whether they had a sense of achievement over what they had accomplished in their lifetime, 79 percent of Christians responded that they did; only 16 percent responded not really or no. For the Jews, the percentages were also weighted on the positive side, but not quite to the same degree; 66 percent felt a sense of achievement while 22 percent did not.

For those who felt they had not achieved, there was no relation between that dissatisfaction and either present or former job status. If people were unhappy, they were unhappy for reasons other than employment. Expectations had something to do with their sense of achievement, but generally most of them were fairly realistic in their job expectations and goals, as indicated in an earlier chapter. Joseph P., who became a successful contractor after starting as a carpenter, remarked that he "never put up any target. I didn't need to be a millionaire. I could not expect better. If you don't have what you like, you have to like what you have. That was an old Jewish saying in Poland and I like to refer to it." One person after another indicated that money did not bring them happiness, that they did not desire great wealth, that they were content with modest circumstances. To own a home, a car, to have some savings, was all they wanted. To have a family and be able to educate their children and give them a better life than they were able to have gave them a tremendous sense of pride and achievement.

For the Christian refugees, whatever job they had was fine, as long as they made a living. Gertrude J., who had come over as a displaced person and worked on a farm in Culpepper, Virginia now worked behind the counter at a fast-food establishment. Her husband was a janitor. Their job status was obviously low, but she was a very proud person. "Our goal was to own a house [which they did, in Lawrenceville]. We do not have a fancy house, but we have savings for our girls' education. We don't believe in insurance—we only have $1,000 for funeral expenses. I never worked in the best job, but we are self-sufficient." John O., who became a blacksmith, felt a strong sense of achievement also. "I don't live extravagantly. I didn't want anything fancy. I was only a steelworker and never pretended to be anything I'm not. A man's job is to support his wife." Fabian and Frances B, too, were satisfied. "I have no complaint," said Fabian. "I have two children who are educated. In thirty years we have had a good life. We have a house and all we need. I worked hard and never refused overtime. We don't have a mortgage the way my daughter does. I don't believe in that." His wife, who had survived Siberia, added how happy she was just to have a roof over her head. Esther L., who had been taken to Germany as a young girl for forced labor, remarked how proud she was also. She had never used a credit card. She and her Polish husband, who she had met after the war in Germany, had raised four children and had bought a lot and built two houses on it so one of her daughters and her family could be close by.

Edmund L., who began in this country as a steel mill laborer, took a course to pass the civil service examination, and was eventually able to become a postal service employee, was satisfied. "I have enough to live on, a nice family, a beautiful home, and all kinds of friends. I worked hard. My parents sacrificed for me so much. I got an education and gave it to my children. That was important." Marion K. had a smile on his face. "I never wanted anything too much. I wanted a shanty and a little wife who doesn't beat me too much. We're comfortable— no debts, and we don't go to bed hungry at night." Maria S. did not worry about money either. "My husband says I should think about myself more, but if it were up to me, we would not save any money. We would send everything to our family in Poland."

For those few women who indicated that they were not completely satisfied with their achievement, they spoke of thwarted ambitions. Krystyna M. felt that if she could change anything, she definitely would have gone to college to get some kind of profession for herself. She was thrilled that her two girls were getting a good education, but now that "I'm looking to go to work, I want to find something that just doesn't waste my time." Other women too complained of not doing enough in their lives—both Jews and Christians. These comments appear to reflect not just the problems of the immigrant experience but the weight of traditional female responsibilities in the home and the modern revolution in female attitudes about careers and the numbers who are working outside the home.

In explaining their feelings about their accomplishments in life, the values of the Christians were clear. In their emphasis upon family, home ownership, savings, hard work, a steady job, they reflected traditional Polish values. In stressing self-reliance, independence, and education, they were also reflecting American values. Yet they were not caught up in the drive for material success, which they and many others have attributed to Americans. Indeed, an accumulation of wealth or the lack of it was rarely mentioned by the respondents as a preoccupation or measure of success. Most often the response was something to the effect that "we have all that we need." This general sense of achievement, expressed by most of the respondents regardless of previous social status, must be weighed in considering the attachment they felt toward America. A personal sense of accomplishment can only facilitate a willingness to assume a new national identity.

The sense of accomplishment felt or not felt by the Jewish survivors was also not related, in most instances, to expectations about economic success. Only one of those who said he had not achieved complained because he had no business or property. Another admitted that, although he was happy with what he had, "as I lived here, I wanted more and more and thought I would be more successful than I am." The rest of the Jews had other reasons for their less-than-complete feelings of achievement. A number were frustrated because they had been unable to go into the career or to get the education they had always wanted. Two women had wanted to be doctors. Melvin Goldman had wanted to go into engineering but never had the opportunity and wound up owning a jewelry store. Harry Friedman, who was a carpenter, had hoped to become a builder or contractor, but never did. He also wanted to have his kids marry and have grandchildren, but that had not happened yet, either.

Others too, expressed dissatisfaction with their personal lives. Albert Levenreich had wanted to raise Jewish children, but he had married a Christian woman (they subsequently were divorced), and his children had no interest in his faith. Another woman was bitter because she was divorced and lonely. Jacob Wolhender, a wealthy proprietor, did not feel he had achieved much either. "I wanted to have a family and never achieved that. Money isn't everything. Before, it was everything—when I didn't have it. But as soon as I got it, it lost all its meaning, because it can't buy what I want with it." Two persons responded that they had not achieved because of something related to the Jewish people as a whole. Morris Manela remarked, "I would like America to get off Israel's back." For him, no job was done until you die. He was going to keep struggling. (He died in 1986.) Rabbi Mordechai Glatstein's frustration was not with his family or circumstances; it too related to his people. He had not achieved, because "I don't see a greater awakening of American Jewry toward their heritage."

Those who felt that they had certainly achieved something in their lifetime were content with family and occupation. In some instances they had long ago reconciled themselves to the obstacles they had had to face and were proud of their accomplishments in the face of such hardships. Isaac Greenberg waxed philosophical; with a twinkle in his eye, he said, "I didn't have any particular goals, so whatever I achieved was fine. I can sit down and read. Some people enjoy other things, but more than a bagel I don't need to eat in a day. Besides, bagels have a hole in the middle! I don't have to demand more and more. Who says more is so good? If I had more hair on my head, it would be better, but then if I looked too handsome, my wife would be in trouble!" His wife, Frances, was more serious. "I think we achieved—material independence, security. . . . We worked very hard. We didn't get any help. We worked with ten fingers and sometimes our toes. . . . We're proud of what we have. My goal was not to work in a cleaning store, but you have to make peace with what happens. It brings you food on the table. Now we can relax, enjoy life, travel, and help others."

Dora Iwler also was content. "I think I have done beautifully. In thirty years we brought up two children—and we came with nothing. We had to go from A to Z. We're grateful to God for this great accomplishment. I was denied an education in Poland, so I was determined to do what I could for my children's education. I'm not afraid to go, because my children can stand on their own feet." David Guss exclaimed "I achieved a million times more than I wanted! I never could believe I could make a living. I just came here to survive. . . . I only wanted bread with

potatoes to make me happy." Bernard Gelman shared his sentiments. "I think I achieved more than I wanted. I never dreamed
I'd have what I do have. I'm not just talking financially, but as a
person, as a member of a community, this country. I built myself
a good life, and I'm very happy with the way my children have
grown up."

The majority of Jewish refugees were happy with the life they
had made for themselves in this country and lived comfortably.
They were content not only with what they had accumulated, but
perhaps even more importantly, with what they had given to
their children and what their children had accomplished. Yet
compared to the Christians, more were less content, less strong
in their sense of accomplishment. This appeared to be related to
a higher level of expectation on the part of the Jews, aims that
were formulated as they lived in this country and not necessarily
when they first came here. The Jews appeared to place greater
demands on themselves and thus suffered more from what they
perceived as personal setbacks and defeats. Whether these
perceptions and goals were a function of their Jewish cultural
values or whether they were related to their wartime experience
is, of course, difficult to determine. Generally, most of these
survivors came out of the war happy to be alive, just wanting to
start life again. They were realistic in what they had lost and
what they could hope to achieve given their deprivation. Their
determination to succeed seems neither more nor less than that
of other Jewish immigrants. But perhaps because of their losses,
as they grew older, the need to somehow make up for the
Holocaust drove them harder and made it more difficult for them
to really feel a strong sense of achievement. There was so much
to overcome and regain.

For both the Jews and the Christians, the maintenance of
either their Polish identity or their Jewish identity was of great
importance. We have seen how often a hyphenated identity was
cited even by those who felt a real love for America. Both groups

sought to maintain their identities either as Poles (in the case of the Christians) or as Jews. To do this they joined ethnic organizations. The Christians overwhelmingly joined Polish organizations over non-Polish ones, listing 111 memberships in Polish organizations, compared to 37 in American ones. While they also did not settle in Polish neighborhoods or go to predominantly Polish churches, they did attempt to communicate a love for the land of their birth to their children.[8] Twenty-six Christians felt that had done this, while seven did not.

A number of social scientists and researchers have suggested that the higher the social class, the lower the ethnic identity.[9] However, this was not borne out in this study. First of all, in response to the question on self-identity, those who considered their identity to be American varied in social class and occupational level. Of the eighteen Christians who indicated they felt they were Americans, there was a wide occupational range, including both blue- and white-collar workers. There were also differences in educational levels and former status in Poland. Most of the most successful Polish professionals identified themselves either as Polish-Americans or even just Polish.

Those Christians in higher social brackets tended to belong more frequently to Polish organizations. The Christians who had attained higher status and came from other countries after the Displaced Persons Act had terminated had twenty-seven ties to various Polish organizations, compared to fifteen ties to American or non-Polish groups. Thus Christian professionals, both by their expressed sentiments and by their affiliations, still felt a very strong commitment to their Polish heritage even as they demonstrated their ability to succeed in American society.

The strong commitment to a Jewish identity by the Jewish refugees paralleled the Polish Christians' loyalty to their cultural heritage. Communicating an identification with the Jewish people to their children was very important. Forty-four people felt they had done this, while five thought they had only to some extent. Only three Jews did not feel they had successfully managed to do that. The group had seventy-three married children, sixty-three of whom had married Jews, a much lower intermarriage rate than the one-out-of-three rate current among young Jews in general.

The Jewish refugees had joined ethnic organizations far more than non-Jewish organizations, belonging to 111 Jewish organizations (the same number as the Christian membership in Polish organizations) and only 23 non-Jewish organizations. Moreover, unlike the Christians, who spread out across the region, the Jews continued to cluster in highly Jewish areas, such as Highland Park, Squirrel Hill, and Greenfield.

While the Christians have gone back to Poland many times and continue to feel a very strong attachment to the country despite the fact most would not like to live there now, Jews felt that same emotional tie to Israel. This great bond with Israel is characteristic of native-born American Jews as well.[10] Yet allegiance and love for America are also very clear among these Jews. As with the Christians, who viewed their national tradition as completely consonant with the American tradition of freedom and justice, so did the Jews see the ideals and democracy of Israel as concurrent with American values and interests. Dual loyalty held true for both Jews and Christians, except that in one case it was to Israel and in the other it was to Poland.

The commitment Jews feel to the State of Israel is related not just to a sense of a universal Jewish family or a religious feeling but to concerns about anti-Semitism in this country and fear of an outbreak of discrimination or persecution. The refugees reached various conclusions on the matter, but the concern was there. As Julius Aussenberg said, "I'm a Jew and very much for Israel, but I'm also very much for the United States. Don't get me wrong. I've very grateful. . . . It's the best country in the world. America gave me a big chance, and I'm very happy. But I think I would like to be in Israel. I'm still afraid it [the Holocaust] could happen again. . . . I see more anti-Semitism now than when I came. I could never believe that I would see painted swastikas in this country."

On the other hand, Sam Shear identified himself as a Jew but one who wanted to live in no other country but America. "I've been in eight different countries, but if you want to do for yourself, the opportunity is here. Freedom is a diamond here. . . . I'm concerned about anti-Semitism, because I know what it means. But I used to hear more anti-Semitism years ago. I don't think the Holocaust can happen again. As long as we have our own state, it can't happen. If there had been an Israel in 1939, it wouldn't have happened. Izak Mikowski, who felt there was open anti-Semitism on the part of too many leaders, also felt that if it was not for Israel, there was the possibility of another Holocaust in the United States. No matter whether individuals wanted to live in Israel or not, the concern about its future was intimately tied to their own concern about their future and that of their children.

These were people who generally could not be blasé about the subject of anti-Semitism. If one were to divide reactions to the topic of anti-Semitism into three broad categories, about one quarter of the respondents expressed little fear or concern about its occurrence in the United States, one quarter saw it as a present or growing threat, while the remaining half thought it might become a threat if conditions were ripe. Sarah Joskowitz, who had spent years in a hospital after the war recovering from her wartime ordeal, believed that anti-Semitic feelings were harbored by a lot of people. "I can feel it. It could happen again if the Jews are not prepared." Fanny Lieberman was scared about the extent of anti-Jewish feeling. "In Poland it started little by little and then came out big. Nobody believed it could happen there." Irene Szulman, like Julius Aussenberg, believed that anti-Semitism was worse now than when she had first come to this country. "I think the situation with the Palestineans and Israel has a lot to do with it." Janina Winkler, who felt comfortable in Poland, deplored the anti-Semitism in this country. "We are too naive. We don't realize what is going on with the KKK and other groups."

The majority of the Jews were somewhat less gloomy in their outlook. Aaron Fox commented that America was not Poland and that in this country there was a variety of groups, so Jews were not singled out. But he felt that if anything happened to Israel, American Jews would be in trouble. Lucy Dafner remarked that Jews always have to be concerned about anti-Semitism. "I think the independence of Israel did a lot for American Jews. People believe more now in the Jew as a hero who can stand up for his rights. They have more respect for Jews. The image of the Jew is different here than it was in Poland. Besides that, you do not have the same religious anti-Semitism as you had there." Sally Melmed was very much concerned. "Coming out of Poland, you have to be. It's a disease that can grow, but we have terrific leaders who speak out and we have access to the White House and Congress." Dora Lipschitz, too, saw the importance of the attitude and policies of government officials, but she had a different point of view. "In Europe we were comfortable; we didn't have fear. And then everything changed suddenly. Everything depends upon the government. Here, it could be just the same thing. It could happen again." Helen Birnbaum agreed. "God, if it happened once—and in Germany—it could happen again. Mass hysteria is very catchy, especially in times of unemployment and when people don't have anything."[11]

Polish refugees in Pittsburgh, both Jewish and Christian, have established themselves within their own communities and within American society as a whole. They count themselves as loyal and patriotic citizens who appreciate the ideals and traditions of this country, perhaps more so than many native born. However, at the same time they are intent on maintaining their ethnic identity and feel a great affinity for either Poland or Israel. They take their citizenship responsibilities seriously and regularly and enthusiastically vote in elections.[12] They have gotten on with their lives, raising their children to be skilled and educated citizens of their adopted society, and making homes for themselves in America. They are comfortable in this country, and most are glad they came here.

Yet they stay to themselves and for the most part have not joined organizations outside their ethnic groups. And particularly with the Jewish refugees, there is still a sense of pain, insecurity, and vulnerability. The Jews are not as sure about their achievement in this country, despite all their outer trappings of success. They still have trouble talking about their experiences during the war. The hurt lingers in the absence of relatives, the loss of a people, of a way of life, a culture. It is manifest in their visceral reaction to the topic of anti-Semitism both in the past and in the present.

Christians and Jews have traveled along somewhat different paths but with the same values of hard work, love of freedom, sacrifice for their children, and commitment to their people and to America. Displaced no longer, they have found a home. But whether one stream of that postwar immigration, the survivors of the Holocaust, can ever be truly at home, in terms of having a sense of security in America and relaxed confidence in the future, is harder to determine and certainly beyond the craft of the historian.

8

Postscript

▶▶▶ IN JANUARY 1987 SIX CHRISTIANS
and six Jews formerly of Poland and now citizens of the
United States and living in Pittsburgh were brought together by
the author at the University of Pittsburgh for a dialogue. Few were
eager to attend; all were wary. It was clear that the perceptions
about the past and the ongoing isolation from one another continued to be real factors in their attitudes and occasioned expressions of reserve, particularly on the part of the Jews. They were
told the purpose of the meeting was to discuss their feelings about
one another after all these years of separation and what they felt
they had shared or had not shared in their long journey from
Poland to Pittsburgh. When they eventually convened however,
the atmosphere was friendly, honest, and intense.

The following introductory statement was made by the author:

Today is an opportunity for you to get to know something about one
another. Perhaps it can be seen as the climax to your experience, a
certain closing of a cycle because you are again side by side, but
this time in Pittsburgh rather than in Poland. You had the same
homeland, participated in a common culture, and today you are all
Americans, sharing despite your diversity a common background.
How have you changed in the long journey you have made? Have
you been molded in similar ways? How have your experiences and
the American scene shaped you in common and yet distinct ways?
In what ways have your lives paralleled one another and how have
they diverged? And beyond this comparative dimension in looking at

where you have come from and where you are today, each one of
you is a fascinating history book. You have witnessed some of the
most profound and disturbing events not only in the twentieth century, but in all of man's history. You have had to confront the fact
that science and technology were harnessed for destruction. You
have had to face deprivation and dehumanization knowing that mankind did and could again unleash such a scourge. How does one
deal with that?

Brief wartime biographies of each of the twelve participants were
read, without any names being given. They were then asked to
discuss how they felt about either their own experience or that of
others.

MORTON *(Jewish):*
How can you tell what happened over six years in such a short
period of time. With the Russians, you had a chance of surviving;
with the Germans, you had none. I was the only one out of 200 who
survived. I'll never forget. They're all dead for no reason at all!
They couldn't understand you could be a Jewish Polack. They
couldn't understand you could be both. Everyday at my school when
I was a kid they would beat me up and call me names. We thought
that was the way things are. We lived as a group, because we felt
safer that way. . . . I still feel hurt how. We could have been
helped, like the Danish Jews were, and there were a lot of Poles
who did try to help. But nobody ever did anything for me. The
neighbors could have done something, but whatever we had, they
just took away.

IRENE *(Jewish):*
The United States is a pluralistic country, but Poland never was.
They were intolerant of all minorities. Unless you were Catholic,
you were not a full-fledged citizen. My father served in the Polish
army, and so did my uncle. He would have been an officer if he
wasn't Jewish. We were all great Polish patriots, but as far as they
were concerned you could only be a Pole if you were a Catholic.
Otherwise, you were not a full-fledged citizen. . . . I was saved by

Polish workers after a death march. They saw us abandoned on the
road with our shaved heads. We could not walk any more, so they
hid us from the Nazis. They gave us shirts and pants. . . . What
hurts is that even here in this discussion you cannot refer to us as
Poles. We are only Jews. This hurts, even though I have lived in
this country many years.

DORA *(Jewish):*
When the Germans came in, I suddenly became a Jew and not a
Pole. Maybe the Poles couldn't help us, but did they have to point
us out to the Nazis? . . . The Ukrainians hated the Poles, the Poles
hated the Ukrainians, and both hated the Jews.

The Jewish hurt was palpable and forthright. The Christians
listened politely, and then responded.

STEFAN:
I was a commander in the Polish underground in charge of the area
south of Warsaw during the war. I was in charge at night, but the
Germans were in charge during the day. I was in control of the
forest, but the Germans were in control of the cities. We sent arms
and men, but we could not save the Jews in the Warsaw ghetto. I
could not even save my own father, who was beaten and murdered
at Maidanek, so how could I have saved the Jews? There were
people [Christians] crying on the streets when the Warsaw ghetto
was fighting. There was shooting, bombs, tanks. There was nothing
we could do. We had one department in our underground
organization whose task it was to provide whatever assistance we
could to the Jews. In May 1943 I personally ordered the execution
of fifteen Poles who had turned Jews into Nazi custody. In my
territory, anybody who cooperated with the Gestapo in any way was
shot. . . . That policy was set from the top.

LIDIA:
When I was growing up in Warsaw, I was aware of the
atmosphere—that Jews were shunned and treated as second-class
citizens—but I never gave it much thought. I never met many Jews;
they seemed to keep to themselves. During the war, I heard about

Auschwitz, and we knew they were in trouble, but quite a few people were helping them, including my father. He was a policeman and could do a lot of things. . . . The Warsaw ghetto uprising was as futile as the Warsaw uprising a year later . . . but I see that there are some hurts which are so deep, so total, and so overwhelming, that no matter what we say, that hurt will still be there.

Other Christians denied that they had ever harbored any anti-Jewish feelings. They were sincere, earnest, and sympathetic to the Jews who were in such pain, recognizing their great suffering. The conversation moved on. John had completed four years of the gymnasium and was going to be an electrical engineer when the war began. He joined an underground student unit and was arrested in 1942 and taken to Plaszow, near Crakow. He was there six months until the Americans bombed close by the camp and he was able to escape and eventually join up with General Wladyslaw Anders in Italy. "You try to forget it, but you cannot. Everyone of us lost so many years as a young person, which will never come back. It's a loss—the best years of your life. Once you were young; then you got old, and something in between disappeared. That's what I think about." The others nodded.

The participants were asked, "What have you each learned from your hardship? Do you share any common values which the wartime experience has given you? How have you incorporated your wartime experience into your outlook?"

Stefen (Christian) believed that he had been taught much from the war and that both Christians and Jews had probably learned the same values. Both people did not want to lose their identity.

I am a Polish-American. You probably call yourself Jewish American. Individuals assimilate, but an ethnic identity can still be preserved, and the culture is richer because of the diversity. . . . We want to preserve certain values, like the value of human life. We all went through the war. My deep thought is, everyone wants to live. You don't feel it until you see the human heart murdered. That's one value. Another is some moral principal. You can take it from the Christian or Jewish religion. But if you look at American society, they look at material things first. The rest is just forgotten. One other thing, and that is the ability to be friendly to another human being.

Mark (Jewish) and others agreed. Mark had been through Plaszow and finally Flossenburg, where he worked in an airplane factory. He had been liberated by the Americans while on a death march near the end of the war. He lost his entire family, with the exception of his brother, who had gone to Palestine to study after being beaten up in riots against Jews at the University of Crakow. He said, "You've got to depend on the person next to you, or you don't survive. You have to share and lean on that person, and they on you. In our house there is nothing fancy. We want to be comfortable, but we appreciate the value of other people. We are different beause we have learned the value of life."

Lidia (Christian), who had been deported to Germany after fighting in the unsuccessful Warsaw uprising, talked about how she had left Poland with a knapsack after the war. "If I had to, I could do it again. Possessions and positions just do not matter that much. They had all seen people who had a lot one day and nothing the next. You have to think about what is really important in life." John (Christian) felt that all of them were better people for what they had gone through. "We understand things better, we value things more than other people who were born here. I was buried twice during my life. My mother had masses for me two times. But I'm still alive today. Thank God, I'm still alive today."

Frances B. (Christian) had struggled all her life, but now her daughter was a vice president at Westinghouse and her son was an engineer. "When I came here, I lived in a place that had no toilet; we took water from the spring. We had nothing, but I was happy. We never were hungry. We never were cold. I knew I could lie down in my own bed and nobody would come and arrest me. The air was free; I could breathe. I am free, not like in Siberia. I never forgot that."

The others, too, appreciated this country. Mark: "When I came to America, one of the goals I set for myself was to teach people what horrors can happen when people disregard the value of life and to have people learn to live with one another and appreciate the freedom that we have. I have spoken a lot about it, and because of this, I feel there is some value in my survival."

"Was there any value in Polish Christians and Polish Jews who are now Americans all coming together to talk as we did today?"

Mark: "In the beginning I felt I was looked at as a Jew. Now I feel I have been accepted as a Polish Jew, that I was a Polack." Irene said she was glad she had come. She said, "I can never forgive the Christian world for wiping out my culture. I love my Christian friends; I love my Polish friends. My best friend is a German. But this thing will go down with me forever, and I cannot forgive the others for not trying to do something to save the Jews. The guilt should stay with the Christian world. You should have it and not just us for surviving. Those who stood by and said nothing are just as guilty."

Stefan, miles apart in background and experience from Mark, said, "I have found a friend—you and I. I'm not asking whether you are Christian or Jewish. When we talk openly, we learn about one another. I didn't know what you went through; you didn't know what I went through. What we did today could be applied on a larger scale—Poles and Jews in the United States, Jewish representatives at the Vatican. It is in our interest, America's interest to do this. The more division, the more prejudices, the more infighting. We need to cooperate."

"We broke the ice," said Frances G. (Jewish), amid the tears. "In a dialogue, we feel closer and we can really relate to one another." She then proceded to recite a Polish poem about the war, which all found very moving.

FOR THE POLISH JEWS (Zydom Polskim)
by Stanislaw Broniewski

No longer are heard their desperate screams
From Polish cities and towns
For they fell as fighting troops,
Defenders of the Warsaw ghetto.

With these words, tainted with blood
And a heart laden with intolerable sorrow
For you—Oh Jews of Poland
This wandering Polish poet writes.

Not people, but bloodthirsty dogs,
And not soldiers, but heathens
They came to terrify you with death.
They came to choke your children and wives in the gas chambers,
And poison with lime, those of you locked in freight cars,
And finally, to scoff at those dying, helpless and in terror.

But you picked up stones
To use against the gunner
Directed at the destruction of your home.

Oh sons of the Maccabees—
You allow yourselves to die,
To undertake a battle, without a trace of hope
A battle begun in September.
Together our homes were destroyed,
As the blood of our brothers was poured.
We are united by the wall of death.
We are united by Dachau and Auschwitz,

By each nameless grave
And every prison bar.

Heaven shines above us all
Looking down upon Warsaw's devastation
To see if we end in victory.

Each person is given freedom,
A piece of bread and rights
And there exists but one. . .
The highest race
People of supremacy!!!

Alina (Christian) perhaps was the most stirring. Her father
had been a wealthy landowner, a chemist, and then a member of
the Polish parliament. When the war broke out, they lost all
their property and moved to Warsaw. She remembered what she
described as her helplessness during the Warsaw ghetto uprising
and then the Warsaw uprising, during which her father was
killed on the street.

We all went through horrible suffering, perhaps some more than
others. I think though that the human spirit is so strong that we can
go forward and overcome our suffering. I can sense that the atmosphere here has melted. I feel that we are becoming friends. If we
spend another day or two together, I think we would really hug each
other, and I would be the first to do it. When we came, the atmosphere was so full of hurt, and maybe it was the leadership that
allowed us to talk about those hurts. I am an optimist, and I think
that this speaking up of the hurts will be a springboard for helping
us all, for using our suffering to help others. That's what I have
tried to do.

When she finished there were tears, applause, and heartfelt
handshakes.

These Polish Christians and these Polish Jews have made long
and difficult odysseys. They started together in the land of

Poland, a land that had witnessed the ravages of three partitions, and that had finally tasted independence and freedom after World War I only to lose them in the aftermath of World War II. Both Jews and Christians suffered through the devastation of a war that unleashed both the Nazi fury and the Soviet terror on a luckless people. Those who survived the ordeal came away from their experience very different from what they had been. All earnestly desired to get far away from the desolation of their homeland, whether motivated by the awful memories it held or the current condition of the nation. They all esteemed the prize of freedom and feared and hated the spoiler. When they came to the United States, their patriotism and appreciation far outstripped the enthusiasm of native-born Americans, who had never experienced the despair of totalitarianism. The belief that the United States had to stay strong and ever vigilant against the menace of communism or anti-Semitism was shared by virtually all who came here after the war, no matter what their backgrounds.

Both the Polish Christians and the Polish Jews suffered and lost because of their powerlessness. The Jews were unable to secure a refuge in a world gone mad, with no state of their own to which to escape. All Poles were forced again to look on while their country became a pawn in an international chess game. This time the players were the United States and the Soviet Union, and the game was the cold war. Both peoples have longed to have their own homeland. The Jews finally achieved a free and independent homeland. Many Polish Christians are still waiting for theirs. Both groups could taste and feel the necessity and hope of freedom. In the aftermath of the most catastrophic war in history, these two groups became pilgrims to the United States. They came to pick up the pieces of their lives and start again and, to a remarkable extent, succeeded. From nothing they built something. Today, their children are poised to continue to take advantage of the opportunities they find in America.

Can a fruitful dialogue between Christians and Jews of Polish descent now be continued? The signs are hopeful. The world has changed radically since that time when hostility between these two groups festered. They are now joined as citizens of a new country, with the same rights, opportunities, and goals. Between the United States and present-day Poland a strong bond and sympathetic understanding has been forged. There is a growing relationship between Israel and Poland. Vatican II has done much to discredit the religious myths that formerly created intolerance.

Because of their past, there persists into the present an open wound. It affects those well-meaning persons who seek to promote intergroup understanding and coalitions among Polish-Americans and Jewish Americans. There is no completely satisfactory way to respond to the allegations and sensitivity on the part of Christians and Jews to the issue of Christian-Jewish relations in Poland during World War II. Historical perceptions and realities cannot be forgotten or overlooked. However, there are common threads, common concerns, common values, and common fears, which can be shared and discussed. In their struggle for understanding and even reconciliation, these two groups realize perhaps more than any others the dangers to all mankind of unbridled bigotry and of a callous disregard of human life. The dialogue can and must be continued for its own sake. Beyond that, it serves as an example and underscores the importance of intergroup exchange in the ethnically, religiously, and racially complex society that is America today. The dream of all immigrants for a new land of freedom and opportunity must not be undermined by indifference, prejudice, and rancor. All postwar Polish refugees can understand that imperative.

Notes

Bibliography

Index

Notes

INTRODUCTION

1. R. L. Duffus, "Is Pittsburgh Civilized?" *Harpers Monthly Magazine*, October 1930, pp. 537–40. Reprinted in Lubove, *Pittsburgh*, p. 160.

2. The table below shows the percentages of displaced persons in each occupation as recorded by the U.S. Government (Displaced Persons Commission, *DP Story*, p. 368).

Major occupational group	%
Farmer and farm laborer	24.7
Operative and kindred worker	16.7
Private-household worker	14.2
Laborer, except farm and mine	14.7
Craftsman, foreman, and kindred worker	11.6
Service worker, except private-household	7.8
Clerical and kindred worker	4.3
Professional, technical, and kindred worker	3.2
Manager, official, and proprietor	0.6
Sales worker	0.6
No occupation (including student)	1.6

These figures have little value in ascertaining the average background of the Poles, particularly the Polish Christians who came to the United States. Many were not officially considered "displaced persons," but came to this country from England and were in some way associated with the Polish Resettlement Corps and benefited from that connection

(see chap. 3). Approximately one-third of the estimated 100,000
Polish Christians who came to the United States were displaced persons from Germany. About one-third of the Pittsburgh sample had also
come from Germany; most but not all had lived in displaced persons
camps. The point is that the Pittsburgh group appears to be representative of the Poles who emigrated to the United States in the decade
following World War II. The only other study of Polish displaced
persons in recent years is Mostwin, *Transplanted Family*, pp. 130,
141, 144, 151–53. She used for her representative population the
results of a mass mailing of 8,700 questionnaires to members of Polish
organizations, community leaders, and individuals who found out
about her survey through Polish-American newspapers. Of that total,
1,290 were returned to her, representing a return of 14.8%. This
research is not comparable to mine, however, for it includes arrivals
from Poland who came up to 1962. Moreover, because of the research
methodology, it would appear that many more professionals and
middle-level people responded than blue-collar workers. Certainly the
36 percent in Mostwin's study who currently consider themselves
professionals or high-level white-collar managers contrasts sharply
with the 19 percent or so in my sample who I placed in those
categories. (See table 2, p. 156.)

3. Feingold *(Politics of Rescue)* and Friedman *(No Haven for the
Oppressed)* have written on America's response to the Holocaust.
However, the best work has been done by Wyman *(Paper Walls;
Abandonment of the Jews).*

CHAPTER 1. PROLOGUE TO BLITZKRIEG

1. K. Bartel, *Mowy Parlamentarne* (Parliamentary Speeches).
Warsaw, 1928. Quoted in Bronsztejn, "Jewish Population of Poland in
1931," p. 5.

2. Watt, *Bitter Glory*, p. 365.

3. Marcus, *Social and Political History of the Jews in Poland*,
p. 16.

CHAPTER 2. BETWEEN SWASTIKA AND SICKLE

1. Central Commission, *German Crimes in Poland*, p. 13.

2. This story is reminiscent of the final chapter in the life of

Janusz Korczak. Korczak, who real name was Henryk Goldszmidt, was a Polish Jewish educator and social worker, and an internationally famous writer. In 1942 he refused offers of rescue in order to remain with the 200 children of his Jewish orphanage in the Warsaw ghetto, knowing full well what the consequences might be. When the Nazis ordered the deportation of the children despite Korczak's protests, he told the children they were going for a picnic in the country; he died with them in Treblinka.

3. Schindler was honored by Israel by the planting of a carob tree for "righteous gentiles" at the Yad Vashem memorial in Jerusalem.

4. Earlier in the chapter, it is mentioned that Borke's father was able to save Harry Feldman, who later came to Pittsburgh.

5. There were Jews in Anders's army, including Menachem Begin. Anders wrote that approximately 4,000 Jews were evacuated with his forces, but it is unclear how many of these were army personnel and how many were civilians. Anders, *An Army in Exile*, p. 112.

6. Davies, *God's Playground*, p. 451.

CHAPTER 3. POINT OF NO RETURN

1. Proudfoot, *European Refugees*, p. 34.

2. Only four Jews in the Pittsburgh group had served in the Polish army. Irwin Lewenstein managed to escape when the Polish army collapsed; he wound up in Russia. Abe Cymerman was called up from reserve in 1939, fought until the Polish surrender, and then went back to his home. Michell Borke worked at a first aid station until the surrender. Albert Levenreich was drafted in 1937 and was still in the army when the war broke out. His orders were to get to Hungary, but once there, the men from the Polish army were kept under guard. A special camp was created in Hungary for the Jews in the Polish army. "The Jews, unlike the others, were not free; we had to work longer hours. If we complained, the Hungarian general said, we'll send you over to the Germans!" After some close calls, Albert was finally liberated by the Americans near Mauthausen in Austria. A number of Jews including Albert insisted that there was discrimination in the army and that either Jews were not accepted or could not become officers. Haskell Nordon in his autobiography *Education of a Polish Jew*, insisted that Jews were deliberately excluded from the army.

3. Bauer, *Jewish Emergence from Powerlessness*, p. 65.

4. Proudfoot, *European Refugees*, p. 341.

5. See Dinnerstein, "U.S. Army and the Jews"; and *American and the Survivors of the Holocaust*, chap. 1.

6. This topic has been given much current publicity as a result of the deportation of John Demjanjuk. See a recent book on the subject by Allan Ryan, former director of the U.S. Justice Department's Office of Special Investigations *(Quiet Neighbors)*.

7. "Harrison Report," in Dinnerstein, *America and the Survivors of the Holocaust*, pp. 300–01.

8. "PAC Selected Documents," p. 67, papers of the Polish-American Congress, Pilsudski Institute.

9. Mostwin, *Transplanted Family*, p. 65.

10. Patterson, "Poles," p. 216.

11. *Displaced Persons Commission, DP Story*, p. 246.

12. Sachar, *Redemption of the Unwanted*, p. 166.

13. See discussion in Korewa, "Casework Treatment of Refugees," p. 33.

CHAPTER 4. "I LIFT MY LAMP"

1. Vernant, *Refugee in the Post-War World*, p. 500. Over half the refugees coming in under Displaced Persons Act were between fourteen and forty-five years of age; 22% were under fourteen.

2. American Jewish Committee, "Immigration and Refugee Aid," p. 219.

3. Davie, "Immigration and Refugee Aid," p. 226.

4. White, *300,000 New Americans*, p. 397.

5. Dinnerstein, "Voluntary Agencies," pp. 5–7.

6. NCWC News Service, 24 Feb. 1947, file 15, "Displaced Persons," National Catholic Welfare Conference, CIS. Carroll had been in Rome for fourteen years and was one of three brothers, all of whom were priests from the Pittsburgh diocese.

7. Davie, "Refugee Aid," p. 213.

8. Dinnerstein, *America and the Survivors of the Holocaust*, p. 204.

9. Mohler to Swanstrom, 18 Sep. 1946, file 15, "Displaced Persons," NCWC.

10. Buckley to Mohler, 30 Aug. 1946, ibid.

11. Reinl to Mulholland, 20 Aug. 1946, ibid.

12. Disco to Mohler, 2 Dec. 1946, enclosing "Immigration Report by Dr. Max Brezezinski," 1 May through 1 Aug., 1946, ibid.

13. Mohler to Mulholland, 21 Sep. 1947, box 9, CCR, NCWC.

14. Dinnerstein, *America and the Survivors of the Holocaust*, p. 201.

15. "Catholic Immigration Program for Displaced Persons," 8 Oct. 1946, p. 3, War Relief Services, 023, box 99, CIS.

16. Mohler to McCarthy, 31 Mar. 1947, file 42, NCWC.

17. Ibid.

18. McCarthy to Mohler, 2 April 1947, ibid.

19. Ibid.

20. Travers to Mohler, 23 April 1946, file 15, "Displaced Persons," NCWC.

21. Mohler to Komora, 12 Aug. 1946, ibid.

22. See Dinnerstein, *America and the Survivors of the Holocaust*, chaps 6–9; and Dinnerstein, "Anti-Semitism in the Eightieth Congress," pp. 11–26.

23. Mohler to Swanstrom, 27 Jan. 1948, enclosing "Information on Legislation to Admit Displaced Persons to the United States," p. 1, file 87, NCWC.

24. Ibid., p. 2.

25. Ibid., p. 3.

26. "Article Sent to *Jewish Criterion* for Publication," 24 Jan. 1947, 63:II:4:3, American Service Institute, AIS.

27. Ibid.

28. Ibid.

29. "Displaced Persons Committee," 63:II:4:3, American Service Institute, AIS.

30. Allegheny County Citizens Committee on Displaced Persons, "Executive Secretary's Report," 13 Mar. 1947, 63:II:4:3, American Service Institute, AIS.

31. Visitors Bureau for New Arrivals, "Background Paper," 13 Apr. 1951, 63: III:3B:1, American Service Institute, AIS.

32. American Jewish Committee, "Immigrant Legislation, DP, 1948, "Memorandum to the State Department in Opposition to Admission of Former Nazis under Our Immigration Laws." The AJC advocated tests to ensure that Nazis or their sympathizers could not apply

under the Displaced Persons Act; the following would have been excluded.

1. Persons who out of political motives committed crimes against victims or opponents of the Nazis.
2. Persons who gave property or other support to Nazis.
3. Persons who were avowed believers of the Nazis.
4. Persons who contributed to establishing Nazi tyranny.
5. Persons who taught Nazi doctrine to youth.
6. Persons in the service of Nazis who agitated against churches, etc.
7. Persons who unjustly enriched themselves in administering formerly occupied territories.
8. Persons who formulated or disseminated militaristic ideas.
9. Persons who trained youth.
10. Persons who were agents or provocateurs.
11. Persons who by word or deed took an attitude of hatred to opponents of the Nazis at home or abroad, prisoners of war, to populations of formerly occupied territory, to foreign civilian workers, or to internees or similar persons.

33. "Catholic Plans for the Resettlement of Displaced Persons in the United States," 1947, pp. 4–5, file 15, "Displaced Persons," NCWC.

34. "Memo on Suggested Catholic Program for Resettlement of Displaced Persons," 1947, ibid.

35. Interview with Zachariasiewicz.

36. Mohler to Mulholland, 6 May 1947, file 5#40, NCWC.

37. Mohler to Mulholland, 8 May 1947, ibid.

38. Mulholland to Mohler, 7 May 1947, ibid. Mulholland wrote that "we have to be alert to see that the tail [the Polish Immigration Committee] does not wag the dog [the CCR]."

39. Ibid.

40. Mohler to Mulholland, 24 June 1947, ibid.

41. Interview with Zachariasiewicz.

42. Krysiewicz, *Polish Immigration Committee*, 28–30.

43. Ibid., p. 27.

44. Mulholland to Mohler, 5 Dec. 1951, file 70, "Pier Work," NCWC.

45. Bernard, "Programs and Concepts in the Resettlement of Immigrants and Refugees," p. 11.

46. Krysiewicz, *Polish Immigration Committee*, p. 18.

47. Lopata, "The Function of Voluntary Associations in an Ethnic Community," p. 112.

48. Ibid., p. 356.

49. Ibid., p. 113. It is unclear how many of those assurances were used. In any event, more research needs to be undertaken on the role of the various Polish organizations, including the American Committee for the Resettlement of Polish Displaced Persons. See Jaroszynska, "American Committee."

50. Krysiewicz, *Polish Immigration Committee*, pp. 32–33.

51. Lopata, "The Function of Voluntary Associations in an Ethnic Community," p. 113.

52. It must be pointed out, however, that Gunther was active on a higher level. He was appointed by Governor James H. Duff in August 1948 to become state chairman of the Pennsylvania State Displaced Persons Commission. He also was elected chairman of a national effort by the Polish American Congress to find employment, housing, and transportation for Polish refugees entering the country under the Displaced Persons Act.

53. Father Lappan to John F. Dearden, Bishop of Pittsburgh, 3 Jan. 1952, file on Displaced Persons, Synod Hall.

54. "Resettlement Report on Blanket Assurances," 1951, File on Displaced Persons, Synod Hall.

CHAPTER 5. A JEWISH COMMUNITY FACES THE REFUGEES

1. Proudfoot, *European Refugees*, p. 341. The percentages of Jewish displaced persons in the assembly center on 26 Sep. 1947 were, by nationality: Polish, 81; Hungarian, 6; Czech, 4; Lithuanian, 3; Russian, 2; German, 1; other, 3. Boris M. Joffe to Lazard Teper, 26 Sep. 1947, quoted in Dinnerstein, *America and the Survivors of the Holocaust*, p. 279.

2. Minutes of the Budget Committee, 1 Oct. 1946, United Jewish Fund, UJF files.

3. *Jewish Criterion*, Pittsburgh, 26 Apr. 1946, p. 11.

4. Report by President Max Rogal, Annual Meeting of the

YM&WHA, 15 May 1949, Young Men's and Women's Hebrew Association files, JCC.

5. Interview with Noven. Mr. Noven was a very active member of the Y board. He talked about the programming at the Y and how busy the building on Bellefield Avenue used to be. In his opinion, the JSSB did not play as important a role in the community as the Y.

6. Report of the Executive Director, 13 Dec. 1949, Young Men and Women's Hebrew Association files, JCC.

7. Ibid.

8. The Friendship Club disbanded in 1979 and was replaced by Club Shalom, the friendship club of the new wave of immigrants to Pittsburgh and America—the recently arrived Soviet Jews. That club now is associated with the Jewish Community Center.

9. *Monthly Bulletin* of the National Council of Jewish Women, Apr. 1949, p. 34.

10. National Council of Jewish Women, *1946–1947 Yearbook*, p. 11.

11. Federation of Jewish Philanthropies, minutes of the Board of Directors, 19 Mar. 1946, UJF. Milton Susman, who was a returning veteran at the time, commented in an interview on the impossibility of finding a home after the war and how lucky he was to finally get one.

12. *Monthly Bulletin* of the *National Council of Jewish Women*, Oct. 1947, p. 7.

13. "Annual Report of the President," *Monthly Bulletin of the National Council of Jewish Women*, June 1948, p. 4.

14. Two typed sheets on "Summary of Ending of NCJW Project for New Americans on February 7, 1952, Service to Foreign Born 1951–1952," National Council of Jewish Women files, AIS.

15. Letter from Pittsburgh Section to National, 6 Apr. 1950, Committee on Service to the Foreign Born, National Council of Jewish Women files, AIS.

16. *Monthly Bulletin* of the National Council of Jewish Women, Apr. 1952, p. 11.

17. Presentation given at Panel of New Americans by Pauline Oseroff, 20 Apr. 1952, Committee on Service to the Foreign Born National Council of Jewish Women files, AIS.

18. The pages of the Pittsburgh Jewish newspaper, the *Jewish Criterion*, were filled with notices and stories of one appeal after another, as a host of organizations tried to raise funds for their projects

on the home front or overseas. An estimate of the conflicting claims for attention, and therefore monies, can also be gauged by the organizational structure in the Jewish community. According to a research report prepared immediately after the war, there were in Pittsburgh at least thirty-five synagogues, ten *landsmanshaften* groups, twenty-one relief and free-loan organizations, two veteran organizations with their auxiliaries, four labor unions, and twenty-six fraternal and auxiliary organizations. See "The Jewish Community in Pittsburgh," p. 3, JFCS. These organizations were in addition to the thirty-five beneficiary agencies of the United Jewish Fund, many of which had their own fund-raising drives. A study done a few years before 1947 indicated that $2.25 million had been raised for communal, religious or other purposes by the Jewish community. See United Jewish Fund minutes of the Board Directors 6 Feb. 1947, UJF.

19. United Jewish Fund minutes of the Board of Directors, 30 June 1947, UJF.

20. Board of Directors files, 25 Nov. 1947, JFCS.

21. Ibid.

22. United Jewish Fund, minutes of the Board of Directors, 11 Sep. 1947, UJF.

23. Ibid. 30 June 1947.

24. *Jewish Criterion*, Pittsburgh, 28 Feb. 1947, p. 5.

25. Ibid., 19 May 1947, p. 7.

26. Ibid., 3 Jan. 1947, p. 7.

27. Ibid., 25 Apr. 1947, p. 10.

28. Ibid.

29. United Jewish Fund 1947, 1948, and 1949 budgets, 25 Oct. 1949, UJF. This figure fell about $100,000 short of the goal, but was more than $700,000 over the intake from the preceding year.

30. *Jewish Criterion*, Pittsburgh, 19 Mar. 1948, p. 4.

31. Budget Committee files, 10 Feb. 1948, United Jewish Fund, UJF.

32. *Jewish Criterion*, Pittsburgh, 20 Feb. 1948, p. 5.

33. A special committee was set up by the Fund "to study duplicating and independent drives in Pittsburgh." This committee discovered one year later that there were nearly fifty separate Jewish fund-raising efforts in the city and that many of the drives were duplications of effort for the same causes and were in direct conflict with the work of the UJA. See minutes of the Committee to Study Duplicating and Indepen-

dent Drives in Pittsburgh, 10 Jan. 1949, United Jewish Fund, UJF. One leader in his frustration was prompted to remark that "the business of fund raising has become so widespread and so continuous, that any organization that submits itself to discipline is to be congratulated." UJF. 24 Jan. 1947, UJF.

34. Report prepared by Gertrude Glick to the Board of the Jewish Social Service Bureau, Annual Meeting, 1948, JFCS.

35. "Federation of Jewish Philanthropies Service Report of Constituent Agencies August 1950 compared with April 1940, December 1949, and August 1949," 12 Oct. 1950, UJF.

36. Budget Committee files 27 Oct. 1949, United Jewish Fund, UJF.

37. Council of Jewish Federations and Welfare Funds, *Jewish Social Service Yearbook, 1950*, table FC-E, "Jewish Family Service, Service and Financial Assistance to Immigrants."

38. Telegram from Edwin Rosenberg, president of the USNA to Maurice Taylor, minutes of the Board of Directors, 29 Dec. 1949, United Jewish Fund, UJF.

39. Board of Directors files, 18 Jan. 1950, JFCS.

40. Board of Directors files, 5 July, 1950, United Jewish Fund, UJF.

41. Federation of Jewish Philanthropies, Board of Directors files, 6 Mar. 1951, UJF.

42. Board of Directors files, 9 Nov. 1950, JFCS.

43. Annual Report to the JFCS Board of Directors director, Feb. 1952, JFCS.

44. Dorothy Blumenthal, a long-time Pittsburgher who herself was a sympathizer of the American Council for Judaism before 1948, felt that the organization was not strong in Pittsburgh. Milton Susman, editor of the *Jewish Criterion*, also felt that the group "never coalesced into anything powerful." He called them "Jewless Jews."

CHAPTER 6. INTO THE PITTSBURGH CRUCIBLE

1. Under the Displaced Persons Act of 1948, New York State gained 31.7% of the newcomers, Illinois, 10.9%, and Pennsylvania 7.5%. Displaced Persons Commission, *DP Story*, p. 367.

2. Pennsylvania Commission on Displaced Persons, "Third Annual Report," 1951, p. 16.

3. Vernant, *Refugee in the Post-War World,* p. 497.

4. Ibid., p. 499. Leonard Dinnerstein in his notes indicates that Jews constituted 16% of those who came in under the act. This percentage, or the Vernant figure of 19%, is still far less than the two-thirds admitted to the country under the Truman directive. Dinnerstein, *America and the Survivors of the Holocaust,* p. 287.

5. The Veterans of the Polish Armed Forces in Exile cite 100,000 Polish (Christian) emigrants to the United States, so there is a discrepancy of about 20,000 people.

6. See White, *300,000 New Americans,* p. 397; and Dinnerstein, *America and the Survivors of the Holocaust,* p. 288.

Year	Total Immigration	Jewish Immigration	Jewish DPs
1948	170,420	16,000	
1949	248,987	37,469	31,381
1950	203,407	14,139	10,245
1951	238,287	16,973	13,580

7. Only 10,487 of the 18,000 stipulated for admission actually entered the United States. Dinnerstein, *America and the Survivors of the Holocaust,* p. 286.

8. Glassman, *Adjustment in Freedom,* p. 30.

9. "Federation" at that time meant the JSSB. It was tied to both the United Jewish Fund and the Federation of Jewish Philanthropies, which in 1955 merged to become the United Jewish Federation.

10. For example, Herble and Hall, *Displaced Persons in Louisiana and Mississippi,* p. 45.

11. Adolf, "Adaptation of Eastern European Refugees," p. 237.

12. Bodnar, Simon, and Weber, *Lives of Their Own,* p. 24.

13. Central Council of Polish Organizations, 63:1:1:3, American Service Institute, AIS.

14. Sypek, "Displaced Polish Persons in the Greater Boston Community," p. 8.

15. In visits by the author to veterans' meetings and in interviews by the author with Polish respondents, the hostility between the two groups was openly expressed.

CHAPTER 7. DISPLACED NO MORE

1. The one exception was a widow who had immigrated to Canada from England after the war and had become a Canadian citizen. Once in the United States she planned to return to Canada, but her husband died and she remained in the United States.

2. Collectively, Christians had made 114 trips to Poland. Sixteen persons had never gone back. Four Jews had made a total of 20 trips to Poland.

3. Jacek Adolf, in a study on Eastern European refugees to Canada in the 1960s and 1970s, found that, while having less success financially than nonpolitical refugees, the political group he was studying evidenced a higher identification with Canada and satisfaction with their lives there. They saw their exile identity as complementary to rather than exclusive of their Canadian identity. He felt that they saw themselves as having a mission to open up the eyes of the West to the danger of the Soviets. Adolf, "Adaptation of Eastern European Refugees," p. 252.

4. At a recent meeting of a clergy dialogue group held in Pittsburgh and sponsored jointly by the American Jewish Committee, Pittsburgh Chapter, and the First Trinity Church, this point was affirmed and agreed upon, interesting enough, by both the Jewish and Christian clergy present.

5. Data from 1972 U.S. Bureau of the Census, *Current Population Report*, cited in Sowell, *American Ethnic Groups*, p. 378:

*Percentage Distribution of Polish-American Males
Employed in 1972*

Professional, technical, and kindred worker	18.1
Manager and administrator, except farm	12.9
Sales worker	6.3
Clerical and kindred worker	7.9
Craftsman and kindred worker	23.3
Operative, including transport	18.3
Laborer, except farm	4.3
Farmer and farm manager	0.9
Farm laborer and foreman	0.4
Service worker, except private-household	7.7

45% of Polish-American males fell within the first four categories, while 26% of the Polish Christian refugees in Pittsburgh did.

6. The question was asked, Have you stayed with the same employer the majority of your working years? Thirty-two Christian males said yes, two said no.

7. Tobin and Chenkin, "Recent Jewish Community," p. 165.

8. Only nine of the Christians lived in the heavily Polish area of Lawrenceville. No one lived on Polish Hill, which got its name because of the number of older Polish-Americans there. As scattered as their residential patterns were, so too was their membership in churches. While those who lived around Lawrenceville joined one of the local Polish churches, the others in the group joined a wide variety of churches.

9. Neil Sandberg writes, "by and large American ethnicity today is working class ethnicity" (*Ethnic Identity and Assimilation*, p. x). Herman Gans and Milton Gordon (ibid., p. 4) both emphasize the importance of social class and its relation to ethnicity. Mostwin (*Transplanted Family*, p. 248) found in her study of Polish-Americans that the higher the income, the lower the family ethnic commitment: "the higher the social status, the greater is the satisfaction from employment and the lesser the need for self-expression through ethnic channels."

10. Cohen, *1984 National Survey of American Jews*, p. 21.

11. In a recent survey on the political attitudes of American Jews, questions were asked about anti-Semitism. When asked whether anti-Semitism in America could become a serious problem for American Jews, 77 percent of the respondents answered in the affirmative, 10 percent disagreed, and 13 percent were not sure. Forty percent felt that anti-Semitism in America was currently not a serious problem for American Jews, while 47 percent disagreed. Ibid., pp. 26–28.

12. In response to a question on voting, only six Christians indicated they did not vote regularly. The great majority, fifty-one persons, indicated they voted in every election. Only one Jew indicated he did not vote regularly. All others responded that they always voted.

Bibliography

INTERVIEWS

Polish Refugees

Aussenberg, Julius, 25 Apr. 1983
A., Robert, 12 Jan. 1983
Birnbaum, Helen, 20 June 1983
Borke, Michell, 22 June 1983
B., Fabian, 23 Feb. 1983
B., Frances, 1 Feb. 1983
B., Helena, 17 Jan. 1983
Cieply, Morton, 9 May 1983
Cymerman, Abe, 14 June 1983
C., Raymond, 16 Nov. 1983
Dafner, Lucy, 25 Apr. 1983
Drucker, Harry, 27 July 1983
D., Francinski, 13 Nov. 1982
D., John, 1 Mar 1983
Enzel, Abraham, 5 July 1983
Federman, Hyman, 29 June 1983
Feldman, Harry, 13 July 1983
Forstenzer, Estelle, 25 June 1983
Forstenzer, Nathan, 22 Apr. 1983

Fox, Aaron, 5 July 1983
Friede, Wolf, 10 May 1983
Friedman, Harry, 15 Apr. 1983
Friedman, William, 10 May 1983
Frost, Samuel, 27 Apr. 1983
Gelman, Bernard, 30 June 1983
Glatstein, Mordechai, 21 Nov. 1983
Goldman, Aron, 15 June 1983
Goldman, Melvin, 20 May 1983
Greenberg, Frances, 7 June 1983
Greenberg, Isaac, 9 June 1983
Grundman, Benjamin, 9 Oct. 1983
Guss, David, 29 June 1983
G., Joanna, 28 Aug. 1983
G., John, 4 Feb. 1983
G., Joseph, 4 Mar. 1983
G., Mieczyslaw, 6 Oct. 1983
G., Stefan, 18 Jan. 1983
Hausler, Dora, 22 May 1983
Hoffman, Gabriel, 14 June 1983

H., Maria, 27 Feb. 1983
H., Viktor, 30 Nov. 1983
Infeld, Norman, 2 June 1983
Iwler, Dora, 20 Apr. 1983
Joskowitz, Sarah, 28 June 1983
J., Alina, 3 Mar. 1983
J., Gertrude, 25 Oct. 1982
J., Stefan, 25 Feb. 1983
Kohane, Abe, 1 June 1983
K., Henry, 13 Jan. 1983
K., Irena, 20 Feb. 1983
K., Janusz, 13 Feb. 1983
K., Jessie, 22 Feb. 1983
K., Maria, 26 Feb. 1983
K., Marion, 6 Dec. 1982
K., Rita, 17 Jan. 1983
K., Stanley, 17 Jan 1983
Levenreich, Albert, 28 June 1983
Lewenstein, Irwin (Izak), 22 Nov. 1983
Lieberman, Fanny, 1 July 1983
Lipschitz, Dora, 28 July 1983
L., Adam, 13 Nov. 1983
L., Edmund, 2 Mar. 1983
L., Esther, 14 Feb. 1983
Manela, Morris, 30 June 1983
Mangurten, Henry, 22 June 1983
Melmed, Sally, 26 Apr. 1983
Mikowski, Izak, 24 May 1983
Morgenstern, Fela, 30 June 1983
M., Jan, 28 Oct. 1982
M., Krystyna, 21 Feb. 1983
M., Lidia, 16 Jan. 1983
M., Rudolf, 14 Jan. 1983
N., Bernice, 7 Dec. 1982

Ni., John, 26 Oct. 1982
No., John, 21 Jan. 1983
O., John, 2 Dec. 1982
O., Zygmunt, 12 Nov. 1982
Perlmutter, Rose, 22 June 1983
P., Henrietta, 4 Feb. 1983
P., Jan, 20 Nov. 1982
P., Joseph, 25 Jan. 1983
P., Marcel, 11 Nov. 1982
P., Stanyslaw, 25 Feb. 1983
Relis, Gusta, 1 July 1983
Rosen, Harry, 11 July 1983
R., Alphonse, 10 Nov. 1982
R., Antoni, 1 Nov. 1982
R., Stefan, 3 Nov. 1982
Salem, Abe, 14 June 1982
Scheingross, Marcia, 17 June 1983
Shear, Sam, 5 June 1983
Sittsamer, Jack, 2 July 1983
Spiegel, Frances, 11 July 1983
Stern, Mark, 20 June 1983
Szulman, Irene, 29 Apr. 1983
S., Adam, 2 Oct. 1983
S., Gabriel, 15 Feb. 1983
S., Jessie, 21 Feb. 1983
S., John, 21 Feb. 1983
S., Louise, 24 Feb. 1983
S., Maria, 27 Oct. 1982
S., Sophia, 5 Feb. 1983
S., Stanislawa, 23 Jan. 1983
Taube, Moshe, 17 June 1983
Turbiner, Bernard, 27 May 1983
Turbiner, Rose, 27 May 1983
T., Kasmier, 8 Jan. 1983
T., Ursula, 19 Jan. 1983
Weitz, Ruth, 29 June 1983

Winkler, Janina, 31 Aug. 1983

Wolhender, Jacob, 24 Apr. 1983

W., Edmund, 21 Feb. 1983

W., Janina, 21 Feb. 1983

W., Miroslaw, 31 Oct. 1982

W., Stanley, 1 Nov. 1982

W., Walter, 3 Dec. 1982

Zimmerman, Dora, 27 June 1983

Zimmett, Joseph, 3 July 1983

Zimmett, Thelma, 3 July 1983

Zweig, Arnold, 19 June 1983

Representatives of Community and National Organizations

Bader, Fred (Friendship Club), Pittsburgh, 11 Feb. 1980

Balter, Marjorie (National Council of Jewish Women), Pittsburgh, 15 Sept. 1980

Binstock, Dorothy (B'nai Brith), Pittsburgh, 6 Apr. 1980

Blumenthal, Dorothy (National Council of Jewish Women, Rodef Shalom), Pittsburgh, 16 June 1980

Borkowski, Joseph (historian in Polish community), Pittsburgh, 10 Oct. 1980.

Fineberg, Herman (United Jewish Fund), Pittsburgh, 25 June 1980

Fisher, Myrtle (National Council of Jewish Women), Pittsburgh, 1 Feb. 1980

Grafner, Alice (Rodef Shalom Temple), Pittsburgh, 2 July 1980

Heymann, Bessie (Rodef Shalom Temple), Pittsburgh, 16 May, 1980

Heymann, Sidney (Rodef Shalom Temple), Pittsburgh, 16 May 1980

Holstein, Lillian (B'nai Brith), Pittsburgh, 8 Mar. 1980

Jendzura, John (Priest, Immaculate Heart of Mary Church), Pittsburgh, 3 Mar. 1981

Landerman, Ethel (Jewish Social Services Bureau, Montefiore Hospital), Pittsburgh, 3 Apr. 1987

Lesser, Robert (Hebrew Free Loan), Pittsburgh, 1 July 1980

Levinson, Aaron (United Jewish Fund), Pittsburgh, 10 July 1980

Levy, Kurt (Friendship Club), Pittsburgh, 5 Apr. 1980

Mallett, Dorothy (National Council of Jewish Women), Pittsburgh, 5 April 1980

Markus, Lotte (Friendship Club), Pittsburgh, 8 Apr. 1980

Mazerov, Paul (Beth Shalom Congregation), Pittsburgh, 20 May 1980

Nachman, Ernest (Friendship Club), Pittsburgh, 30 May 1980

Noven, S. J. (Young Men and Women's Hebrew Association), Pittsburgh, 21 June 1980

Pervin, Abraham (Young Men and Women's Hebrew Association), Pittsburgh, 30 June 1980

Poupko, Baruch (Rabbi, Shaare Torah Congregation), Pittsburgh, 24 June 1980

Saul, Joseph (brother of Zena Saul, director of Committee on Service to the Foreign Born), Pittsburgh, 3 July 1980

Sidransky, Hannah (social worker, Jewish Family and Children's Service), Pittsburgh, 7 Apr. 1980

Silverblatt, Gertrude (National Council of Jewish Women), Pittsburgh, 28 May 1980

Siwicki, Hatti (Central Council of Polish Organizations), Pittsburgh, 4 Feb. 1981

Stoltzer, Shirley Lederman (social worker, Jewish Family and Children's Service), Pittsburgh, 4 May 1980

Susman, Milton (editor, *Jewish Criterion*), Pittsburgh, 5 Feb. 1980

Treibel, Ronnie (Friendship Club), Pittsburgh, 2 July 1980

Weitzman, Leonard (United Vocational and Employment Service), Pittsburgh, 7 July 1980

Zachariasiewicz, Walter (Polish Immigration Committee), Washington D.C., 27 Nov. 1984

ARCHIVES

American Jewish Committee (AJC), New York.

Archives of Industrial Society (AIS), Hillman Library, University of Pittsburgh. Contains the papers of the American Service Institute, the Friendship Club, the Jewish Community Relations Council, the National Council of Jewish Women, and Tree of Life Congregation.

Center for Immigration Studies (CIS), Staten Island, NY. Papers of the National Catholic Welfare Conference (NCWC).

Jewish Community Center (JCC), Pittsburgh, Pa. Merger of the Young Men's and Women's Hebrew Association and the Irene Kaufmann Settlement.

Jewish Family and Children's Services (JFCS), Pittsburgh, Pa. Formerly the Jewish Social Service Bureau.

Pilsudski Institute of America, New York, NY. Contains archives of the National Committee of Americans of Polish Descent, and of the Polish-American Congress.

Rodef Shalom Temple, Pittsburgh, Pa.

Synod Hall, Pittsburgh, Pa. Records of the Catholic Diocese of Pittsburgh.

United Jewish Federation (UJF), Pittsburgh, Pa. Has records of the Federation of Jewish Philanthropies and the United Jewish Fund.

PUBLISHED AND UNPUBLISHED MATERIAL

Adolf, Jacek A. "Adaptation of Eastern European Refugees and Political Emigrés in Toronto, with Special Reference to Immigrants from Poland and Czechoslovakia." Ph.D. diss., York University, Ontario, 1977.

Amerian Jewish Committee, "Immigration and Refugee Aid," *American Jewish Yearbook 1946–1947*. Philadelphia: Jewish Publication Society of America, 1947.

Apenszlak, Jacob. *The Black Book of Polish Jewry*. American Federation for Polish Jews, 1943.

Anders, Wladyslaw. *An Army in Exile*. London: Macmillan, 1949.

Barton, Josef J. *Peasants and Strangers*. Cambridge: Harvard University Press, 1975.

Bartoszewski, Wladyslaw. *The Blood Shed Unites Us*. Warsaw: Interpress Publishing, 1970.

Bauer, Yehuda. *Flight and Rescue BRICHAH*. New York: Random House, 1970.

———. *The Jewish Emergence from Powerlessness*. Toronto: University of Toronto Press, 1979.

———. *A History of the Holocaust*. New York: Franklin Watts, 1982.

Bernard, William S., "Programs and Concepts in the Resettlement of Immigrants and Refugees by American Voluntary Agencies." American Immigration and Citizenship Conference, AICC Committee on Integration 1969.

Bernstein, David. "Europe's Jews: Summer, 1947." *Commentary* 4 (1947): 101–09.

Bernstein, Philip S. "Displaced Person." *American Jewish Yearbook 1947–1948*. Philadelphia: Jewish Publication Society of America, 1948.

Black Book of Poland, Polish Ministry of Information, United States, 1942.

Blejwas, Stanislaus A. "Old and New Polonias: Tensions within an Ethnic Community." *Polish American Studies* 38 (1981): 55–83.

Bodnar, John, Simon, Roger, and Weber, Michael. *Lives of Their Own.* Urbana: University of Illinois Press, 1982.

Boehm, Werner. "State Programs for DP's." *Social Service Review* 23 (1949): 485–94.

Bronsztejn, S. "The Jewish Population of Poland in 1931." *Jewish Journal of Sociology* 6 (1964): 3–29.

Burstin, Barbara S. "The Response of the Pittsburgh Jewish Community to Holocaust Survivors, 1946–1951." Seminar paper, History Department, University of Pittsburgh, 1981.

Castellan, Georges. "Remarks on the Social Structure of the Jewish Community in Poland between the Two World Wars." In Bela Vago and George Mosse, eds., *Jews and Non Jews in Eastern Europe 1918–1945.* Jerusalem: Keter, 1974.

Central Commission for Investigation of German Crimes in Poland. *German Crimes in Poland.* Vol. 2. New York: Howard Fertig, 1982.

Ciechanowski, Jan. *Defeat in Victory.* Garden City, N.J., Doubleday, 1947.

Chrobot, Leonard F. "Ethnic Awareness and Self-Identity," Orchard Lake Center for Polish Studies and Culture, no. 6, April 1971.

Cohen, Steven M. *The 1984 National Survey of American Jews.* New York: American Jewish Committee, 1985.

Conzen, Kathleen Neils. "Immigrants, Immigrant Neighborhoods, and Ethnic Identity: Historical Issues." *Journal of American History* 66 (1979): 603–15.

Council of Jewish Federations and Welfare Funds. *Jewish Social Service Yearbook 1950.* New York: CJFWF.

Dark Side of the Moon. New York: Chas. Scribner's Sons, 1947.

Davie, Maurice R. "Refugee Aid." *American Jewish Yearbook 1947–1948.* Philadephia: Jewish Publication Society of America, 1948.

————. "Adjustment of Refugees to American Life." *Annals of the American Academy of Political and Social Sciences* 262 (1949): 159–65.

————. "Immigration and Refugee Aid." *American Jewish Yearbook*

1948–1949. Philadelphia: Jewish Publication Society of America, 1949.

Davies, Norman. *God's Playground: A History of Poland.* Vol. 2. New York: Columbia University Press, 1982.

Dawidowicz, Lucy S. *The War Against the Jews.* New York: Holt, Rinehart and Winston, 1975.

DeGroot, Dudley Edward. "Assimilation of Postwar Immigrants in Atlanta, Georgia." Ph.D. diss., Ohio State University, 1957.

Des Pres, Terrence. *The Survivor.* New York: Oxford University Press, 1976.

Dinnerstein, Leonard. "Anti-Semitism in the Eightieth Congress: The Displaced Person Act of 1948." *Capitol Studies* 6 (1978): 11–26.

———. "The U.S. Army and the Jews." *American Jewish History* 68 (1979): 353–66.

———. "The Voluntary Agencies and the Resettlement of the Displaced Persons." Paper presented at the Duquesne University History Forum, Pittsburgh, 1980.

———. *America and the Survivors of the Holocaust.* New York: Columbia University Press, 1982.

Dinnerstein, Leonard, and Jaher, Frederic. *Uncertain Americans.* New York: Oxford University Press, 1977.

Dinnerstein, Leonard; Nichols, Roger; and Reimers, David. *Natives and Strangers.* New York: Oxford University Press, 1979.

Displaced Persons Commission. *The DP Story: Memo to America.* Washington, D.C.: Government Printing Office, 1952.

Divine, Robert A. *American Immigration Policy, 1924–1952.* New Haven: Conn.: Yale University Press, 1957.

Evans, Jon. *The Nazi New Order.* London: Victor Gallancz, 1941.

Feingold, Henry. *The Politics of Rescue.* New Brunswick, N.J.: Rutgers University Press, 1970.

Fishman, J. A., ed. *Studies on Polish Jewry 1919–1939.* New York: YIVO Institute for Jewish Research, 1974.

Friedman, Paul. "The Road Back for Displaced Persons." *Commentary* 6 (1946): 502–10.

Friedman, Saul. *No Haven for the Oppressed.* Detroit: Wayne State University Press, 1973.

Gilbert, Martin, *The Macmillan Atlas of the Holocaust.* New York: Macmillan, 1982.

Glassman, Helen L. *Adjustment in Freedom*. Cleveland: United HIAS Service, 1956.

Gonka, Joseph. "They Thought We Could Be Trusted." Ms.

Gordon, Sarah. *Hitler, Germans and the Jewish Question*. Princeton, N.J.: Princeton University Press, 1984.

Gottlieb, Amy Zahl. "Refugee Immigration: The Truman Directive." *Prologue* 13 (1981): 5–18.

Gringauz, Samuel, "Our New German Policy and the DP's." *Commentary* 5 (1948): 508–14.

Gross, Jan Tomasz. *Polish Society Under German Occupation*. Princeton, N.J.: Princeton University Press, 1977.

Grossman, Kurt R. *The Jewish DP Problem*. New York: Institute of Jewish Affairs, 1951.

Gunther, John. *Inside Russia Today*. New York: Harper and Bros., 1957.

Handlin, Oscar. *The Uprooted*. Boston: Little, Brown, 1951.

———. *Boston's Immigrants*. Cambridge: Belknap Press, Harvard University Press, 1959.

Hansen, Marcus Lee. *The Atlantic Migration, 1607–1860*. Cambridge, Mass.: Harvard University Press, 1940.

Heberle, Rudolf, and Hall, Dudley. *Displaced Persons in Louisiana and Mississippi*. Baton Rouge: Louisiana State University, 1950.

Heller, Celia S. *On the Edge of Destruction*. New York: Columbia University Press, 1977.

———. "Assimilation: A Deviant Pattern Among Jews of Interwar Poland." *Jewish Journal of Sociology* 15 (1973): 221–37.

Himmelfarb, Milton, and Singer, David, eds. *American Jewish Yearbook 1985*. New York: American Jewish Committee, 1984.

Homze, Edward L. *Forced Labor in Nazi Germany*. Princeton, N.J.: Princeton University Press, 1967.

Horak, Stephen. *Poland and Her National Minorities 1919–1939*. New York: Vantage, 1961.

International Refugee Organization. *Facts About Refugees*. Geneva; IRO, 1948.

Iwanska, Alicja. "Values in Crisis Situation." Ph.D. diss., Columbia University, 1957.

Jaroszynska, Anna Dorota. "The American Committee for Resettlement of Polish Displaced Persons (1948–1968) in the Manuscript

Collection of the Immigration History Research Center." *Polish American Studies* 44 (Spring 1987): 67–74.

Karski, Jan. *Story of a Secret State.* Boston: Houghton Mifflin, 1944.

Katsh, Abraham I., ed. *The Warsaw Diary of Chaim A. Kaplan.* New York: Collier Books, 1965.

Katz, Steven T. "The 'Unique' Intentionality of the Holocaust." *Modern Judaism* 1 (1981): 161–83.

————. *Post Holocaust Dialogues.* New York: New York University Press, 1983.

Kishinka, Joyce Williams. "A Study of Assimilation Experiences of Jewish, Latvian and Ukrainian Displaced Persons." Ed.D. diss., Rutgers University, 1979.

Kleeman, Janice. "Polish-American Assimilation: The Interaction of Opportunity and Attitude." *Polish American Studies* 42 (Spring 1985): 11–27.

Klein, Philip. *A Social Study of Pittsburgh.* New York: Columbia University Press, 1938.

Kolm, Richard. "The Change of Cultural Identity: An Analysis of Factors Conditioning the Cultural Integration of Immigrants." Ph.D. diss., Wayne State University, 1965.

————. "The Identity Crisis of Polish Americans." *Quarterly Review,* April–June 1969, pp. 1–4.

Korbonski, Stefan. *Fighting Warsaw.* London: Allen and Unwin, 1956.

————. *The Polish Underground State, 1939—1945.* New York: Eastern European Quarterly, 1978.

Korewa, Maria B. "Casework Treatment of Refugees: A Survey of Selected Professional Periodicals from January 1939–1956." Master's Thesis, Wayne State University, 1962.

Krakowski, S. "The Slaughter of Polish Jewry: A Polish Reassessment." *Wiener Library Bulletin* 121 (1973): 293–401.

Krueger, Nancy. "Assimilation and Adjustment of Post-War Immigrants in Franklin County, Ohio." Ph.D. diss., Ohio State University, 1955.

Krysiewicz, Thaddeus, Theodore. *The Polish Immigration Committee in the United States.* New York: Roman Catholic Church of St. Stanislaus B.M., 1954.

Kulischer, Eugene M. *Europe on the Move: War and Population*

Changes, 1917–1947. New York: Columbia University Press, 1948.

Kusielewicz, Eugene. *Reflections on the Cultural Condition of the Polish American Community*. New York: CZAS Publishing, 1969.

Lane, Arthur Bliss. *I Saw Poland Betrayed*. Indianapolis: Bobbs-Merrill, 1948.

Leslie, R. F., ed. *The History of Poland Since 1863*. Cambridge, U.K.: Cambridge University Press, 1980.

Lestchinsky, Jacob. "The Jews in the City of the Republic of Poland." *YIVO Annual of Jewish Social Science* 1 (1946): 156–77.

———. "The Industrial and Social Structure of the Jewish Population of Interbellum Poland." *YIVO Annual of Jewish Social Science* 11 (1956–57): 243–69.

———. "Aspects of the Sociology of Polish Jewry." *Jewish Social Studies* 28 (1966): 195–211.

Lopata, Helena Z. "The Function of Voluntary Associations in an Ethnic Community: Polonia." Ph.D. diss., University of Chicago, 1954.

———. *Polish Americans: Status and Competition in an Ethnic Community*. New York: Prentice Hall, 1976.

Lubove, Roy, ed. *Pittsburgh*. New York: New Viewpoints, 1976.

Lukas, Richard C. *The Strange Allies: The U.S. and Poland, 1941–1945*. Knoxville: University of Tennessee Press, 1978.

———. "The Polish American Congress and the Polish Question 1944–1947." *Polish American Studies* 38 (Autumn 1981): 39–53.

Madaj, M. J. "The Polish Community—A Ghetto?." *Polish American Studies* 25 (July–Dec. 1968): 65–73.

Mahler, R. "Jews in Public Service and the Liberal Professions in Poland, 1918–1939." *Jewish Social Studies* 6 (1944): 291–350.

Marcus, Joseph. *Social and Political History of the Jews in Poland, 1919–1939*. Berlin: Mouton, 1983.

Martin, Jean I. *Refugee Settlers: A Study of Displaced Persons in Australia*. Canberra: Australian National University, 1965.

Mendelsohn, Ezra. *The Jews of East Central Europe Between the Wars*. Bloomington: Indiana University Press, 1983.

Meyer, Peter. "Polish Jews under Soviet Rule." In Bernard D. Wein-
ryb, *The Jews in the Soviet Satellites*. Syracuse, N.Y.: Syracuse
University Press, 1953.

Morton, Malvin. "Development and Structure of the War Relief Agencies." Bureau of Social Research, Federation of Social Agencies
of Pittsburgh and Allegheny County, Pittsburgh, May, 1945.

Mostwin, Danuta. "Post World War II Polish Immigrant in the U.S.."
Polish American Studies 26 (August 1969): 5–14.

———. "Profile of a Transplanted Family." *Polish Review* (1974),
19:77–90.

———. *The Transplanted Family*. New York: Arno Press, 1980.

Murphy, H. B. M. *Flight and Resettlement*. Paris: UNESCO, 1955.
National Council of Jewish Women. *1946–1947 Yearbook*. New
York: NCJW.

Nowak, Jan. *Courier from Warsaw*. Detroit: Wayne State University
Press, 1982.

Nordon, Haskell. *The Education of a Polish Jew*. New York: D.
Grossman Press, 1982.

Obindinski, Eugene. *Ethnic to Status Groups*. Buffalo: State University
of New York, 1968.

———. "Polish Americans in Buffalo: The Transformation of an
Ethnic Subcommunity." *Polish Review* 14 (1969): 28–39.

———. "American Polonia: Sacred and Profane Aspects." *Polish
American Studies* 32 (Spring 1979): 5–18.

———. "Beyond Hansen's Law: Fourth Generation Polonian Identity." *Polish American Studies* 42 (Spring 1985): 27–43.

Pachner, Alfred. "The Political Exile of Poland, Czechoslovakia and
Yugoslavia." Master's thesis, Northwestern University, 1957.

Patterson, Sheila. "The Polish Exile Community in Britain." *Polish
Review* 6 (1961): 69–97.

———. "The Poles: An Exile Community in Britain." In James L.
Watson, ed., *Between Two Cultures: Migrants and Minorities in
Britain*. Oxford: Basil Blackwell, 1977.

Pennsylvania Commission on Displaced Persons, *Third Annual Report*.
1951.

Peszke, Machael A. "The Polish Armed Forces in Exile." *Polish
Review* 26 (1981): 67–113.

Pinchuk, Ben-Cion. "Jewish Refugees in Soviet Poland, 1939–1941." *Jewish Social Studies* 40 (1978): 141–57.

Pine, Kurt. "The Jews in the Hill District of Pittsburgh, 1910–1940." Master's thesis, University of Pittsburgh, 1943.

Pinson, Koppel S. "Jewish Life in Liberated Germany." *Jewish Social Studies* 9 (1976): 101–26.

Proudfoot, Malcolm. *European Refugees, 1939–1952*. Evanston, Ill.: Northwestern University Press, 1956.

Rawley, Callman. "The Adjustment of Jewish Displaced Persons." *Journal of Social Casework* 29 (1948): 316–21.

Ray, Helen E. "Problems Confronting Displaced Persons in the Areas of Employment, Family and Neighborhood Life, and Social and Recreational Activities." Master's thesis, University of Pittsburgh, 1952.

Richmond, Anthony H. *Postwar Immigrants in Canada*. Toronto: University of Toronto Press, 1967.

Rifkind, Simon H. "I Lived with the Jewish DP's." *The Congress Weekly* 13 (1946): 9–12.

Ringelblum, Emmanuel. *Polish-Jewish Relations During the Second World*. New York: Howard Fertig, 1976.

Rischin, Moses. *The Promised City*. New York: Harper, Torchbooks, 1962.

Rothchild, Sylvia, ed. *Voices from the Holocaust*. New York: New American Library, 1981.

Rothschild, Joseph. *East Central Europe Between the Two World Wars*. Seattle: University of Washington Press, 1974.

Rubin, Gary. "The Process of Immigrant Acculturation: Recent Findings and Policy Implications." *Migration Today* 8 (1980): 18–22.

Ryan, Allan A., Jr. *Quiet Neighbors*. Orlando, Fla.: Harcourt Brace Jovanovich, 1984.

Sachar, Abram L. *The Redemption of the Unwanted*. New York: St. Martins/Marek, 1983.

Sandberg, Neil C. *Ethnic Identity and Assimilation: The Polish American Community*. New York: Praeger, 1974.

Schwarz, Leo. *The Redeemers*. New York: Farrar, Straus, and Young, 1953.

Segal, Simon. *The New Poland and the Jews*. New York: Lee Furman, 1938.

————. *The New Order in Poland.* New York: Knopf, 1942.

Shapiro, Leon. "Poland." *American Jewish Yearbook 1947–1948.* Philadelphia: Jewish Publication Society of America, 1948.

Social Planning and Research Department. *Survey of Greater Pittsburgh's Jewish Population, 1984.* Cleveland: Jewish Community Federation of Cleveland.

Sowell, Thomas, ed. *American Ethnic Groups.* Washington, D.C.: Urban Institute, 1978.

Srole, Leo. Why the DP's Can't Wait. *Commentary* 3 (1947): 13–24.

Swick, Phyllis. "Participation of Jewish New Americans at the YM&WHA of Pittsburgh from 1949–December, 1951." Master's thesis, University of Pittsburgh, 1950.

Sypek, Stanislaw. "The Displaced Polish Persons in the Greater Boston Community." Ph.D. diss., Fordham University, 1953.

Syrkin, Marie. "I Met a Black Marketeer." *Jewish Frontier* 14 (August 1947): 13–14.

Taylor, Maurice. "The Jewish Community of Pittsburgh, December 1938—A Sample Study." Federation of Jewish Philanthropies, Pittsburgh, 1941.

Thernstrom, Stephan. *Poverty and Progress.* Cambridge, Mass.: Harvard University Press, 1964.

————. *The Other Bostonians.* Cambridge, Mass.: Harvard University Press, 1973.

Thomas, W. I., and Znaniecki, Florian. *The Polish Peasant in Europe and America.* Boston: Richard G. Badger/Gorham Press, 1918–1920.

Tobin, Gary A., and Chenkin, Alvin. "Recent Jewish Community Population Studies: A Roundup." In Milton Himmelfarb and David Singer, eds., *American Jewish Yearbook 1985*, pp. 154–79. New York: American Jewish Committee, 1984.

Vernant, Jacques. *The Refugee in the Post-War World.* London: Allen and Unwin, 1953.

Watt, Richard. *Bitter Glory: Poland and Her Fate, 1918–1939.* New York: Simon and Schuster, 1979.

White, Lyman C. *300,000 New Americans.* New York: Harper Bros., 1957.

Wischnitzer, Mark. *Visas to Freedom: The History of HIAS.* Cleveland: World Publishing, 1956.

Wycislo, Aloysius J. "The Catholic Program for the Resettlement of DP's." *Polish Review* 8 (1948): 6–7.

Wyman, David S. *Paper Walls*. Boston: University of Massachusetts Press, 1968.

―――. *The Abandonment of the Jews*. New York: Pantheon, 1984.

Wytrwal, Joseph A. *Poles in American History and Tradition*. Detroit: Endurance Press, 1969.

Zand, Helen S. "Polish American Profile." *Polish American Studies* 18 (1961): 90–100.

Zubrzycki, Jerzy. *Polish Immigrants in Britain*. The Hague: Martinus, Nijhoff, 1956.

Zweig, Ferdynand. *Poland Between Two Wars*. London: Secker and Warburg, 1944.

PERIODICALS

American Jewish Yearbook, 1946–53, 1985. American Jewish Committee, New York.

Jewish Criterion, 1945–52. (At Rodef Shalom Temple, Pittsburgh, Pa.)

Jewish Social Service Yearbook, 1947–52. Council of Federation and Welfare Funds, New York.

Notes on Immigrant Care, 1950–53. United Service for New Americans, New York.

Index

A., Robert, 130
Adolf, Jacek, 130
AJC. *See* American Jewish Committee
American Committee for the Resettlement of Polish DPs, 82–83
American Council for Judaism, 109, 192n44
American Jewish Committee (AJC), 71–72, 74, 77
American Relief for Poland, 78–79, 81, 82
American Service Institute (ASI), 73–74, 76
Anders, Wladyslaw, 24, 32, 35, 39, 43, 80, 174
Anti-Semitism: condemnation of, by Catholic church, 152; in postwar Poland, 46–47, 48, 50, 61; in prewar Poland, 7, 8, 15; in U.S., 72–73, 167–69, 195n11
Anti-Zionism, 108–09
ASI. *See* American Service Institute
Association of Polish Combatants (SPK), 137
Association of Veterans of the Polish Army (SWAP), 137
Auschwitz concentration camp: personal experiences at, 12, 17, 18, 20, 21; gas chamber at, 15, 16; survivors of, 48, 64
Aussenberg, Julius, 4, 16, 123, 167

B., Fabian, 31–32, 128, 161
B., Frances, 32, 143, 151, 161, 175–76
B., Helena, 5, 25, 59
Bader, Fred, 108
Balter, Marjorie, 97, 110, 111
Bartel, Kasimierz, 3
Battle of Britain, 43
Belzec death camp, 15, 23
Ben Gurion, David, 53
Bergen Belsen concentration camp, 24
Berling, Zygmunt, 47
Bernard, William S., 74, 81–82
Binstock, Dorothy, 111
Birnbaum, Helen, 7, 36, 169
Bisholovitch concentration camp, 36
Blue and White Club, 137
Blumenthal, Dorothy, 109, 110, 192n44
B'nai Brith, 111
Borke, Michell, 17, 36–37, 38, 154, 185n2, 185n4
Borkowski, Mieczyslaw. *See* Borke, Michell

Braunschweig labor camp, 20

Brichah, 49, 52

Broniewski, Stanislaw, 177

Buchenwald concentration camp, 16, 22, 51

Burant, Felix, 79, 81, 82

Bureau of Immigration of the National Catholic Welfare Conference, 98

C., Raymond, 64, 151

Carroll, William, 67

Catholic Committee for Refugees (CCR), 67, 69–71, 73, 78–80

Catholic Daughters of America, 70

Catholics (Polish): and aid for displaced persons, xi–xii, xiii, 67–70, 73, 78; discrimination against Jews by, 6–7; in displaced persons camps, 67; efforts to encourage immigration of, 79, 80–84; number of, among Christian Poles, x; as victims of Nazis, 15. *See also* Christians; Immigrants (Christian)

Catholic War Relief Service, 69–70

CCDP. *See* Citizens Committee for Displaced Persons

CCR. *See* Catholic Committee for Refugees

Central Council of Polish Organizations, 84, 85, 131

Chelmno death camp, 15

Christians (Polish): after World War II, x, 42–43, 45–46, 118; anti-Semitism of, xi, 61; compared with Jews, x, xiv–xv, 4–8; effect of loss of homeland on, 118; as emigrants to U.S. and England, 46, 55–58; experiences of, in Poland, xiii, 7–8, 10–11, 18, 22–

26, 40, 41; as survivors of concentration camps, 22–26, 45–46. *See also* Catholics (Polish); Immigrants (Christian)

Churchill, Winston, 58–59

Cieply, Morton, 45, 119, 124, 138, 146

Citizens Committee for Displaced Persons (CCDP), 72, 73–74, 75–77, 84, 88

Club Shalom, 190*n8*

Committee on Service to the Foreign Born. *See* National Council of Jewish Women

Communism, xiii, 46, 48, 49

Communist criminal code, 28

Community Relations Council of Pittsburgh, 77

Concentration camps: Christians in, 22–26, 45–46; Jews in, 15–16, 18, 22, 23; liberation of, 12, 16, 18, 20, 26, 49–50; medical experiments at, 24

Conrad, Joseph, 130

Council of Churches of Christ, 75

Council of New Americans, 137

Cymerman, Abe, 124, 138, 185*n2*

D., Francinski, 9, 127, 143

D., John, 23–24, 56

Dachau concentration camp, 12, 21, 22–23, 26, 49

Dafner, Lucy, 4, 145, 151, 169

Dearden, John, 84

Death marches, 16, 20, 21, 22–23, 49

Demjanjuk, John, 186*n6*

Dinnerstein, Leonard, 69

Displaced persons (Polish): aid for, 69–70, 74, 78, 83–85; Catholic, 67–70, 73, 85; Jewish, 67–69,

85, 87, 106–07; movie about, 76; postwar condition of, 45; statistics on, 84–85, 183n2; U.S. legislation on, 50, 72–73, 88–89. *See also* Immigrants; Refugees (Polish)

Displaced Persons Act (1948): criticism of, xiii–xiv, 76–77, 103; and denial of immigration to Nazis, 187n32; effect of, on PIC, 80; expiration of, 85, 97, 107; explanation of, 76; immigrants entering U.S. under, 55, 58, 65, 77, 103–04, 115–17, 133, 186n1; and marriage figures, 62; 1950 amendment to, 106, 117; revisions to, 77

Displaced persons camps: children born in, 63; Christians in, 65–66, 67; conditions of, 49–52; in Europe, 102; immigrants from, 65, 115

Displaced Persons Commission, 81

Drucker, Harry, 123, 154

Einsatzgruppen, 12, 15

Eisenhower, Dwight D., 51, 101

England: immigration laws of, 53–54, 87; resettlement programs in, 55–58, 60–61

Enzel, Abraham, 45, 124

Falk, Louis, Jr., 100

Farben, I. G., 16

Federal Council of Churches, 73

Federman, Hyman, 149

Federation of Social Agencies, 75

Feldman, Harry, 16–17, 54, 149, 185n4

Felgheber. *See* Fox, Aaron

Final Solution, the, 12, 15

Fineberg, Herman, 110

Fisher, Myrtle, 93, 108–09, 111

Flossenberg concentration camp, 18, 22, 25–26

Forced labor, 10–11, 20–21, 42

Forstenzer, Estelle, 22, 124, 154

Forstenzer, Nathan, 54, 124

Fox, Aaron, 4, 154, 169

Frank, Hans W., 9–10, 15

Freehof, Solomon, 113

Friedberg, Lillian, 74

Friede, Wolf, 33, 47, 120, 137, 154

Friedland camp, 21

Friedman, Harry, 6, 16, 121, 163

Friedman, William, 16, 49, 53, 120, 122, 123–24

Friendship Club (Pittsburgh), 92–93, 97, 123, 190n8

Frost, Samuel, 4, 121, 122, 124, 137, 146

G., Frances, 177

G., Joanna, 18, 130, 134

G., Joseph, 5, 10, 135, 153

G., Mieczyslaw, 5, 58, 128, 153, 154

G., Stefan, 43, 57, 60, 141, 153

Gas chambers, 15, 17, 18

Gelman, Bernard, 37–38, 47, 51–52, 120, 165

Generalgovernment, 15–16

Germany: invasion of Poland by, x, 9, 26; invasion of Ukraine by, 38; Jews' attitudes toward, 39–40; and partition of Poland with Russia, 12; treatment of Jewish survivors by, 108; violation of pact with Russia by, 28

Ghettos, 11, 12, 16, 18–19, 21. *See also* Warsaw ghetto uprising

Glatstein, Mordechai, 11–12, 50, 52, 120–21, 150, 164

Glick, Gertrude, 106

Goldman, Aron, 19–20, 45, 121, 125, 147

Goldman, Melvin, 20, 45, 121, 163

Goldszmidt, Henryk, 185*n2*

Green, Helen, 74

Greenberg, Frances, 54, 147, 164

Greenberg, Isaac, 34, 147, 164

Gross Rosen camp, 21

Grundman, Benjamin, 147

Gunther, Blair, 82–83, 84, 189*n52*

Guss, Daivd, 35–36, 44–45, 124, 164–65

H., Maria, 30–31, 135

H., Viktor, 5, 30–31, 56, 59, 151

Harrison, Earl, 50–51, 53, 73, 75

Hausler, Dora, 7

Hebrew Free Loan Association, 120

Hebrew Immigrant Aid Society (HIAS), 65, 66, 80–81, 88

Heymann, Bessie, 108

Heymann, Sidney, 108

HIAS. *See* Hebrew Immigrant Aid Society

Hitler, Adolf, ix–x, 9, 15

Hoffman, Gabriel, 4, 119–20, 124, 147–48

Immigrant Aid Committee (Pittsburgh), 94

Immigrants (Christian): adjustment problems of, 126–29; arriving under Displaced Persons Act, 116–17, 133; children of, 156–57, 159; effect of war on religious beliefs of, 151–53; employment of, 155–56, 195*n6*, 195*n9*; ethnic identity of, 141–43, 165–66; expectations of, for U.S., 130–31, 142–44; feelings of, for Poland,
118, 141; feelings of, toward Jews, 174; lack of aid for, 78, 80–81, 127, 128–29; relationship of, with Polish-Americans, 132–36; residential patterns of, 195*n8*; sense of achievement of, 161–63, 165; social organizations for, 131–32, 136–37

Immigrants (Jewish): adjustment problems of, 111, 112, 124, 125; aid to, xi–xii, 3, 88–89, 113–14, 119, 120, 121; and anti-Semitism, 167–69; anti-Zionism among, 108–09; arriving under Displaced Persons Act, 115–16; attitude of American Jews toward, 110–11, 122, 123–24; attitude of, toward German Jews, 123; attitude of, toward Polish Christians, 145–46; children of, 125, 159–60; clothing provided for, 95–97, 106, 110–11, 112; effect of war on, 118, 146–48, 149, 150–51, 154–55, 163–64, 165; employment for, 90, 111, 157–58; ethnic identity of, 144–46, 166–67; feelings of, for Poland, 144, 145–46; feelings of, for U.S., 124–25, 145–46, 164–65; housing for, 89, 94, 100–01, 111, 121–22; number of, arriving in Pittsburgh, 100, 103–04, 107; to Palestine, 86; quotas on, 99, 100, 101–02; reasons of, for leaving Poland, 44–45, 46–48; search for relatives by, 90, 94; social programs for, 90–93, 137–38; support for Palestine by, 98, 102, 167–69. *See also* Jews (Polish)

Immigrants (Polish): adjustment problems of, 117–19, 138; aid to, 65–

68, 74–75, 79–80, 85, 191*n18*, 191*n33*; and area of Pittsburgh settled in, ix, 138; background check on, 77; children of, 63; countries favored by, 54, 57, 58, 86, 115, 191*n1*, 194*n3*; dialogue between Jewish and Christian, 171–80; effect of Truman directive on, 99, 115; employment for, 138–39, 189*n52*; figures on, entering U.S., 55, 57, 62–63, 64–65, 77; housing for, 79, 189*n52*, 190*n11*; identity problem of, 140–42, 165–67, 174–75, 176; present-day experiences of, xiv, 174–75, 195*n12*; problems encountered by, in entering U.S., xiv, 49, 53–58, 83–84; proportion of, by religion, 70–72, 77; quotas on, 65, 76; reasons of, for leaving Poland, 44, 46–48; reception of, in U.S., xiv, 135–36; sense of achievement of, 160–61, 165. *See also* Displaced persons; Immigrants (Christian); Immigrants (Jewish); Refugees

Immigration laws, 51, 53–54, 70–71

Infeld, Norman, 22–23, 123

International Refugee Organization, 67

Iwler, Dora, 12–13, 53–54, 62, 154, 164

J., Alina, 5–6, 56

J., Gertrude, 127, 141, 151, 161

Janowska labor camp, 13

Jaslo concentration camp, 24

Jewish Criterion, 93, 101–02, 114

Jewish Family and Children's Service (JFCS), 106. *See also* Jewish Social Service Bureau

Jewish Organization for Rehabilitation and Training (ORT), 52

Jewish Social Service Bureau (JSSB): aid to immigrants in Pittsburgh by, 66, 89–90; budget of, 99, 103–04, 105; and care for orphans, 100; and housing for immigrants, 121–22; sponsorship of immigrants by, 119–21. *See also* Jewish Family and Children's Service

Jewish Vocational Agency, 158

Jews (Polish): and anti-Semitism in Poland, 5, 6–7, 8, 172–73; attitude of, toward Russia and Germany, 39–40; background of, in Poland, xiii, 4–5; and Communism, 48; compared with Christians, x, xiv–xv, 4–8; deportation of, to Siberia, xiii, 37; as displaced persons, 67–69, 106–07; effect of Depression on, 7–8; effect of Nuremberg War Trials on, 109–10; in postwar Europe, x, 3–4, 33–38, 43–44, 45, 88, 101, 102, 106–07, 108, 118–19; forced labor seizures of, 11; as inmates of concentration camps, 15–16, 18, 22, 23; as members of Polish army, 185*n2*; and Operation Barbarossa, 12. *See also* Immigrants (Jewish)

JFCS. *See* Jewish Family and Children's Service

Joint Committee on Service to New Immigrants, 89, 99, 100, 104–05, 106–07

Joint Distribution Committee, 66

Joskowitz, Sarah, 45, 148, 168

JSSB. *See* Jewish Social Service Bureau

K., Henry, 142, 153
K., Irena, 134–35, 153
K., Janusz, 28–29, 56, 57, 59, 60, 151, 153
K., Jessie, 64
K., Marion, 26–27, 29–30, 56, 162
K., Rita, 153
K., Stanley, 18–19, 58, 126–27, 132, 141–42
Klagenfurt concentration camp, 25
Kohane, Abe, 120, 123, 125, 137, 148
Komora, Emil N., 67, 71, 79
Korczak, Janusz. *See* Goldszmidt, Henryk
Kovarsky, Marcel, 106
Kreta, Peter M., 74
Krysiewicz, Thaddeus, 83
Krystallnacht, 7

L., Adam, 128, 130
L., Edmund, 162
L., Esther, 140–41, 161
Landerman, Ethel, 112, 113
Lappan, Thomas, 84
Lawrence, David L., 88
Lesser, Robert, 111
Levenreich, Albert, 51, 121, 163, 185*n2*
Lewenstein, Irwin, 47, 52, 185*n2*
Lieberman, Fanny, 4, 168
Lipschitz, Dora, 148, 169
Lowenthal, Mrs. Alex, 74, 75

M., Krystyna, 141, 162
M., Lidia, 56–57, 59, 134, 141
M., Rudolf, 56, 142
McCarthy, Sarah, 70–71
Maidanek death camp, 12, 15, 17, 47

Mallett, Dorothy, 93, 96–97, 110–11, 112
Manela, Morris, 4, 21–22, 53, 54, 125, 137, 147, 164
Mangurten, Henry, 20, 21, 64
Markus, Lotte, 92
Mass graves, 14, 15, 37, 40
Mazerov, Paul, 110
Melmed, Sally, 33–34, 47, 119, 121, 125, 169
Mengele, Joseph, 20, 147
Mielec concentration camp, 4, 17, 22
Mikowski, Izak, 125, 148, 168
Minorities Treaty, 6
Mohler, Bruce, 67–71, 79, 98
Molotov-Ribbentrop Pact (1939), xiii, 12, 26, 37
Montefiore Hospital (Pittsburgh), 90, 91, 112
Morgenstern, Fela, 7, 14, 149–50
Mulholland, Thomas, 67–69, 79–80, 81

N., Bernice, 56, 58, 134, 142
Nachman, Ernest, 92–93
National Catholic Committee for Refugees, 65
National Catholic Welfare Conference (NCWC): aid to displaced persons by, 78; Bureau of Immigration of, 67–69, 71, 73; immigrants' dissatisfaction with, 126, 127, 128–29; and PIC, 79
National Council of Jewish Women (NCJW): aid to refugees by, 75, 93–94; budget of, 97; and clothing for immigrants, 95–97, 106, 110–11, 112; and Committee on Service to the Foreign Born, 90,

94–95, 97; Pittsburgh chapter of, 75
National Democrats, 7
National Resettlement Council, 78, 80, 84
Nazis: attempts to prevent admittance of, to U.S., 77, 187n32; effect of, on Jewish Poles, 46–47, 48; medical experiments of, 24; and occupation of Poland, x, 25–26; propaganda of, 8. *See also* Germany
NCJW. *See* National Council of Jewish Women
NCWC. *See* National Catholic Welfare Conference
Nuremberg War Trials, 10, 109–10

O., John, 161
Operation Barbarossa, 12
Operation Carrot, 46
ORT. *See* Jewish Organization for Rehabilitation and Training
Oseroff, Pauline, 96

P., Henrietta, 10, 129, 135
P., Jan, 14, 59
P., Joseph, 29, 59, 142, 152, 160
P., Marcel, 25–26, 151–52
P., Stanyslaw, 27–28, 59, 134
PAC. *See* Polish American Congress
Palestine: aid to Jews in, 98; Jewish immigrants' ties to, 102, 167–69; Jewish immigration to, 53–54, 86, 87; turmoil in, in 1947, 101
Passamaneck, Herman, 90–91
Passport to Nowhere (movie), 75
Perlmutter, Rose, 7, 54
PIC. *See* Polish Immigration Committee
Pilsudski, Jozef, 3

Pittsburgh: aid to immigrants in, 74–75, 84–85, 89, 94; and area immigrants settled in, 138; financial support for Israel in, 102–03; financial support for Jewish immigrants in, 88–89, 91–92, 99, 102, 106–08, 191n33; immigration figures of, 65–66, 100, 107; sympathy for Jewish immigrants in, 110–12, 122, 123–24
Pittsburgh Diocesan Resettlement Council, 84
Plaszow concentration camp, 22, 23
Poland: anti-Semitism in, 5, 6–7, 8, 172–73; army of, 36–37, 43, 47, 185n2; and census of 1931, 6; Depression in, 3–4, 7–8; economy of, 3–4, 8; forced labor in, 42; German invasion of, x, 9, 26; partition of, between Russia and Germany, xiii, 12; postwar death toll in, x, 42; refugees' postwar attitudes toward, ix–x, xii, 48, 61; Russian occupation of, x, 29–30, 31–32, 39–41; and Sikorski Agreement, 37; surrender of, 43; underground army of, 14, 25, 40
Polish American Congress (PAC), 51, 73, 81, 189n52
Polish-Americans, 132–36, 194n5
Polish Falcons, 131–32
Polish Immigration Committee (PIC), 65, 78–79, 80–81, 83, 126–27, 128
Polish National Alliance, 84, 85, 132
Polish Resettlement Corps, 56, 60–61, 130, 132, 183n2
Polish Roman Catholic Union of America, 132

Polish Women's Alliance, 128, 132
Pope John XXIII, 152
Poupko, Baruch, 109–10, 111

R., Alphonse, 141
R., Antoni, 141
R., Stefan, 59
Ravensbruck concentration camp, 20, 24, 25, 45
Red Cross, 17, 25
Refugees (Polish): American policy on, xiii–xiv, 186n1; and displaced persons camps, 54–55; emigration of, 46–48, 49, 53–57; feelings of, toward England and U.S., 58–61; as members of armed forces, 38, 43; postwar attitude of, toward Poland, xii, 48, 55, 61; postwar statistics on, 42; resettlement programs for, 56–58, 69, 74; in Russia, 27, 29, 33–38, 39. *See also* Displaced persons; Immigrants (Polish)
Relis, Gusta, 13–14, 125
Rice, Charles Owen, 74
Rodef Shalom Temple, 109, 113
Roosevelt, Franklin Delano, 58–59
Rosen, Harry, 4, 125, 155
Rozmarek, Charles, 73
Rumkowski, Chaim, 21
Russia: army of, 38; attitude of Poles toward, 39–40; escape of refugees from, 39; invasion of, by Germany, 12; invasion of Poland by, x, 26, 29–30, 31–32, 39–41; Jewish refugees in, 27, 29, 33–38, 39; as Polish ally, 28–29, 40; refugees as citizens of, 34, 36, 37; and Sikorski Agreement, 37. *See also* Siberia
Ryan, Hermione Braunsteiner, 24

S., Adam, 59, 128
S., John, 142
S., Louise, 58
S., Maria, 5, 24–25, 57, 162
S., Stanislawa, 5, 31, 58–59, 129, 142, 151, 153, 154, 157
Salem, Abe, 45, 122, 137, 148
Saul, Zena, 90, 92, 94
Scheingross, Marcia, 38, 121, 125, 154
Shear, Sam, 45, 52, 137, 158, 168
Siberia, 27, 29, 30, 32, 36, 37
Sidransky, Hannah, 110
Sikorski, Wladyslaw, 43, 59–60
Sikorski Agreement (1941), 37, 64
Silverblatt, Gertrude, 97, 110
Sittsamer, Jack, 4, 17–18, 121, 137, 148
Smith, John C., 74
Sobibor death camp, 15
Spiegel, Frances, 120, 151, 154–55
SPK. *See* Association of Polish Combatants
Steinfirst, Donald, 99, 107
Stern, Mark, 23, 125, 149
Stratton bill (1947), 72–73, 75–76
Susman, Milton, 101–02, 103, 110, 111, 190n11, 192n44
SWAP. *See* Association of Veterans of the Polish Army
Szebnie labor camp, 16
Szulman, Irene, 49–50, 145, 148, 154, 168

T., Ursula, 136–37
Tarnow concentration camp, 24
Taube, Moshe, 23, 150
Travers, Howard, 71
Treblinka death camp, 11–12, 15, 18, 34
Tree of Life Congregation, 113

Truman, Harry S., 50–51, 64, 67–68, 76–77

Truman directive: immigrants entering U.S. under, 65, 67–68, 70–71, 77, 99, 115; failure of, 88–89; and proportion of Jews to Catholics, 70–72

Turbiner, Bernard, 119

Turbiner, Rose, 12, 119, 154

Twardy, A. M., 85, 127, 128

UJA. *See* United Jewish Appeal

UJF. *See* United Jewish Fund

Union of St. Joseph of North America, 132

United Jewish Appeal (UJA), 88, 98, 100–03

United Jewish Fund (UJF), 88, 98–99, 100–04, 108, 120, 191*n18*

United Nations Relief and Rehabilitation Agency, 46, 49

United Palestinean Appeal, 98

United Service to New Americans (USNA), 65, 66, 88, 99, 105, 107

U.S. armed forces, 49–52

United States Committee for the Care of European Children, 65

U.S. Congress, 55, 72–73

U.S. Department of State, 71

U.S. House of Representatives, 75–76

U.S. Immigration and Naturalization Service, 68

United Vocational and Employment Service (UVES), 90, 103

USNA. *See* United Service to New Americans

UVES. *See* United Vocational and Employment Service

Veterans of the Polish Armed Forces in Exile, 55

W., Edmund, 58, 127

W., Janina, 10, 127

W., Stanley, 58, 128, 133, 135, 143

W., Walter, 29, 128, 141

Wannsee conference, 15

Warsaw ghetto uprising (1944), 12, 40, 178

Weitz, Ruth, 14, 125, 154

Weitzman, Leonard, 90, 111, 113–14

Wiesel, Elie, 110, 150

Winkler, Janina, 54, 121, 144, 149, 168–69

Wolhender, Jacob, 154, 163

Wyman, David, xiv

Yalta Agreement, 58, 59

Yashkar Ola concentration camp, 37

YM&WHA, 90–91, 137

Zachariasiewicz, Walter, 80–82, 83, 126–27

Zaslaw labor camp, 13

Zimmerman, Dora, 62, 158

Zimmett, Joseph, 14–15, 54

Zimmett, Thelma, 13, 14–15, 54

Zweig, Arnold, 20, 21, 48, 137, 154